Neighborhood
Organizations

Recent Titles in Contributions in Political Science
Series editor: Bernard K. Johnpoll

The Myth of Inevitable Progress
Franco Ferrarotti

A Philosophy of Individual Freedom: The Political Thought of F. A. Hayek
Calvin M. Hoy

Roots of Failure: United States Policy in the Third World
Melvin Gurtov and Ray Maghroori

Disarmament Without Order: The Politics of Disarmament at the United Nations
Avi Beker

The Liberty Lobby and the American Right: Race, Conspiracy, and Culture
Frank P. Mintz

The Liberal Future in America: Essays in Renewal
Philip Abbott and Michael B. Levy, editors

A Change of Course: The West German Social Democrats and NATO, 1957–1961
Stephen J. Artner

Power and Policy in Transition: Essays Presented on the Tenth Anniversary of the National Committee on American Foreign Policy in Honor of Its Founder, Hans J. Morgenthau
Vojtech Mastny, editor

Ideology and Soviet Industrialization
Timothy W. Luke

Administrative Rulemaking: Politics and Processes
William F. West

Recovering from Catastrophes: Federal Disaster Relief Policy and Politics
Peter J. May

Judges, Bureaucrats, and the Question of Independence: A Study of the Social Security Administration Hearing Process
Donna Price Cofer

Party Identification, Political Behavior, and the American Electorate
Sheldon Kamieniecki

Without Justice for All: The Constitutional Rights of Aliens
Elizabeth Hull

Neighborhood Organizations

Seeds of a New Urban Life

Michael R. Williams

Contributions in Political Science, Number 131

G P

Greenwood Press
WESTPORT, CONNECTICUT • LONDON, ENGLAND

Library of Congress Cataloging in Publication Data

Williams, Michael R., 1938–
  Neighborhood organizations.

  (Contributions in political science, ISSN 0147-1066 ;
no. 131)
  Bibliography: p.
  Includes index.
  1. Community development, Urban—United
States.   2. Citizens' associations—United States.
3. Urban renewal—United States—Citizens participation.
4. Community organization—United States.   5. Neighbor-
hood—United States—Case studies.   I. Title.
II. Series.
HN90.C6W466   1985   307′.3362   85-9948
ISBN 0-313-24749-8 (lib. bdg. : alk. paper)

Library of Congress Catalog Card Number: 85-9948
ISBN: 0-313-24749-8
ISSN: 0147-1066

First published in 1985

Greenwood Press
A division of Congressional Information Service, Inc.
88 Post Road West
Westport, Connecticut 06881

Printed in the United States of America

10 9 8 7 6 5 4 3 2 1

to

Mary Alice,
Christa, and
Cara

CONTENTS

Figures and Tables   ix

Preface   xi

Acknowledgments   xv

I. The Setting for Neighborhood Organization

1. Redefining Urban Decline and Revitalization   3
2. The Meanings of *Neighborhood*   29
3. Democratic Culture and Leftist Ideological Remnants   51

II. The Dynamics of Neighborhood Organization

4. Historical Antecedents and Present Characteristics   71
5. Leadership: The Driving Gear in the Neighborhood Organization   83
6. Other Group Process Variables in the Neighborhood Organization   107

III. The Tasks of Neighborhood Organizations

7. Neighborhood Reinvestment Strategies   125
8. The Energy Crisis   157
9. Crime: The Biggest Neighborhood Issue   173
10. Neighborhood Schools   185

IV. The Promise of Neighborhood Organizations

11. The Organization as Conflict Manager   205
12. The Organization as Mediating Institution   223
13. The Promise of Neighborhood Organizations for Urban
    Vitality   249

    Bibliographic Essay   261

    Index   271

FIGURES AND TABLES

Figures

1.1	Urban Influence Levels of Jurisdictional Bodies	15
2.1	Proposed Comprehensive Model of Neighborhood Change	49
5.1	The Leadership Continuum	86
5.2	The Decision-Making Grid	87
5.3	Varieties of Group Membership Among Leaders by race	94
7.1	The Golden Mean Diagram	142
7.2	The Matrix of Housing Dynamics	143

Tables

2.1	Description of Six Types of Neighborhoods	38
2.2	Neighborhood Characteristics According to Neighborhood Type	42
11.1	Two Models of Institutionalizing Protest	217

PREFACE

Across America, groups of urban residents, especially since World War II, have organized to fight for the betterment of conditions in their neighborhoods. Now, thousands of such organizations, from small city block clubs to big city coalitions, face an uncertain future. They have gained spot successes in halting or reversing urban decline, but can they do much more? How realistic is it to think that these "Havenot" organizations will gain significant influence in the political arenas of our cities?

My answers to these questions flow from the combination of my own experience in neighborhood activism since the late 1960s and the research and experience of countless others, which are distilled in the literature on neighborhood organizing. I helped create and operate an alternative school in a low-income neighborhood of Milwaukee; along with others I confronted various institutions that affected my neighborhood and others nearby; I was involved in local political campaigns, supporting neighborhood-oriented candidates for city, county, and state offices. Yet the more involved I became in neighborhood organizations, the more I wondered what they were about. Endless and frequent meetings required great stamina. Attendance at meetings, probably for these very reasons, was sporadic. Lack of sophistication, lack of funds, lack of commitment at times all discouraged us. Much of the effort was quiet detail work; the organization was intangible, invisible—perhaps not even there, it seemed.

Yet in the last fifteen years, during which neighborhood organizations began sprouting up in my home city (Grand Rapids, MI; population:

185,000), citizen participation has virtually become part of the cultural core. Evidence abounds. The United Fund has begun to explore ways to fund neighborhood associations in low-income areas. Some successful candidates for the City Commission either have been neighborhood activists themselves or have relied heavily on neighborhood activists in their campaigns. City Hall bureaucrats now regularly consult neighborhood groups whose areas would be affected by some pending action. Laws and ordinances have been created and enforced by organized citizen pressure.

Some neighborhood organizing in this city, I must admit, has had anti-progressive effects, too. Middle-class neighborhoods have organized to keep subsidized housing or home-like institutions for the mentally ill out of their areas. Considerable physical improvement in other sections has led to higher tax assessments that have squeezed fixed- and low-income residents. Some neighborhood organizations have naively avoided conflict at all costs. Activists themselves have disagreed cantankerously on the basis of their conservative or liberal ideologies.

Yet overall the impact of neighborhood organizing in my city has been beneficial. The repair and preservation of many physical structures in the older neighborhoods has paralleled improvement in public services, especially police-community relations. Perhaps most important has been the blossoming of numerous grassroots leaders, without whom threatened neighborhoods cannot claim viability.

This book is not primarily an analysis of neighborhood organizations in Grand Rapids, however. It attempts to draw general conclusions from the many particular and very different neighborhoods of our nation that have witnessed neighborhood organizing. It begins with a section that examines the settings for neighborhood organizations, follows with a section analyzing their internal dynamics, adds a third on their tasks, and concludes with a section on their promise for change.

The first part, "The Setting for Neighborhood Organization," begins with a chapter that departs from traditional catalogs of urban ills by emphasizing how they arise from our very political and economic systems. Havenot neighborhood activists typically redefine these urban problems as issues and are likely to envision their solutions differently from city bureaucrats and other powerbrokers. The second chapter explores several conceptions of "neighborhood" and proposes a model of how neighborhoods change that includes the variable of the neighborhood organization itself. Chapter 3 examines the seemingly contradictory ideological tendencies of progressivism and conservatism that the typical neighborhood organization embodies.

Part II, "The Dynamics of Neighborhood Organization," opens with a bridge chapter on the historical antecedents of these groups; this chapter also attempts the difficult task of describing their general characteristics. Chapter 5 draws the research literature on leadership to a sharp focus on the attributes of Havenot neighborhood leaders. Chapter 6 studies other variables in the group life of neighborhood organizations, such as members' motivations, group goals, issues, and norms, and life-cycle patterns.

Part III, "The Tasks of Neighborhood Organizations," dwells on how such groups have defined problems in housing and commercial redevelopment, energy, crime, and education by devoting a chapter to each of the four. Solutions tried and available research on the effectiveness of these solutions are staples of each chapter.

The final part, "The Promise of Neighborhood Organizations," examines the concepts of conflict manager and mediating institution as appropriate roles for these groups in their relations with City Hall, other institutions, and their own constituencies. Chapter 11 uses a theoretical model of conflict and a contrast between the neighborhood organization conflict process and that of a labor union to make suggestions about the best ways to utilize conflict with outside institutions. Chapter 12 elaborates on the two functions of mediation—internal education and external advocacy—as bases for a "tense partnership" relation with municipal government as well as nongovernmental institutions. The last chapter argues that neighborhood organizations can play a key role in revitalizing their neighborhoods. In doing so, they will enhance the autonomy of the city itself, and hence its viability.

My first-hand experience in the near west side neighborhoods of Milwaukee and the southeast side neighborhoods of Grand Rapids leads me to believe a hope for revitalization is not mere academic speculation but is grounded in a reality that has tenacious grassroots. This difficult process of reversing urban decline is the route by which neighborhood organizations become seeds of a new urban life.

ACKNOWLEDGMENTS

As any author comes to realize upon honest reflection, a book is never the product of a single mind. I owe debts to so many people who over the past two decades have influenced my thought on the matters in this book that I could not begin to name them all. They were people in the civil rights and anti-war movements of the 1960s and people in schools and anti-poverty agencies. They were organizers and street people, students and professors. Some have written about their experiences; Saul Alinsky heads my list. They were extraordinary ordinary people: parents, children, and neighborhood residents struggling and taking risks.

There are four, however, whom I would like to acknowledge specially. Tom Edison and Linda Easley were colleagues with whom I collaborated to write the book *Eastown!*. Norbert Hruby, as President of Aquinas College, provided the vision that enabled the college to support the Eastown Community Association (ECA) in its infancy. Most important by far, however, in my education about cities and their neighborhoods has been my spouse, Mary Alice, a former president and executive director of ECA and a City Commissioner of Grand Rapids. Her understanding of and compassion for "little people" and her considerable political skills have demonstrated repeatedly for me that local political activism can be successful. If the reader discovers a sense of realistic hopefulness in these pages, much of it is due to Mary Alice.

Those who helped produce the book also deserve mention. The people at Greenwood Press and the staff of Aquinas's Learning Resource Center were all more than cooperative. Robbi Osipoff and Sandy Savina typed the final manuscript. Thank you to everyone.

PART I

The Setting for
Neighborhood Organization

1

REDEFINING URBAN DECLINE AND REVITALIZATION

> The struggle for power over one's own life situation always begins with an awareness that one does not have such control and that someone else does.
>
> Michael R. Williams

In its opening credits, a popular TV show originating from New York satirically boasts it as "the most dangerous city in America," while scenes of nighttime mayhem, complete with a snarling dog, flash on the screen. As an informal barometer of the mass mind, the label is not far from wrong. New York is *the* city; other American cities merely participate in its characteristics, like the manner in which, as Plato suggested, material realities are mere shadow copies of the ultimate reality of the Idea. New York as the prototype embodies all that is wrong with cities, and what is wrong, it seems, far outstrips what is right.

A quieter, more realistic scene, however, is being played out in America's urban neighborhoods. Residents committed to coping with "what's wrong with cities" are forming local organizations at an unprecedented rate. Many leaders of these groups, especially those in low- to moderate-income neighborhoods, take a view of urban problems that differs drastically from the conventional wisdom. All sides may *describe* urban decline in the same terms, but they will disagree, often vehemently, over the *causes* of such decline.

This chapter therefore is brief in first describing the symptoms of decline, but it lingers over distinctions in *why* they occur. How we see the causes of problems affects how we solve them. Accordingly, this chapter carries these perspective distinctions into a discussion of solutions, and it closes with comments on the role of perception in urban problem-solving.

SYMPTOMS OF URBAN DECLINE

Sidewalk surveys, block club meetings, and barroom conversations about "what's wrong with life in the city" oscillate between two major themes: the *antisocial people* one hears about and sometimes meets who inhabit the city, and certain *structural* problems that are directly felt in one's daily life. The first broad category is *urban incivility*; the second is *systematic contradiction*.

Examples of incivility range from street crime and public impropriety to the unruliness of youths (in and out of school) and the alienation people seem to feel from each other and from themselves. Problems in the "system" include unemployment and underemployment, governmental inefficiency, and technological harassment, everything from air, water, and noise pollution, to escalating energy costs to the slaughter, maiming, and inconvenience due to the automobile. The breakdown of social concord is a more easily understood concept, as the conventional wisdom would have it, but the inadequacies of the systems that have been created to sustain organized urban life are not so clearly analyzed. They are, nonetheless, sources of grave concern to all, especially as they make urban life more precarious.

Social science has brought breadth and precision to these popular generalizations about incivility and systemic evils. For example, Katherine Bradbury, Anthony Downs, and Kenneth Small studied urban deterioration in 153 cities and the 121 Standard Metropolitan Statistical Areas (SMSAs) in which those cities were located.[1] The investigators began by distinguishing between *descriptive* and *functional* decline. By descriptive decline they meant losses of population and jobs. Functional decline meant undesirable changes that reduced a city's ability to perform its social functions effectively. In short, a city's loss of jobs and people was related to its becoming less livable.

Bradbury and her associates also connected certain large demographic trends with an overall reduction in the urban growth rate over the past several decades. For instance, the fertility rate fell after 1965; the migration rate from farm to city, especially for blacks, dropped off; auto and air travel increased in volume; and the number of suburban housing units rose. All these changes were associated with the growth of suburbs as their central cities declined.

Further data analysis showed the central cities as either stagnant (with population loss just balancing the increase in the number of households) or declining in 63 percent of the metro areas. Several factors were associated with big-city population decline:

1. SMSA decline
2. Cold January temperatures
3. High city-SMSA disparities with regard to
   —the percentage of older housing in the total area
   —the percentage of blacks in the total area
   —local tax rates
4. A large number of separate municipalities in SMSA
5. A high SMSA unemployment rate
6. A low percentage of Hispanics, SMSA or city
7. A public school system not extended past the city limits

In other words a large central city was likely to have lost population (and jobs) if it was in a metropolitan area in the northern United States that also lost people and jobs. Furthermore, if the city had disproportionately large numbers of blacks and older houses together with high taxes, it was in serious trouble. Currently, however, most SMSAs (78 percent) are growing, even though the majority of their central cities are not.

CAUSES OF URBAN DECLINE

An Overview

Dozens of theories have competed to explain urban decline. Bradbury and her associates clustered them into six categories: (1) *disamenity avoidance* theories, which focus on motivations to leave the city because of perceived or actual incivility, the concentration of poor persons, and consequent neighborhood decline or inconvenience due to pollution, congestion, or high costs; (2) *tax avoidance* theories, which emphasize the "push" out of the city due specifically to high tax burdens on residents and firms; (3) *positive attraction* ("pull") theories, which underscore the deeply rooted American desire for new low-density housing and the amenities of suburban living made available through cheap gas, cheap mortgages, and new highways in the post–World War II era; (4) *economic evolution* theories, which point out that current industrial mixes in central cities, the rise in white-collar employment, and density of development, are all factors favoring suburban growth at the expense of the central city; (5) *biased policy* theories, which claim that federal home construction, homeownership, and income tax policies have favored the suburbs and the South and West; and (6) *demographic trend* theories, which hypothesize that the demographic composition of an urban population, especially its age structure, is a primary influence on its population growth.

Each of these groups of theories has its evidence and its adherents. The investigators tested most of these hypotheses using the data they had gathered on the 153 cities and their SMSAs to see how each theory correlated with either SMSA growth or suburbanization. They found *strong* support for the following assertions:

1. Race discrimination played an active role in suburbanization. The more blacks were concentrated in the central city, the more rapid was suburban growth.

2. Economic opportunity for firms in the suburbs led to their relocation there. This movement correlated with overall SMSA population growth, so that where the people were, jobs followed. Conversely, there was also evidence that people followed job opportunities to the suburbs.

3. High population densities in the central city spurred suburban growth.

Some support for several other specific theories appeared, but the authors suggested that the most effective policies to counter SMSA decline should be aimed at deterring the loss of both business firms and households, since there appeared to be a close interplay between job and population movement. In summary, overall SMSA growth and decline were a function of the area's entire economy. Strictly suburban growth, however, resulted more from disparities between central cities and suburbs in such attributes as housing age, racial distribution, and economic opportunity.

Entrenched attitudes and trends have showed little change. People still desire new, low-density housing; and they tend to segregate themselves racially and socioeconomically. In addition, cars are in ever increasing use; homeownership retains certain economic advantages; and rising real incomes in SMSAs promote central city population loss.

The objectivity of the Bradbury study, in which the complexity of the urban dynamic is couched in terms of manifold variables and in which correlations are tested for, may obscure the undercurrent of oppression in troubled cities. *Urban decline* is a sanitized way of speaking about the losers in a drawn out scramble for the good life. The reasons ordinary city dwellers are likely to bring up the rear in the race for resources have been eloquently told in literature and song, in textbooks, and in sermons. Bradbury and other social scientists are not wrong in their analyses, but a perspective on urban decay that comes from central city neighborhood organizations must be added. Leaders of such organizations speak with a political edge; they stand conventional wisdom on its head. A few have written or been interviewed for books. Their message is clear: where public perception lays blame for urban problems on the unruly victims, they would chiefly fault those systems that only too efficiently drain the lifeblood of cities and help people who do not need help. In other words, neighborhood organizations redefine the problems of cities.

Causes of Urban Decline Redefined by Neighborhood Organizations

That many city dwellers suffer a variety of indignities and pains from their environment is not in question. An organizer does not have to sound the alarm that problems abound; the people are only too aware already. People are also cognizant of the immediate sources of many of their difficulties: slumlords, hustlers, retail ripoff artists and commercial conmen, petty bureaucrats and politicians, and often some of their neighbors. What remains is a broader and deeper analysis of the causes of their grievances. The work of the neighborhood organization is to place these problems within a larger framework of meaning. In his analysis of The Woodlawn Organization in Chicago, John Fish described this redefinition of concerns:

Most people in Woodlawn have an ''interest'' in slum housing, poverty, unemployment, poor schools, inadequate medical facilities in the sense that they are affected by these social problems and have an attitude toward them. But these problems are not issues until the interests are lifted up by a group which interprets them, places them in a more comprehensive framework, furnishes them with tactics in order that they might be pursued to a successful outcome, and hence, presses them onto the public agenda. Community organization is, in this sense, an attempt to convert interests into politically relevant issues.[2]

The reconsideration of the causes of urban decline that follows springs from the point of view of those community organizations that this book is about, although not all these groups are equal in political awareness. Since their central concern is the readjustment of power relations, at least to the extent that citizen involvement in decision making becomes more democratic and effective, this perspective cuts across ideological lines.

Neighborhood leaders often hold to a progressive or even radical left ideology because it provides a more useful explanatory base for their purposes than would a conservative view, although elements of conservative concern for local autonomy come into play. One difficulty with the conservative ethos is that its emphasis on traditional values—harking back even to the agrarian origins of the United States in the time of John Adams and later the self-reliance of Ralph Waldo Emerson—blind it to the vast power and control exerted by the megastructures of society, particularly by the giant corporations. Contributing to this blindness, of course, is the access of such corporations to the media, which they use to present an image of themselves as much less threatening than they actually are. For example, a recent Exxon television commercial shows a man dressed as a blue-collar worker. The voice-over announces that "Exxon is Joe Doaks." Somehow Exxon becomes as familiar as your next-door neighbor. AT&T made itself known not as the world's largest company, but as good old "Ma Bell." The point can be extended. Leaders of community organizations in poor neighborhoods know that corporate control of the economy, and the corresponding lack of economic democracy, must be a basic consideration in any analysis that seeks to move more people into positions of control over their own lives.

Even thoughtful conservatives can see the folly of maintaining the status quo, because of the enormous social costs it imposes. Environments that cause pain, in the form of hunger, cold, or violence (or that injure self-esteem through unemployment and prejudice) cannot be condoned. Life no longer need be "nasty, brutish, and short." Where it is so, the resources of society must be mobilized to end these conditions. The issue is neither abstract nor merely metaethical: it is eminently practical. Studies of families under severe economic stress confirm higher incidences of antisocial behavior, from fighting to child and spouse abuse. Social pain begets social pain. In our complex, mobile societies, we cannot afford rejects and outcasts. They will hurt each other and us, either directly or by requiring a huge and expensive social service bureaucracy. A harmonious society and a civil city demand that the vast disparities between the Haves and the Havenots be reduced. Thus will justice be served and wise public policy prevail.

Haves and Havenots

Since the concept of Haves and Havenots is central to the argument of this work, it deserves elaboration. The large middle class of U.S. society suggests that there is a continuum of power across classes and that the boundaries are difficult to draw. At one extreme are either the very wealthy or the top public or corporate managers, whose decisions affect the lives of most of us in various ways. At the other extreme are the members of the underclass, whose very existence is constantly threatened by the vagaries of life. They may be addicts, bag ladies, or derelicts, but they share a common powerlessness. They scarcely control their own lives, let alone influence anyone else's. Between these extremes lie many degrees of power and influence.

What distinguishes Havenots is their actual as well as perceived incapacity to change their living conditions by themselves. These living conditions are unduly constraining in some way. For example, employment opportunities are limited, housing is inadequate, the neighborhood is unpleasant, crowded, and unsafe, or schooling is ineffective. Havenots' basic needs are not fully met, and their unorganized potential to meet these needs by their own efforts is minimal.

Class status is germane to the definition of Havenot. The poor, according to Frances Fox Piven and Richard Cloward, are not a stratum below the working class "but rather a stratum within the working class that is poor by standards prevailing in society at the time."[3] They may be welfare mothers, displaced Southern farm workers, urban immigrants, industrial workers, the elderly, the unemployed.

Although traditional class demarcations are usually accurate in distinguishing Havenots from Haves, the residents of central city neighborhoods, particularly ethnic or racial ghettos, are rarely homogeneous in their class characteristics. As later chapters will show, leaders in Havenot neighborhood organizations will often have acquired more education and somewhat higher incomes than their fellow residents, though these differences do not necessarily place them in a higher class status, unless one admits those subcategories of upper working class or lower-middle class. Some middle-class residents of the same neighborhoods may also be in sympathy with the goals of the neighborhood organization. They share a sense of solidarity with the Havenots, particularly a sense of powerlessness and isolation *vis-a-vis* urban systems.[4]

Havenot, then, refers especially to the poor within the working class. But it includes some of the non-poor who share their condition of powerlessness and isolation to an extent. By defining Havenot more broadly, organizers have tried to prepare the ground for the construction of coalitions that could span the traditional lines of race, class, and ideology. Where such coalitions have sprung up, they have usually aimed in specific ways at reducing the Have-Havenot gap, a maze of inequities produced by those systematic contradictions to which we now turn our attention.

Systematic Contradictions Leading to Urban Decline

Systematic contradictions are an insidious cause of urban decline because they underlie the "people problems." The term *contradiction* denotes "opposition between factors inherent in a system," according to Webster. Where these oppositions occur, the system either fails to function or produces outcomes quite different from the ones the builders of the system intended. A third possibility is that systems function efficiently to maintain gaps between Haves and Havenots. Virtually every urban system contains such polarities, due to economic processes, bureaucratic complexities, or technological imperatives. Political malice and greed exploit and exacerbate these systemic faults, which arise also from contradictions in our very culture, in which, for example, the value of equal economic opportunity clashes with the desire by Haves for socioeconomic segregation.[5] Since these overlapping contradictions form a good part of the progressive analysis of urban decline, they require further explanation.

Contradictions Due to Corporate Capitalism

The capitalist form of our economy promotes attainment of individual wealth, regardless of subsequent effects on the public good. The grosser injustices due to capitalistic exploitation at the turn of this century have been mitigated by government intervention at all levels, particularly at the federal level, and also by labor unions. But the hard fact remains that economic power is increasingly concentrated in the hands of the few. Big business, now in the form of multinational conglomerates, threatens national democracies far more than did the Rockefellers, Mellons, Morgans, Carnegies, DuPonts, and Vanderbilts of a century ago. *Why* they are a threat requires further analysis.

To put it at its simplest, the capitalists own and control capital (i.e., the means of production), and they hire workers to produce. The workers sell their labor at certain rates, which the capitalists seek to minimize in order to make profits as large as possible when they sell what is produced. When the pie of all that is produced is continually getting larger, as it did after the second World War (at the rate of 4.3 percent per year), corporate profits increase, and workers' demands for higher wages can be met to a degree.[6] The 1970s, however, saw a decline in the profitability of the world's largest industrial and commercial corporations.

Barry Commoner's analysis of the contradictions of our present economic system summarizes why it is breaking down.[7] Capitalist decision-makers have consistently tended to introduce labor-saving machinery to increase the output of labor. This technological growth has not increased the need for labor; it has decreased it, leading to ever higher unemployment levels, which become accepted as natural. Thus, the first major contradiction of modern capitalism is that economic growth requires unemployment in a high technology society.

At the same time, the capital formed by production has not been reinvested in sufficient quantities. If I make profits in my business, I have to reinvest a part of them in the business to keep competitive. At least three new forces in the past decades have added to this reinvestment burden: the need for pollution control, rising costs of energy, and competition from other highly industrialized nations. The rate of return on investment, related to profit, has been declining since World War II, and especially since 1966 (when great quantities of capital began to be diverted into the Vietnam War). The recent spurt of business mergers and acquisitions has also concentrated power while simultaneously proving to be a drain on job-producing reinvestment. The second contradiction of capitalism, therefore, is that the desire for profit wars with the demand for reinvestment.

Economic growth, the counterbalance to this skewed approach to productivity, has slowed considerably under the pressures of ballooning energy and raw materials costs. Since growth can no longer mask the more basic process of decline, Commoner contends, the diversion of capital to support huge weapons buildups and the domestic high technology of nuclear power is nonsensical. This capital drain only aggravates the tendency of capitalism to swallow its own tail. The third contradiction of capitalism, then, is that, on the one hand, economic growth in a capitalist system is necessary for the Havenots to gain the material basics of life. Where growth cannot be sustained, gross imbalances in distribution create severe hardships for the Havenots, and their numbers increase significantly. Yet, on the other hand, conditions indicate that fossil-fuel-based economic growth cannot be sustained far into the future.

For the past decade, the major corporations have acknowledged the decline in their profits. Their solution to this problem has been predictable; they have looked to government for new sources of capital. Their "welfare for the rich" strategy has succeeded in two ways.[8] First, they have gotten public officials elected who would widen their tax loopholes and subsidize their capital-intensive approaches to production. Second, they have convinced the public that government is the enemy and that business is the salvation of a depressed economy. Slogans such as "Get Government off the Backs of the People" and "Big Government Is the Problem," paid for with billions of dollars in advertising (to be written off at tax time, of course), created the impression that government social programs were a waste of money. This exploitation of many citizens' racial and class prejudices, their xenophobic fear of communists, particularly Russians, and their historic distrust of state intervention in economic affairs distracted them at election and budget times. The federal government is now more in synchrony with the wishes of big business, its needs for capital, and its pursuit of profit at the expense of the public good. Although a countervailing mistrust of big business is blossoming among the U.S. public, the contradictions of our capitalist economy are still present and profoundly affecting the fate of our cities.

Contradictions Due to Government Policy

A brief history of relations between local, state, and federal governments should preface discussion of current urban problems due to government policies. Early in U.S. history, state governments dominated civic affairs; city governments served at their whim until the crowded conditions of the larger cities bred health problems that had to be addressed.[9] Urban reformers in the nineteenth century, armed with the new technologies of smooth ceramic tiles, electric water pumps, and the germ theory of disease, prodded city governments to build sanitary sewers. Because the pipes required a straight line layout, the cities had to interfere with private property rights in order to get them laid. The huge capital expenditures required massive municipal borrowing, which in turn spurred the growth of political machines to accomplish it.

The last three decades of the nineteenth century saw the urbanization of America as immigrants poured into cities, searching for work in the factories powered by the new steam engines. The city bosses built roads, docks, and water lines to go with their sewers. The states' reaction to this urban growth was to increase their interference in civic decision making, right down to the naming of streets and the closing of alleys.

States rearranged districts to insure urban underrepresentation in the state legislature. Corporate trusts, mergers of many small businesses under the control of a single large one, grew rapidly before the turn of the century. Under their influence, state governments began to see themselves as the promoters of business, rather than as its regulators. Thus emerged a powerful coalition with business against the interests of the cities.

At the dawn of the new century, however, cities were fighting back. Many lobbied successfully for home-rule legislation, which stipulated that the city could decide for itself in those matters not specified by the state. Prior to this idea, cities had to ask state legislatures' permission in the smallest matters. Professional municipal management techniques became popular as a reaction to the corruption of the boss-systems and their resulting inefficiency and incompetency.

Just before the Great Depression, city governments had reached a peak in their struggle for autonomy and local control. Two factors in the second quarter of the twentieth century combined to reverse this trend. The New Deal policies of the federal government began a tendency (that has not yet abated) of federal control of city governments through policies attached to transfer payments. In addition, cheap gasoline and natural gas underwrote the flight to the suburbs, a demographic hemorrhage that has recently slowed but not yet stopped. Municipal governments, aware that their resources were being sapped by corporate relocation decisions, became more involved in economic planning for their cities, but remained mostly on a competitive basis with sister cities for location of new plants. Public Authorities, creatures of the New Deal, borrowed money for public construction through tax-exempt bonds. These unelected governments also wielded considerable influence on patterns of urban development.[10] In general, the authority of municipal governments has eroded since the 1930s, although it has resurged somewhat in the past decade as a result of growing awareness that urban problems are to a large extent due to the city's economic dependence on distant governments and corporations.

The legitimate jurisdictional bodies at local, state, and federal levels have vied with one another for control over the shape and function of cities. They have reeled under the impact of technological innovation and the demands first of the great corporate trusts and then of the multinational corporations. Figure 1.1 somewhat fancifully summarizes the relative amounts of influence of these governing institutions in municipal affairs since the mid-nineteenth century. Also included is the influence of neighborhood groups on city policy, a point to which we will return in Chapter 13. The term *fanciful* underscores the idea that this chart is meant only as a visual aid to present the gross direction of changes over time. The amounts of influence never total 100 percent because they have been affected by developments in the private sector, international events, and cultural value changes.

Of particular concern now are federal government policies that, since World War II, have exacerbated the decline of U.S. cities, particularly those in the Northeast and Midwest. A former controller for the City of New York, Richard Morris, details how a number of federal programs, some that were well-intended and some that were the result of special interest lobbies, have hurt older urban areas by accelerating withdrawal of capital.[11] He contends, for example, that a side effect of the push to eradicate poverty in the mid–1960s was the creation of a large welfare bureaucracy, from foster home inspectors to Medicaid doctors, that absorbed up to 80 percent of all welfare funds. Another boondoggle that accelerated the population shift to the Sunbelt was the disproportionate awarding of defense contracts to firms in those parts

Figure 1.1
Urban Influence Levels of Jurisdictional Bodies

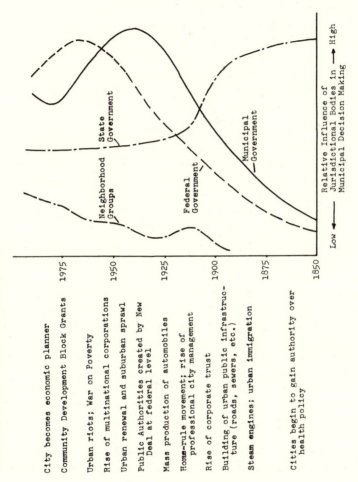

of the country. Social Security laws unduly benefit the South and the Southwest because they do not adjust for the higher cost of living in Northern cities. The North has lost 300,000 federal jobs to the South in recent years. Even trucking regulations boosted costs to the cities because of bans on carrying full loads both ways.

Morris is not alone in his critique. Northern politicians have become fond of pointing out the net tax drain on Northern states. The government that is supposed to adjudicate imbalances in U.S. society is in fact accelerating them, through these and other policies (especially energy pricing and distribution policies, which effectively enrich some states at the expense of others).[12]

After World War II, federal policy encouraged the flight of the middle class from the cities, by funding massive highway projects that sliced whole neighborhoods to bits and by making suburban mortgages easier to obtain through the Federal Housing Administration (FHA) and the Veterans Administration (VA). In addition, cheap natural gas contributed to the rapid expansion of suburban tracts so that the large houses at the end of those highways were easier to purchase.

Urban renewal projects of the early 1960s accelerated the deterioration of inner city communities by bulldozing block after block of older housing and replacing it with high-rise apartments (perhaps envisioning the residents as urban cliff-dwellers), with institutional usages, or by simply letting it lie fallow. Crowding and allied social problems increased as a result. A 1980 study of 130 large cities burst the bubble of a popular myth: that urban renewal, the razing of slums near the central business district (CBD), was an attempt to improve poor neighborhoods for their residents.[13] On the contrary, urban renewal was most likely to occur in cities where the CBD was already in the process of revitalization and where large corporations, headquartered in the CBDs, exerted influence on city policymakers to help them expand into adjacent (razed) areas.

Policy may now be somewhat more enlightened, allowing for more local input into the overall planning for adequate housing of a city's low-income population. But there are still many vacant weed-choked blocks of land at the hearts of America's large cities.

The federal government's current position of influence over urban development cannot be understood apart from the analysis of our capitalist economy presented earlier. The industrial firms based in cities, particularly in the North, have seen their costs of production balloon over the past 50 years, as unions have gained economic leverage and as energy and materials costs have risen. A standard strategem used to counter these trends has been to relocate in areas of the U.S. where labor unions were less powerful or to forsake the country entirely (for less developed nations whose workers are more amenable to the needs of the organization).

When an industry leaves a city, it takes with it the taxes it would have paid and leaves its workers unemployed. The local government thus has less money to provide services for its people. In order to regain the lost revenue, it has to raise the taxes of those people and firms remaining behind, inadvertently creating pressure on them to leave also. And some do. As they leave in turn, the cycle repeats itself, and the city declines even more. Those who flee the city have too often been replaced by people less able to pay for the services they are even more in need of.

Most of the people and firms that leave the cities, however, do not leave the country. They have in fact been migrating to the suburbs where taxes have been lower and land has been cheaper.[14] When the urban crisis burst into America's living rooms in the form of the ghetto riots of 1964–67, the U.S. government began making block grants to cities for everything from bridge construction to support of welfare payments. The federal portion of municipal government budgets increased exponentially, in some rare cases to as much as 70 percent. Without the federal dole, America's cities would be bankrupt. And with the purse came the pursestrings. When the federal government jerks them, the cities, particularly the Northern industrial cities, twitch spastically. The federal government became a powerful broker for capital that local governments could not retain.

Although federal policy carries the most influence in urban development, state and local governments also shape the face of the cities. These bodies are even more at the mercy of the corporations, however, and the scramble is on to attract business with tax abatements and other incentives.

The rebuilding of U.S. urban centers was postponed by a series of events: the Depression of the 1930s, World War II, the federal emphasis on suburban development, and the 1960's preoccupation with urban riots.[15] In the 1970s, a new focus on downtown development emphasized cultural, commercial, and corporate reinvestment. The rationale offered in most cases was that the city needed an identifiable center to attract convention business, to service corporate office operations, and to offer entertainment, from festivals to opera, for all ranks of the citizenry. The larger cities also encouraged luxury housing development downtown. Unfortunately, neighborhood residential and commercial areas of the city were often sorely neglected as capital reinvestment was concentrated at the heart of the city. The construction of the gigantic Renaissance Center in Detroit, for example, left nearby decaying neighborhoods virtually untouched. Reinvestment in the city must meet the needs of all its citizens, not just a privileged few.

Contradictions due to government policies are related to the government's service of the class-based economic system. The cities, increasingly seen as storage depots for Havenots, have been unable to compete for their share of the tax pie, particularly in the form of jobs and contracts. Where tax money has returned, it has taken the form of politically vulnerable grant programs that have shored up sickly municipal budgets. The current position of city governments is not unlike that of poor welfare recipients: they are stuck in ruts of dependence on government handouts with less and less autonomy over their affairs. City governments must defer the repair of their capital stock (bridges, streets, sewers) until they can rebuild their tax base by attracting new business and higher-income residents. But they cannot attract these resources unless the amenities and infrastructure are already present, a *Catch–22* situation. Thus the fiscal crisis of U.S. cities can only be resolved by a national commitment to urban reinvestment. Cities must be seen for what they are, resource centers that must be constantly replenished.

Contradictions Due to Bureaucracy and the Technological Imperative

Urban centers are interrelated webs of highly complicated organizations. The physical geography of the city makes this organization visible, for example, in the transportation systems of streets, spaces given over to autos and trucks, or the zoning of land for commercial or residential usage. Other organizational aspects of the city are much less visible, such as the operations of city government or business interactions. To live in the city is to encounter constantly the effects of big and complicated organization. That these effects often seem irrational, chaotic, or violent should not surprise anyone familiar with the contradictions of bureaucracy.

On the positive side, a large organization emphasizes reliability, functional rationality, coordination of complex activities, and minimization of personal (nonrational) considerations in decision making. But there are well-known negative aspects as well. The regulations established to see that the service goals of the organization are met can become ends in themselves. Red tape then snarls efficiency and occasionally prevents the original objectives from being met. Impersonality, in which the formal functions of organization replace the treatment of individuals as unique human beings, leads to alienation among workers and between themselves and clients. A bureaucratic mentality sets in that emphasizes acquiescence to authority as a means to security in the organization. Buckpassing and deliberately keeping communications unclear are other techniques employees use to avoid responsibility while repossessing a little personal power.

Bureaucratic structures, as a principal phenomenon of our technological civilization, have enabled cities to grow to the size and complexity they have. Nonetheless, such structures have brought with them the seeds of much of the alienation found in urban life. The technological imperative, according to Langdon Winner, is that aspect of high technology, in this case complex bureaucracies, that seems to turn the ends of the technological system into the service and maintenance of the system itself.[16] Reformers who seek the levers of power in organizations see, once they are in power, that the system as established is not easy to change. In fact they find that they are forced to acquiesce to its demands, in effect becoming its servants to an awesome degree.

Imagine, for example, that you are superintendent of a big city school system and that you believe wholeheartedly in sharing control of local schools with the parents who send their children to them. You want to develop a policy that matches your ideal. That principals, teachers' unions, and central office personnel will resist you is to be expected. The very structure of the current school organization provides each of its functionaries with an idea of where they fit in it. To change the system, even if everyone acknowledges (privately) that it is inefficient, is to threaten the security of hundreds or thousands of individual people who make it work. The system, as each of them perceives it, must maintain itself, or the people who service it will suffer somehow. The system is the true master; its servants are its employees. They will defend it in spite of their awareness of its flaws, content only to make minor adjustments even when egregious flaws are evident.

Of course the tendency to reify or make separate entities out of systems has drawbacks, the principal one of which is to convince people that nothing can be done to bring about change for the better. But it would be a serious error to minimize the contradictions of bureaucracy as a source of urban oppression.

This chapter has followed a different road. Social commentators have traditionally classified urban problems as somewhat isolated phenomena—"crime," "inadequate schools," or "ineffective government"— or attempted to describe them in terms of correlated variables. The present analysis builds onto this work a perspective of systematic criticism from within the Havenot sector itself. The mark of this critique is that it describes the urban malaise much less in terms of people problems and much more in terms of contradictions in our economic system, governmental policies, and the nature of bureaucracy. These systems in turn embody a U.S. culture that emphasizes competition, success, and individualism, and prejudices based on racial, sexual, economic class, age, and other nonessential differences. The concentration of Havenots in central cities has been one result.

The redefinition of urban problems as systematic contradictions is what grassroots leaders mean by raising issues, and it is in the raising of these issues that the proper solutions become clear. Havenots often mean something different when they speak of urban revitalization than do Haves. The next section outlines these divergent concepts of urban revitalization as they exist in the minds of disparate urban actors.

THE MEANINGS OF URBAN REVITALIZATION

What may be urban revitalization to one person may be the imposition of blight to another. Revitalization means considerably different things depending on which sector of society is doing the defining.

To the *longtime resident* of the neglected or threatened neighborhood, the signs of urban revitalization are connected to the insertion of capital into the local area. Houses get fixed up or new ones are built, key retail businesses move in (or at least do not move out), and public spaces, such as parks and streets, are repaired and made usable again. Improvement means better control of traffic flow, fewer trucks and cars, more convenient bus service. It means more jobs are available; it signals that the streets are safe to walk, houses are free from potential intruders, and there are fewer transients passing through the area. For families with growing children, the local school appears to be doing a good job. For every resident, the image of the neighborhood has improved; it feels better to live there.

Neighborhood rebirth, perceived by certain members of the middle or upper-middle class, may also mean that the area is becoming fashionable. Stately old homes, once in disrepair and split into several crowded apartments, begin to sell at high prices to two-career young couples with money and no children. These newcomers want to live a grander lifestyle in a restored older home, near the amenities of downtown. The *new gentry* (as they were first termed in London twenty years ago), often displace former residents unable to finance the increased costs of living there. There is some doubt that the newcomers have moved back into the city; they are much more likely to have moved from another part of the city.[17] Arguments that gentrification is the answer to urban revival are specious. Studies also indicate that most middle and upper-middle income people move back *into* the city only *after* the area to which they move has been completely revitalized.[18]

To *local government officials*, revitalization means rebuilding the tax base. Downtown redevelopment, attraction of new business, and retention of business already there are of the highest priority. The prospect of new jobs and capital is the conventional antidote for the continual loss of tax base that older cities are experiencing. In fact, jobs and capital are so important that whole neighborhoods can be sacrificed in order to have them. The Poletown neighborhood of Detroit is an example. To make way for a new Cadillac plant 4,500 structures were razed between 1980 and 1981. Mayor Coleman Young justified the city's action in condemning the property for sale to General Motors as necessary because the city was so desperate for the 6,000 jobs that would be created. The spirit of urban "removal," so prevalent two decades ago, is still with us.

Further evidence of local government's thirst for new capital is its willingness to ease taxes for new or expanded corporate ventures as an incentive for them to stay, even though research suggests that tax abatements have not affected business relocation decisions. The justification for such largesse is that the new capital generated will fill city coffers through property, income, and sales tax expansions, and pump new blood into the tired urban economy by adding jobs and, in the case of development of cultural or convention facilities, by augmenting tourist or conference revenues.

Corporations have a stake in urban improvement as well, particularly as it promotes a productive work force. Although the major corporate activity in some cities is confined to maintenance of corporate headquarters, whose workers are clerical, managerial, or professional, most cities can still be legitimately viewed as concentrations of industrial workers. And while cynics sometimes compare contemporary corporations to the meatpacking moguls of Chicago at the turn of the century in their ruthless exploitation of immigrant labor, the conditions for production have changed considerably. It is true that large businesses can be bad neighbors, either because they pollute, dominate a local economy, or throw it into chaos by relocating. But most businesses need the sort of skilled, even expert, and stable help that flourishing urban communities provide. Nevertheless, when profit margins dip too low, to save the company top management can make decisions that might seriously hurt the urban community it is in.

Nonprofit institutions' particular interest in urban improvement has often been self-serving.[19] One example in my experience of this tunnel vision was exhibited by a small college on the near west side of Milwaukee. Years ago this institution bought more than 125 duplexes adjacent to its campus in an older, stable neighborhood. Its intent was to expand the campus at some future time. About a decade ago, the college tore down a dozen of these large well-built homes to build an athletic field, which was fenced off and became unused most of the year. In 1981 the college announced plans to raze all its remaining houses for "green space" around its campus. The college as landlord had allowed these structures to deteriorate to the point where the city condemned some of them. But the residents who owned homes in the once-elegant area were outraged; they joined with tenants and local city officials to protest the move. The outcome resulted in the houses remaining but the college relocating to a new campus north of the city. This example illustrates how even a nonprofit service-oriented organization can define revitalization in a way harmful to its neighbors. To improve the college's campus was at the same time to perpetrate a blight on its neighbors. It was clear that the neighborhood was already blighted from the college's perspective.

Are there common threads to these various outlooks on urban improvement? Most people would probably agree that making urban service systems function more efficiently is important. The reinvestment of capital, however, must be accomplished in an equitable way, producing the least possible harm and disruption. Agreement on what is equitable is not easy to achieve, even if there is to be reinvestment. Therefore, the decision-making process ought to be as broad-based as it can, involving all elements of the community. Havenots have begun to organize in earnest so that their voices will be heard above the din. It is impossible to avoid disruption when reinvesting in or rebuilding sections of the city. Poor neighborhoods often suffer the worst upheavals, however, although even affluent residential areas can be affected by the quest for equity in urban revitalization. A current source of contention in some cities is the building of multiunit housing for the elderly and for moderate-income families, at a time of exorbitant housing prices. The largest tracts of developable land are usually adjacent to newer subdivisions of detached (expensive) single-family homes. Subdivision residents resent the denser zoning near them, yet the pressure on urban housing increases with growth in the number of households. The greater good sometimes demands sacrifice on the part of a few, though all too often this utilitarian principle has become a slogan used by the powerful to bully the powerless.

THE ROLE OF PERCEPTION IN URBAN REVITALIZATION

Cities are not just physical places. They are also spaces with which their inhabitants identify. Lewis Mumford, in *The Myth of the Machine*, calls them "containers" of human culture, likening them to a kind of skin, just as one's house, car, or clothing are sorts of skins.[20] They define us, even as we define, construct, or raze them. They are extensions of ourselves. What happens to our cities happens to us.

Many theories of urban decline mentioned earlier imply that change in urban patterns is a result of perceptions that combine to "push" people and businesses away from declining areas while "pulling" them toward growth areas. The more affluent members of older, central city neighborhoods were considered to be pushed out by the migration of lower-class workers into their area. At the same time, the development of new residential properties at the edge of the city lured these people of means away from the heart of town. Although there have been variations on this view, and questions remain as to whether it is still a useful explanatory model, it has operated with different degrees of intensity over the past hundred years.

The push-pull model is self-reinforcing. The perception that one's turf is threatened by decline on nearby land often leads to behavior likely to promote further decline: selling out and moving from the area, deferring maintenance on one's property, or retaining the property but renting to more transient residents. Conversely, if it appears that an area is coming back, demand can heat up quickly. People of much higher income, perceiving that this neighborhood may offer unique amenities, such as stately turn of-the-century homes and proximity to the central business district with its particular retail, entertainment, and business opportunities, rush to grab the choicest properties. More and more of the Havenots who live there are forced out. The area becomes fashionable and commercial enterprises catering to the whims of the new residents blossom: boutiques, wine and cheese shops, and other specialty stores. Rolf Goetze has brought the perception factor into the discussion of urban change, especially at the neighborhood level.[21] His insights, along with those of other observers, have helped flesh out our understanding of how neighborhoods change. Chapter 2 describes that topic more specifically.

The current situation is that the edge of the city has become suburbia and the heart of the town is all too often now, in Anthony Downs' phrase, a "crisis ghetto."[22] Downs' book, *Opening Up the Suburbs*, published in 1973, put forth proposals to improve city neighborhoods, based on the assumption that central city decline could be reversed only by a national policy of dispersal of low-income households to the suburbs. While his theoretical analysis had much merit, few neighborhood organizations focus on this long-term concept. They tend to emphasize localized improvement while discouraging precipitous movement. The push-pull model may describe a natural phenomenon, they reason, but it is one that can be influenced by their localized collective action. Whether the potential for Havenots to improve their own neighborhoods for themselves is illusory, as Downs seemed to imply, remains for the reader to judge after finishing this book. I shall argue that it is not illusory.

Urban revitalization is thus not merely a rebuilding of the seedy sections of the city or the construction of a new downtown center. It is the reconstitution of the urban psyche. This subjective regeneration means more than merely making the city attractive to its residents and increasing their satisfaction with it. It requires a more basic belief that the decline of the present can be reversed, a belief rooted in personal and group commitment to bringing that reversal about. An extensive study of Pittsburgh neighborhoods draws this distinction between mere satisfaction with neighborhood life and commitment to its improvement.[23]

If perception plays a role in urban decline, it must also be an essential element of strategies for revitalizing change. If cities are to become more livable, the people who live in them must see that those changes are possible and want them badly enough to struggle to bring them about.

Some commentators have used the term *therapeutic* to describe the less tangible effects of this work to revitalize the city. Although the term denotes recovery from a disease, here it means that when citizens join the fight to save the city, they themselves are brought toward a healthier outlook. They develop confidence that they can control their future in the place. The involvement of more and more citizens in urban problem solving is really the rekindling of the fragile and abused ideal of democracy. How neighborhood organizations may be a vehicle for this cooperative push is what this book seeks to understand.

Most of the central cities of the U.S. are in decline. Jobs and people have fled to the suburbs, while, on a larger scale, population and resources have migrated toward the South and the West. Although a typical person-in-the-street point of view on central cities may lay the blame for their deterioration on the people now inhabiting them, leaders of Havenot organizations have diagnosed the pathology of the cities and neighborhoods quite differently. Havenots see that U.S. economic and political systems serve to deprive them of the means of living a normal life, a standard the rest of the country takes for granted. These systems, beginning with corporate capitalism itself and including government and most other institutions, are the manifestation of cultural contradictions in the United States—fairness vs. competitive individualism, meritocracy vs. egalitarianism. Urban problems to the Havenots are not merely malfunctions of an otherwise sound system. They are the inevitable result of the *effective* operation of often *un*sound, *un*fair systems.

The people problems that spring from these injustices are real, but how they arose and how they are to be solved are questions to be answered by changing the systems that foment and exacerbate them.

There is also an internal dynamic that changes cities, the self-reinforcing cycles of behavior based on perceptions of that change. Organized attempts to revitalize urban centers must, therefore, confront the institutions and systems that exploit them. At the same time, the process of standing up for their rights should stiffen Havenots' commitment to improvement and short-circuit the cycle of pessimism that leads toward despair.

Certainly, not all Havenots agree to or understand this analysis. Many, taking their cue from the systems oppressing them, blame only themselves for their condition. But many others have crystal clarity about why they are Havenots. Periodically in this century, Havenots have organized to demand redress. The past two decades, however, have seen an exponential increase in organized attempts at the neighborhood grassroots (perhaps we should say at the pavement) level to translate Havenot grievances into demands for change. To begin to understand this relatively recent burst of energy, we must first try to define what a neighborhood is, how a neighborhood changes, and what ideological shifts are occurring that would encourage neighborhood organizing.

NOTES

1. Katherine L. Bradbury, Anthony Downs, and Kenneth A. Small, *Urban Decline and the Future of American Cities* (Washington, DC: The Brookings Institution, 1982).

2. John H. Fish, *Black Power/White Control: The Struggle of the Woodlawn Organization in Chicago* (Princeton, NJ: Princeton University Press, 1972), 106.

3. Frances Fox Piven and Richard A. Cloward, *Poor People's Movements: Why They Succeed, How They Fail* (New York: Pantheon, 1977), xiii.

4. Rodman Webb, *Schooling and Society* (New York: Houghton Mifflin, 1981).

5. Anthony Downs, *Neighborhoods and Urban Development* (Washington, DC: The Brookings Institution, 1981).

6. Harry C. Boyte, *The Backyard Revolution: Understanding the New Citizen Movement* (Philadelphia: Temple University Press, 1980), 10.

7. Barry Commoner, *The Poverty of Power: Energy and the Economic Crisis* (New York: Bantam, 1977).

8. This "welfare for the rich" strategy is documented at length in Boyte, pp. 1–15.

9. David Morris, *Self-Reliant Cities: Energy and the Transformation of Urban America* (San Francisco: Sierra Club Books, 1982), chap. 3.

10. See, for example, J. Clarence Davies, *Neighborhood Groups and Urban Renewal* (New York: Columbia University Press, 1966), chap. 2, for a detailed

description of the influence of Robert Moses in New York's public works projects.

11. Robert Morris, *Bum Rap on America's Cities: The Real Causes of Urban Decay* (Englewood Cliffs, NJ: Prentice-Hall, 1980).

12. Midwest Governors' Conference, *Energy and the Economy*, Lansing, MI, 1981.

13. Roger Friedland, "Corporate Power and Urban Growth: The Case of Urban Renewal," *Politics and Society* 10 (1980), 203–24.

14. T.D. Allman, "The Urban Crisis Leaves Town and Moves to the Suburbs," *Harper's*, December 1978, 41–56.

15. Ed Marciniak, *Reversing Urban Decline* (Washington, DC: National Center for Urban Ethnic Affairs, 1981), chap. 1.

16. Langdon Winner, *Autonomous Technology: Technics-out-of-Control as a Theme in Political Thought* (Cambridge, MA: MIT Press, 1977).

17. Shirley Bradway Laska and Daphne Spain, *Back to the City: Issues in Neighborhood Renovation* (New York: Pergamon Press, 1980), xi.

18. See Dennis Gale, "Middle-Class Resettlement in Older Urban Neighborhoods: The Evidence and Implications," in *Neighborhood Policy and Planning*, ed. Phillip L. Clay and Robert M. Hollister (Lexington, MA: Lexington Books, 1980), 35–54. See also Tim Pattison, "The Stages of Gentrification: The Case of Bay Village," in Clay and Hollister, pp. 77–92.

19. William Worthy, *The Rape of Our Neighborhoods* (New York: William Morrow, 1976).

20. Lewis Mumford, *The Myth of the Machine: Technics and Human Development* (New York: Harcourt, Brace, Jovanovich, 1967), 5.

21. Rolf Goetze, *Understanding Neighborhood Change: The Role of Expectations in Urban Revitalization* (Cambridge, MA: Ballinger, 1979).

22. Anthony Downs, *Opening Up the Suburbs: An Urban Strategy for America* (New Haven, CT: Yale University Press, 1973).

23. Roger S. Ahlbrandt and James V. Cunningham, *A New Public Policy for Neighborhood Preservation* (New York: Praeger, 1979).

2

THE MEANINGS OF
NEIGHBORHOOD

No social movement can be fully understood outside the context of its culture and history. How one thinks about the city, its people, and its institutions forms the basis for one's actions. One's views, however, are often colored by prevailing cultural values, themselves subject to a historical dialectic of ideologies. *Neighborhood* has not been a static concept for the past century in urban America; even now it is undergoing change as debate waxes on what should be done to save and preserve it.

The perspective of this book falls within the political activist tradition, but that is by no means the only view that has attracted followers in recent years. To provide a broad introduction to the question of what a neighborhood is, this chapter divides the discussion into three parts: The first part is a recent history of the meanings of *neighborhood*, the second summarizes different ways contemporary authors describe neighborhoods, and the third models a neighborhood change dynamic that encompasses these different views.

HISTORICAL DEVELOPMENT OF THE CONCEPT OF *NEIGHBORHOOD*

The idea that the neighborhood is a basic urban unit first appeared in America in the latter part of the nineteenth century, according to urban historian Zane Miller.[1] According to his analysis, the idea flourished in the decade following the turn of the century, then disappeared until around 1950, when it began a resurgence that continued into the present.

Prior to the late 1800s, cities were viewed primarily as commercial entities. Geographical groupings were not residential but rather defined by the city-as-commerce-center. Observers divided up territory in terms of the central business district and various manufacturing centers in town. Neighborhoods were not yet distinctly different residential areas interacting as units in an urban system.

Between 1880 and 1920, however, innovations in rapid mass transit did away with the *working city* and began urban sprawl. The organic model of organization in which urban systems were differentiated yet integrated rose to preeminence as a result, leading to the view of the city as a cluster of interlacing communities. There was a sorting of land uses by function and of people by race, class, and ethnicity. Settlement houses existed in every city by 1910, although they did not seek to organize their communities for political action. Neighborhood and community appeared to merge for a time. Progressive thinking about the direction of neighborhood groups was severely counterbalanced by ingrown defensiveness. For example, the white Neighborhood Improvement Associations of Detroit used violence regularly to keep blacks from residing in their communities.[2]

In the period following World War I, there was a reemphasis on the concept of the metropolis as itself a community of distinctive characteristics. The idea gained credence that neighborhood was not possible, given the cultural and economic mosaic that existed in any given section of a large city. Intraurban strife and transition were the hallmark of this era, it was thought. Attention shifted to ways to govern this maelstrom in view of the failures of ward politics. Reform strategies, such as a professional city manager hired by the elected governing council, smaller governing councils elected at large on a nonpartisan basis, and civil service examinations as a way to hire municipal employees all became popular. The depoliticization of city governments accompanied the deemphasis on the neighborhood as an important urban unit.

Even Alinsky, in his earlier work, held that people's organizations should not be based on physical location. "The program of a People's Organization," he wrote in 1946, "knows no boundaries, whether geographical, philosophical, or social."[3] He held that view throughout his career, offering this comment in 1972:

you must understand that in a highly mobile, urbanized society the word "community" means community of interests, not physical community. The exceptions are ethnic ghettos where segregation has resulted in physical communities that coincide with their community of interests, or, during political campaigns, political districts that are based on geographic demarcations.[4]

From 1920 to 1950, the emphasis was on the metropolitan view and regional planning as antidotes to the rapid transitions occurring in U.S. cities. The neighborhood faded to the broadest possible level of identification; it became effectively moribund.

By 1950, however, students of urban change had abandoned the biological model of the city-as-organism and had begun to adopt a more mechanistic view in which the individual was the fundamental analytic unit. Each citizen of the city, in this perspective, worked out terms of mutual accommodation, thereby creating a kind of equilibrium called the social order. The drive of each individual for autonomy and self-expression was the cause of contemporary arrangements. It implied a new respect for diversity and tolerance for separatistic land-use mixes.

Not all observers at the time agreed with this focus on the urban individual. Although they acknowledged that America had become a mass society, they felt that local community still existed within it. This rediscovery was labeled the community of limited liability, because individuals and families with ties and commitments to other communities, such as churches or fraternal and labor organizations, could still identify and interact with each other in varying ways. The individual was still locally, though only partially, interconnected with others.

The idea of the neighborhood as a community of limited liability combined with some unexpected consequences of urban renewal to give a new push to community organization. The slashing of expressways through residential areas, the razing of thousands of slum buildings, and the refurbishing of central business districts produced resentment among the central city residents whose neighborhoods were being wrecked. As early as 1953 the idea of mobilizing public opinion for more responsible urban renewal found fertile ground at the local level. Citizen participation began to be the watchword in renewal activities. Those who were convinced that citizen involvement was a basic ingredient in effecting urban improvement saw individual people as responsible citizens who brought improvement about and benefited by it. Such individuals were a prerequisite for the democratic functioning of mass society. The community of limited liability linked the individual, the local community, and the metropolis. Individuals may be the basic unit of social order, according to this view, but they were also able to be integrated into the civic network of communities.

Until 1968 observers had conceived of the city as a system capable of meeting the demands of most of its groups organized for the welfare of their constituents. Under these conditions people would behave in conformity with civic responsibility. The community of limited liability had a safety valve if one group's needs were not met: one could withdraw to another group to find security. After 1968 a crisis of confidence shook the metropolis; it was apparent the existing system was not working. First blacks, then white ethnics, women, gays, blue-collar and white-collar workers, consumers, taxpayers, seniors, and myriad others became aware of how the system seemed no longer to work to their advantage. In an age of less, it became harder to gain access to scarce resources and jobs; autonomy was harder to achieve. Community became a name for advocacy. Pluralism gave way to separatism. Each group sought to make itself self-sufficient. *Neighborhood* meant a group turned in upon itself.

Though we may be too close to recent events to divine trends now in the shaping stage, current thinking about neighborhoods builds on those earlier concepts of the city as a cluster of interlacing communities, the nongeographical community of limited liability, and the self-determining neighborhood. Some observers distinguish neighborhood from community, others focus on neighborhood social functions, still others on marks of viability. This chapter attempts to integrate these views into a more comprehensive understanding of *neighborhood*.

CONTEMPORARY PERSPECTIVES ON NEIGHBORHOOD

The Community vs. Political Unit Debate and Self-Definition

Some writers emphasize resident consciousness or identification with the physical place as a starting point in defining neighborhood. Others seek a more precise conceptualization based on numerous characteristics of the neighborhood as a social entity. The first set of views is more subjective and may be more compatible with a political perspective on the neighborhood; the second genre of studies is more objective and correlates with a concern for understanding neighborhood as community. Subjectivist and objectivist methods of defining neighborhood are not mutually exclusive, however, because even the hardest data is imbedded in perceptions of place and social mobility. These approaches are a matter of emphasis. In the former case, definition of the neighborhood is an imprecise consensus on its location by those who live there. More objective approaches look for homogeneous characteristics such as race, ethnicity, or socioeconomic status.

Milton Kotler provides a concise and often-quoted statement of how one might subjectively approach a definition of neighborhood:

The most sensible way to locate the neighborhood is to ask people where it is, for people spend much time fixing its boundaries. Gangs mark its turf. Old people watch for its new faces. Children figure out safe routes between home and school. People walk their dogs through their neighborhood, but rarely beyond it. Above all the neighborhood has a name: Hyde Park or Lake View in Chicago; Roxbury, Jamaica Plain, or Beacon Hill in Boston.[5]

This estimation of where one's neighborhood is includes more obvious boundaries such as expressways, major streets, or rivers, and a center, such as a park, a commercial district, a school, or a community center. Kotler puts the population range between 2,500 and 75,000 residents and the size of area between half a square mile and six square miles.

The matter of the neighborhood's exact geographic location is important for the same reason that municipalities require exactness in their boundary lines. Formal planning and governmental power, for example, to levy taxes, to make and implement public policy, or to provide services, extends to these lines and no further. Similarly, neighborhood organizations define their boundaries with precision primarily for political and logistical purposes.

The debate referred to in the heading, therefore, is rooted in differing concepts of what the neighborhood *ought to become*, rather than what it *is*. But common usage may hide these underlying differences; people frequently speak of *community* and *neighborhood* as if they were synonyms. Many turf-based associations, seeking to promote greater cohesiveness, call themselves community organizations instead of neighborhood organizations. *Community organizing* is an acceptable phrase for what neighborhood organizers do.

If we look first at the meaning of urban *community* we can see that it is something more than *neighborhood*. Whereas neighborhood has more neutral connotations, community summons up the deepest feelings and yearnings of the human soul. The neighborhood is often the place where people find community; this may be the source of the confusion. But the misunderstanding is more likely to flow from a view of the neighborhood as the mosaic of conflicting interests mentioned earlier, a condition that demands organization to bring about social cohesion and unification of ideals. In the words of Minneapolis writer and activist David Rubenstein, "that's what the neighborhood movement is about, a conscious attempt to build and preserve communities in the city." He continues on this theme:

Community is a word that has been overworked and exploited, but it remains the best word available to describe something basic about the way human beings traditionally have lived together. There are different ways of understanding community. Children understand it; the church understands it; it enters one's dreams, even the dreams of those who are born, live, and die without it . . .

Firsthand experience of community has become increasingly rare in the industrialized West (and East), but it is still common among ethnic groups in the city, in certain enclaves, among the poor when they are not totally beaten, and among various groups of people who have fallen into it or gotten it together for themselves.

It is essential for the development of community that there be some long-term security, that a specific terrain be securely held by the community.[6]

That *neighborhood* and *community* are not necessarily synonymous becomes clearer as one turns to observers who emphasize the neighborhood as a political unit. Besides Kotler, David Morris and Karl Hess are aware of this distinction. "There can be community without neighborhood consciousness," they write, "and there can also be neighborhood consciousness but little community."[7] Edward Schwartz, in commenting on value-conflicts in the neighborhood movement, describes adherents of the political view as "madisonian" in their outlook.[8] They assume a degree of homogeneity of social values among those in powerless neighborhoods. Therefore, the primary goal of organizing is not to create social cohesion but to gain power for the neighborhood: to establish economic reciprocity between citizens and institutions, efficiency and responsiveness in government services, and broadened participation in urban politics.

These differences in emphasis are not minor; they have led to considerable divergence in organizing strategies. The community view avoids conflict with outside institutions if possible; the political unit perspective recognizes conflict as inevitable and useful in bringing change about. Organizations that emphasize community are most concerned about their own processes of interaction, particularly as these enhance cooperative citizen involvement. They are limited historically to the social work approach to community organizing and are currently thought of as "mediating institutions."[9] Politically oriented organizations focus more on issues and less on building community. They hark back to the traditions of political activism, such as Saul Alinsky and the Communist party in depression-era Harlem.[10]

For a neighborhood to be a political entity, its residents must view it as a base from which to exert power. It must then be organized to exert power. This book presents evidence that many Havenot residents, with few other choices available in exploited declining neighborhoods, hold such a viewpoint, even though they may doubt their own potential to change things. But sociopolitical organization is rooted in the social structure and physical proximity. A political definition of *neighborhood* must therefore include a general analysis of neighborhood social function and type.

Neighborhood Social Functions and Typology

Rachelle Warren and Donald Warren analyze data from two major studies in Detroit's neighborhoods.[11] The data includes responses from 4,500 households in 59 local neighborhoods and interviews with 400 local activists. The Warrens dub their research method *neighborhood ethnography*, a "comparative-research technique based on face-to-face interaction and social network analysis within and outside of the neighborhood setting."[12]

According to their analysis, *neighborhood* performs six kinds of functions. The first is the opportunity for *sociability*, from front-porch visiting to block parties. A second function is the exertion of *interpersonal influence* through opinion-sharing, a sort of low-key, informal leadership. A third almost universally understood role of *neighbor* is the provision of *mutual aid* in time of need or emergency. A neighborhood also provides a setting for *organizing* to meet common concerns, on the block or beyond. Two other related functions of the local place are the opportunities for the *development of local pride* and the *achievement of status* among one's neighbors.

Common parlance often associates these functions with the people on the block or just around the corner. Fully one half of the people in the Warrens' studies thought of their neighborhoods primarily in this limited way. For the rest, the neighborhood was far larger than their block. It often coincided with the local elementary school district or reached beyond it. One-third of the Warrens' interviewees said they considered their neighborhood to extend "beyond walking distance." And even those who thought first only in terms of that which they see every day—their own block—were aware of their connections to the larger neighborhood setting. The six major functions are then by no means confined to the block but probably operate over a span of many blocks, for most people.

The Warrens' data leads them to the conclusion that although each neighborhood is unique, certain similar threads exist that allow them to be classified into types. They develop a typology of neighborhoods using three dimensions: identity, interaction, and linkage. *Identity* is a psychological dimension; it refers to how much people feel they belong to a neighborhood and share a common destiny with their neighbors. *Interaction* is a behavioral dimension; it describes how often and with how many neighbors people interact. *Linkage* is a more abstract structural dimension; it outlines the bridges that cross the neighborhood's boundaries, both in terms of local people's memberships in outside groups and in terms of those who bring news about the larger community back into the neighborhood.

These three main dimensions or variables can range in value from "low (-)" to "high ( )." For example, a single neighborhood could be scored as low in identity, low in interaction, and high in linkage. Using this descriptive procedure, the Warrens' data allows them to identify six basic types of neighborhoods. This analysis better approximates the richness and diversity of urban neighborhoods and avoids the stereotyping that often accompanies descriptions that use only class or ethnicity variables. While these latter dimensions may be vitally important, they do not provide the neighborhood organizer with enough insight to choose appropriate strategies.

On the other hand, these are neighborhood *types* or idealized abstractions. By no means do they exhaust the reality of actual neighborhoods, nor do they intend to. A given neighborhood may, in fact, partake of the characteristics of several of these categorizations.

The description of the six types of neighborhoods in Table 2.1 is arranged in a matrix, with each type scored on the three dimensions of identity, interaction and linkage.

These neighborhoods are different not only in superficial aspects, but also in the way their internal and external life reinforces or fails to reinforce the social functions necessary for neighborhood vitality. If a neighborhood organization is to be successful in promoting local defense, autonomy, and improvement, it must adapt its strategies to the type of neighborhood it serves. In a truly anomic neighborhood, for example, a local organizing effort would have to start by building internal interaction, whereas in a parochial type, construction of linkage or bridges outside the community would take high priority. In general, however, if the neighborhood organization chooses issues that flow from either turf-consciousness or feelings of powerlessness, it stands a chance of becoming a vehicle for meeting those important social needs itemized earlier: to socialize and to extend mutual aid, to feel local pride and achievement of status, to exert influence among one's fellows, and to cooperate in organizing to address commonly felt concerns.

The Continuum Approach: Marks of Viability

A third way to think about a neighborhood is to gauge its potential for revitalization or viability along a continuum. Anthony Downs categorizes neighborhoods as being in one of five stages: (1) stable, (2) minor decline, (3) clear decline, (4) heavily deteriorated, and (5) unhealthy and nonviable.[13] This surface approach emphasizes the visible character of the neighborhood. It assumes that neighborhood viability is closely correlated with its outward appearance. Although this assumption may be warranted, there are more sophisticated marks of viability.

According to Sandra Schoenberg and Patricia Rosenbaum, the word *viable*, applied to neighborhoods, means "those in which residents can control the local social order."[14] Kotler emphasizes self-governance, Morris and Hess focus on self-reliance, Warren and Warren outline a variety of social modalities as a basis for distinguishing types of neighborhoods. Schoenberg and Rosenbaum, in their study of five diverse

Table 2.1
Description of Six Types of Neighborhoods

TYPE	IDENTITY	INTERACTION	LINKAGE
Integral: This means that the neighborhood meshes with other institutions in the larger community. It is a cosmopolitan as well as a local center where residents are in close contact with each other and share many concerns, they also participate in activities of the larger community. Although it often has a number of middle-class professionals, it may also be an inner-city or blue-collar industrial community. This type of neighborhood is relatively rare. It exerts a good deal of control over directions in which it changes.	+	+	+
Parochial: This neighborhood has a strong ethnic identity or homogeneous character. It is self-contained and independent of the larger community. It has ways to screen out what does not conform to its own norms.	+	+	-
Diffuse: This is an often homogeneous setting, such as a new subdivision or an inner-city housing project. The residents have much in common, but there is no active internal life because neighbors are not involved with each other. And, as a corollary, there is little connection to the life of the larger urban community. This is a neighborhood vulnerable to decline.	+	-	-
Stepping-Stone: The activity of this more uncommon neighborhood resembles "musical chairs." People participate in neighborhood activities not because they identify with the neighborhood, but because they want to "get ahead" in a career or some other non-local point of destination.	-	+	+
Transitory: This type of neighborhood is commonly understood. It is a place where population change has been or is occurring. Residents break up into clusters of "old timers" and "new comers" and view each other with suspicion or hostility. As a result little collective action or organization takes place. On the other hand much neighborhood organizing has been successful in such locales.	-	-	+
Anomic: This is really a nonneighborhood. There is great social distance between people. There are no protective barriers whereby it can resist change from outside influences. It lacks a capacity to mobilize from within for common actions. This is not necessarily a poor neighborhood. It could be housed in luxury condominiums or exist in a fast-growing suburban area. This neighborhood is the most vulnerable of all to decline, because it is the most difficult to organize.	-	-	-

Source: Reprinted with permission from Rachelle Warren and David Warren, *The Neighborhood Organizer's Handbook* (Notre Dame, IN: University of Notre Dame Press, 1977), pp. 96-97. Copyright © 1977.

neighborhoods in the heart of St. Louis, provide indicators of the degree to which the residents exert control over the social order of their neighborhood. The more these indicators are present, the more viable is the neighborhood. The authors state that the viability of a neighborhood requires four things:

1. Resident agreement on public behavior
2. Development of an organizational network
3. Creation of linkages to outside economic and political resources
4. Internal exchange relationships to resolve conflict

What are the indicators of these conditions? Resident agreement on public behavior is measured by increased public surveillance, perception of the existence of social networks, agreements on garbage disposal, and shared use of public space, indoors as well as out. The existence of formal organizational networks is marked by a rise over time in the number of new neighborhood organizations, such as block clubs or historic preservation committees, and by stability or rise in membership in older organizations. Linkages to outside resource givers are demonstrated by increases in applications for outside funding (public and private), and increases in actual private funding to neighborhood organizations. The development of internal exchange among conflicting groups is proven by the existence of a neighborhood organization over at least two years, its accomplishment of at least one goal as defined by residents, and the congruence of goals between neighborhood organizations and outside resource givers.

Emphasis on marks of neighborhood viability has ramifications for those organizing for its rebirth. According to this view, the neighborhood association should target those tasks that will most enhance the residents' sense that they exert social control where they live. Issue areas, then, will tend to be crime, schools, and family disorganization. Such a focus is more compatible with the *community* perspective mentioned earlier and may lead to strategies that emphasize internal cooperation and deemphasize external conflict with institutions. One last point on the continuum approach merits mention: how should we think about neighborhoods on the low end, the well-publicized disaster areas? Should we throw up our hands and leave them to the bulldozers, or can they be resuscitated somehow?

Schoenberg and Rosenbaum remark that some urban residential areas are *not* neighborhoods. They are merely "collections of streets with no associational ties." To be a neighborhood, they assert, an area must be a "unit with some level of social intergration." It must be

an area in which a common bounded territory is named and identified by residents, at least one institution is identified in the area, and at least one common tie is shared. This common tie may be shared by commercial facilities, public spaces, or social networks.[15]

Warren and Warren also allow that certain areas are nonneighborhoods. Such a position can overlook the *potential* of these areas to develop social linkages or associational ties. It also neglects to tell us how many of these types of areas we can expect to find.

The public mind sees many more such nonneighborhoods, particularly in inner cities, than there actually are. The temptation is to write them off, as the updated guidelines for designation of Community Development Block Grant target areas have done. The model applied was that of *triage*, in which attention is given to the warwounded who appear able to respond to treatment while the worse off are left to die.

The triage analogy limps because there are basic differences between a person's life cycle and a neighborhood's. The Schoenberg and Rosenbaum marks of neighborhood viability do not provide exact measures of the point at which a neighborhood becomes a nonneighborhood. The Downs model of neighborhood health, proceeding along a continuum from stable to severely deteriorated, implies that the worst areas can be reborn. People die, but neighborhoods can be recycled with more or less effort. There is no justification for an either-or dichotomy in defining neighborhood. While there are residents, there is hope.

Neighborhood Typed by Levels of Identification

In an attempt to type neighborhoods utilizing both quantitative and perceptual indicators, William Hojnacki classifies them by "levels of identification."[16] His review of recent studies leads him to acknowledge that quantitative statements about inhabitants or territory are incomplete. In his view, these variables are "dependent on a set of residential attitudes that (in turn) determine a particular level of neighborhood identification."[17]

What are these residential attitudes? A first one is the distinction residents make between their own and nearby neighborhoods which they perceive as different from and usually less desirable than theirs. A second attitude has to do with the future of their area as they see it. A third attitude, the degree of threat they perceive, correlates with their willingness to defend their turf. All of these feelings can be summarized under satisfaction with one's own neighborhood and perception of threat to that neighborhood. These attitudes, then, both affect and are affected by the physical characteristics and demographic makeup of the neighborhood.

Hojnacki identifies three types of neighborhoods: emergent, traditional, and immediate. Levels of resident identification with these neighborhoods differ according to the interplay between attitudes and area characteristics. The emergent neighborhood is thus a large, diversely populated area with no commonly accepted boundaries, no need for mediating institutions, and low threat coupled with high optimism about the area's future.

The traditional neighborhood is smaller, encompassed by clearly defined boundaries, homogeneity of population, high threat levels and moderate satisfaction. The immediate neighborhood may be thought of as a pocket within the first two. It is the smallest neighborhood, is homogeneous in population, and has a high threat level to go with low optimism about its future. Table 2.2 summarizes these types.

While Hojnacki's classification scheme lacks descriptive variety, it does link quantitative data and resident attitudes together in a way that enables one to predict whether any given area would organize to gain political power. The whole analysis is predicated on the idea that neighborhood is a place that protects individual choices of lifestyle; it implies built-in "defense mechanisms against threats to commonly identified life-styles of the neighborhood residents."[18] The words *protect, defense,* and *threat* conjure a military image, a fortress against undesirable change. If too much negative change occurs, the neighborhood is said to be defeated, a place "where the defense mechanisms have broken down, the strategies have failed, and the territory has been overrun."[19] Where the level of identification implies a feeling of threat, boundaries are clarified and organizing begins to build an *esprit de corps*. Apparently Hojnacki feels that neighborhood organizations ("mediating institutions") are likely to exist only in traditional neighborhoods and that

Table 2.2
Neighborhood Characteristics According to Neighborhood Type

Neighborhood Type By Level of Perception	Neighborhood Physical Characteristics	Resident Social Networks	Resident Attitudes
Emergent	Very large area No defined boundaries Diverse population	No mediating institutions (neighborhood organizations) Not much subgroup inter-action	Low threat High optimism about future of neighborhood
Traditional	Medium size Defined boundaries More homogeneous in population charactics Fairly rare islands within metropolitan area's emergent neighborhoods	Neighborhood organizations Organized subgroup inter-action "We-They" feelings about other neighborhoods	High threat Moderate optimism about future of neighborhood
Immediate	Very small pockets within other two types Homogeneous population characteristics	Little subgroup interaction No formal neighborhood organization Personal interactions	Very high threat Pessimism about future of neighborhood

Source: Adapted from William Hojnacki, "What Is A Neighborhood?," *Social Policy*, September/October 1979, pp. 47-52.

their tactics by implication will be conflictive. Such a view squares with the idea of neighborhood as a political unit but it also encompasses *community* in its emphasis on internal *esprit de corps*.

We have considered several ways of understanding what a neighborhood is. It can be envisioned as a locus for community-building or as a basic unit in the governance of our society. One can use its diverse social functions and interaction to differentiate neighborhood types. Neighborhood can be visualized along a spectrum ranging from physically well-maintained to rundown and blasted out, viable to unlivable, or defensible to defeated. It can be typed by level of resident identification with it.

All of these perspectives act as overlays which, when placed upon each other, give a coherent picture of the neighborhood as a setting for neighborhood organization. The kinds of neighborhoods most likely to see formally active neighborhood organizations will be those which exhibit the following characteristics:

1. They are of moderate size in the urban environment, several square blocks to perhaps a square mile.

2. Their boundaries are fairly clear.

3. Their inhabitants are somewhat homogeneous in background, lifestyle, and income.

4. Residents perceive the neighborhood as a good place to live, at least more desirable than bordering neighborhoods. Their neighborhood in fact may be quite deteriorated, however.

5. Residents feel threats to their neighborhood's stability.

6. Residents are somewhat optimistic about the future of their neighborhood; this optimism is based on a sense that they control the neighborhood social order to an extent.

7. There are preexisting organized subgroupings, although they may interact very little with each other.

Neighborhoods are not frozen in time. They are as dynamic as the cities they comprise. No perspective on what a neighborhood is would be complete without an understanding of the ways it changes in response to internal and external forces. The next section draws an explanatory model of neighborhood change that includes demographic and perceptual, social, political, and economic variables.

TOWARD A COMPREHENSIVE MODEL OF
NEIGHBORHOOD CHANGE

Limits on Local Control

A model is a way to explain the structure or the function of a complicated phenomenon. A physician uses a mental model of the human body when making a physical examination; upon discovering something that does not fit that model, the physician is alerted to investigate further. Social scientists used to think of the city in terms of a biological organism that had different parts integrated with one another. These vital organs first were the industrial and commercial centers of town. Later, residential neighborhoods took on some importance as parts of the city. Then cities grew rapidly in size, sent sprawling over the landscape by new highways and autos traveling on them. The faces of urban populations were of every hue and class. The social order seemed to arise more from the interplay of all these different individuals rather than the groups, such as one found in neighborhoods, that they belonged to. The biological model went out of favor. The past three decades have witnessed the rediscovery of local community within the city. Current views emphasize the viability of a city's neighborhoods as a precondition for the viability of the city itself. The biological model has returned.

Yet there are new complexities. Some neighborhoods are clearly distinctive; most are not. The ways of describing how neighborhood communities fulfill social needs have multiplied. Cultural changes have brought uncertainty to the discussion of political arrangements; ideology seems out of focus. The economic systems of yesteryear have undergone mutation from the pressure of technological innovation.

If the biological approach to modeling has any utility at the municipal level, it should retain its validity at the neighborhood level. The word *viable*, however, shifts its meanings when applied to city and to neighborhood. A city is more clearly self-contained. Granted current urban dependencies on national and international politics and economics, one can envision a city on a plain, standing alone. At the same time, one has difficulty envisioning a neighborhood in such a condition. By analogy one can easily visualize the human individual alone, but not just a human liver. Yet given this difference in functioning, there is a reciprocity. While the life of every person depends on the life of her or his liver, the liver depends on the person as well. If the person dies, for whatever reason, the liver dies, too.

Although this comparison may seem odious in its simplicity, it has meaning for neighborhood change. Even where residents' perception of their neighborhood and the commercial activity there is highly localized, the neighborhood cannot be self-sufficient. The most clearly accepted boundaries and the most homogeneous internal populations still do not make the neighborhood independent. It is much more a dependent entity than the city itself. It is more sensitive by a large factor to lending and business decisions, market perceptions, and cultural prejudices than cities are.

The case is made obvious by the fact that people and businesses can migrate across the neighborhood borders and still receive the benefits of inclusion in the metropolis. When the excursion of such resources occurs in certain neighborhoods, they decline. In turn, they become a drain on the city's resources. The city hurts. Conversely, if the city itself is injured by overall job or population losses, the neighborhoods feel the effects painfully.

This understanding of the particular sensitivity of neighborhoods to larger influences must inform concepts of neighborhood power and control. As the neighborhood is more dependent, then resident control over its social, political, and economic order is more tenuous. On the other hand, there must be some degree of local control. Neighborhood associations have experimented in recent years with ways to extend this control where they claim that it has eroded. The first assumption leading to a comprehensive model of neighborhood change owes a debt to biology. It holds that neighborhoods cannot be self-reliant entities. The second assumption appears a paradox. Because neighborhoods possess some characteristics of small community, such as turf identification, social networks, and internal commerce, they can function *analogously* as political units; they can organize inhabitants formally to exert influence on neighborhood social and economic order. Certainly not all neighborhoods form associations for such purposes, but a useful model of the neighborhood dynamic should include an analysis of factors that lead to the emergence of neighborhood associations. Probably most neighborhoods in the U.S. have seen some such organization develop over the past decade or so.

Previous Models of Neighborhood Change

Any model that seeks to interpret or explain some data is shaped by the data chosen for study. That is, every model has a particular perspective, a built-in bias related to the type of data selected. It could not be otherwise. The value of the ongoing discussion is that it builds an increasingly comprehensive view. The psychological and sociological dimensions of shared sense of belonging to a neighborhood and social interaction within that community offer one set of variables. The political, economic, and social bridges linking the neighborhood to the world outside provide another set. The abstract institutional forces that shape land use, just as subterranean geologic powers push up mountains and rive valleys, form a third set. All of these energies surge within a swirling galaxy of cultural and technological change. The literature on neighborhood revitalization that has emerged in the past decade has sought this comprehensiveness in its paradigms.

Roger S. Ahlbrandt and James V. Cunningham outline three classical models of neighborhood change in their 1979 study of six neighborhoods in Pittsburgh.[20] The first general model is the *ecological*, which emphasizes socioeconomic status and demographic characteristics of a population within a larger geographic area. Three submodels exist under this heading: (1) the *spatial*, which plotted these characteristics along lines stretching outward from a point at the city's center; (2) the *sociological*, which concentrated on such indicators as density, invasions, and segregation; and (3) the *economic*, which focused on real estate prices and transportation costs. A second traditional model, the *subcultural*, analyzed social networks that affected resultant coping behaviors and neighborhood stability. The third classical model, *neighborhood decline*, examined the institutional forces, particularly lenders, that affected the neighborhood.

A Proposed Comprehensive Neighborhood Change Model

Contemporary conceptions of *neighborhood* add nuances to these models, such as a neighborhood life cycle implied by a continuum and the mutuality between perception and physical maintenance implied in levels of identification. A comprehensive paradigm of change should incorporate all these views and the evidence on which they are based.

The following untested model, therefore, includes several derived elements. First, there is reciprocity between the neighborhood's physical condition and the inhabitants' perception of it. This interaction can influence a neighborhood in either direction toward decline or recovery.

Second, the neighborhood is extraordinarily sensitive to outside economic, political, and cultural forces, especially as these forces manifest themselves in local institutions. Third, levels of resident identification do not necessarily result in organization for defensive purposes. Only when the area is of a particular size and resident attitudes combine commitment with feelings of being threatened—a "critical" state of consciousness—is formal organization likely to occur. Fourth, the outside forces mentioned above must be able to provide the resources that the neighborhood organizes to obtain. For example, lenders must have capital to reinvest, local government must have public dollars to meet demands, and cultural values must support localized organizing.

Traditional models of neighborhood change would be complete with only the first two elements, internal reciprocity and external sensitivity. The comprehensive model adds resident *critical consciousness* and a supportive environment as essential to a fuller understanding of the mechanisms of neighborhood revitalization. These latter ideas deserve elaboration.

Resident critical consciousness is a complicated phenomenon. It is not mere awareness of the potential decline of one's neighborhood nor a combination of this with satisfaction in living there. It involves these and more, such as the belief that the neighborhood is defensible. But the main ingredient is what Ahlbrandt and Cunningham point out in their Pittsburgh neighborhood study: commitment.

Ahlbrandt and Cunningham were concerned with how to build or repair the social fabric of the community. Therefore, they examined the relation between citizen attitudes about their own neighborhoods and change or stability in those neighborhoods. Assuming that the former and the latter influence each other to some extent, the researchers sought further, to learn what factors increased commitment to and satisfaction with the neighborhood. They discovered that *commitment to* does not imply *satisfaction with* the neighborhood.

Conversely, satisfaction, with either neighborhood conditions or public services, did not mean that the resident was committed to staying in the neighborhood. This finding held true despite differences in race and income, and regardless of whether one owned a home. One's willingness to stay went hand in hand with one's sense of community and the health of the social fabric.

Another important finding of the Ahlbrandt and Cunningham study is that *willingness* to invest in the neighborhood by making home repairs is conditioned not only by adequacy of income, but also by commitment to the neighborhood. They conclude that public policy should support the neighborhood organization as the promoter of social fabric, especially since public resources, on which public investment strategies are based, appear to be on the wane.

Critical consciousness, the foundation of effective neighborhood organizing, is then a function of the social fabric of the community, the connectedness one has with it and the tenacity one has to stay and protect it. Yet this posture is also a function of the neighborhood's defensibility: its human resources, social networks, and degree of overall health.

An environment that supports neighborhood organizations extends well beyond that neighborhood. There are enough dollars to revitalize neighborhoods; the social surplus of the United States is staggering. Cultural values, however, have supported gross inequities in its distribution. Chapter 3 investigates whether this most basic but intangible outside force will evolve to allow enough redistribution of resources to bring back the nation's declining neighborhoods.

Figure 2.1 summarizes the proposed comprehensive model of neighborhood change. At the center is the neighborhood itself, pictured as a wheel that can revolve in two directions. One way is decline; the other is revitalization. Outside conditions can send it spinning either way, but once in motion the internal interaction between resident perceptions and physical area characteristics tend to exaggerate that motion. They also can hold it stable, however, when external forces are in abeyance. Levels of resident identification appear as a function of both physical environment and resident feelings about their place in it. If it is home, appears threatened by decline, and is relatively defensible, its inhabitants will reach a stage of critical consciousness that may lead to creation of a formal neighborhood organization. This organization will then operate on local institutions embodying outside forces to redirect more of their resources into the neighborhood. The activities of such organization reinforce the social fabric and lead to economic and physical revitalization to the extent that the outside forces, particularly cultural values, support them. Since these latter cultural crosscurrents are so important to the nascent neighborhood organization, they will be discussed in Chapter 3, as a conclusion to our discussion of settings for community organizing.

Figure 2.1

Proposed Comprehensive Model of Neighborhood Change

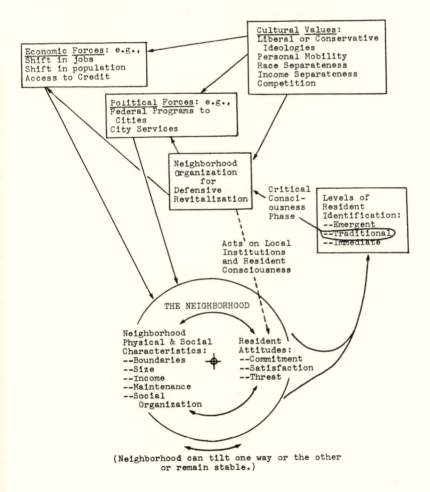

Economic Forces: e.g.,
Shift in jobs
Shift in population
Access to Credit

Cultural Values:
Liberal or Conservative
  Ideologies
Personal Mobility
Race Separateness
Income Separateness
Competition

Political Forces: e.g.,
Federal Programs to
  Cities
City Services

Neighborhood
Organization
  for
Defensive
Revitalization

Critical
Consci-
ousness
Phase

Levels of
Resident
Identification:
--Emergent
--Traditional
--Immediate

Acts on Local
Institutions
and Resident
Consciousness

THE NEIGHBORHOOD

Neighborhood
Physical & Social
Characteristics:
--Boundaries
--Size
--Income
--Maintenance
--Social
  Organization

Resident
Attitudes:
--Commitment
--Satisfaction
--Threat

(Neighborhood can tilt one way or the other
  or remain stable.)

NOTES

1. Zane Miller, "The Role and Concept of Neighborhood in American Cities," in *Community Organization for Urban Social Change: A Historical Perspective*, ed. Robert Fisher and Peter Romanofsky (Westport, CT: Greenwood Press, 1981), 3–32.

2. B.J. Widick, *Detroit: City of Race and Class Violence* (Chicago: Quadrangle Books, 1972).

3. Saul D. Alinsky, *Reveille for Radicals* (New York: Vintage, 1965), 184.

4. Saul D. Alinsky, *Rules for Radicals* (New York: Vintage, 1972), 120.

5. Milton Kotler, *Neighborhood Government: The Local Foundations of Political Life* (Indianapolis: Bobbs Merrill, 1969), 64–65.

6. David Rubenstein, "The Neighborhood Movement," *The Progressive*, March 1981, 27.

7. David Morris and Karl Hess, *Neighborhood Power: The New Localism* (Boston: Beacon Press, 1975), 22.

8. Edward Schwartz, "Neighborhoodism: A Conflict in Values," *Social Policy* 9 (March-April 1979); 8–14.

9. For an overview of the social work vs. political activism debate, see the Introduction in Fisher and Romanofsky, pp. xi-xviii. Mediating institutions are treated in Peter Berger and Richard Newhaus, *To Empower People: The Role of Mediating Structures in Public Policy* (Washington, DC: American Enterprise Institute, 1977). See also James Stever, "Contemporary Neighborhood Theories: Integration vs. Romance and Reaction," *Urban Affairs Quarterly* 13 (March 1978), 263–84.

10. Mark Naison, "Harlem Communists and the Politics of Black Protest," in Fisher and Romanofsky, pp. 89–126.

11. Rachelle Warren and Donald Warren, *The Neighborhood Organizer's Handbook* (Notre Dame: University of Notre Dame Press, 1977).

12. Warren and Warren, p. 4.

13. Anthony Downs, *Neighborhoods and Urban Development* (Washington, DC: The Brookings Institution, 1981), 5.

14. Sandra Schoenberg and Patricia Rosenbaum, *Neighborhoods That Work: Sources for Viability in the Inner City* (New Brunswick, NJ: Rutgers, 1980), 6.

15. Schoenberg and Rosenbaum, pp. 5–6.

16. William P. Hojnacki, "What Is a Neighborhood?," *Social Policy*, September-October 1979, 47–52.

17. Hojnacki, p. 47.

18. Hojnacki, p. 5o.

19. Hojnacki, p. 5o.

20. Roger S. Ahlbrandt and James V. Cunningham, *A New Public Policy for Neighborhood Preservation* (New York: Praeger, 1979), chap. 3.

3

DEMOCRATIC CULTURE AND LEFTIST IDEOLOGICAL REMNANTS

The emergence of the neighborhood movement and allied citizen initiatives during the past decade represents the return of the citizen to public decision making. Yet to make this interpretation is to rely on a set of assumptions about American beliefs, values, and cultural trends that may or may not be warranted. As the model of neighborhood change (developed in the last chapter) implied, cultural values and ideals form a background for embryonic neighborhood organizations every bit as important as their cities and neighborhoods. Just as water is basic to swimming fish, the beliefs and attitudes of mainstream America are essential to an understanding of the rise of the neighborhood organization. Furthermore, its future cannot be imagined without this gestalt.

Democratic culture is not merely a background, however. It is the warp and woof of the neighborhood organizations themselves. To investigate the attitudes on Main Street is to look simultaneously at the ideals of the people organizing Main Street's block clubs. One assumes some degree of congruence between the two; successful organization demands it. Therefore, one approach to the matter of the current cultural climate for neighborhood organizing is to pose two fundamental questions with which grassroots activists continually struggle. First, is their belief in people fortified by an emerging New Populism? Second, how can organized protest be used as a tactic to bring about progressive change within the constraints of U.S. culture? The first question investigates whether there are trends in mainstream U.S. culture that are incubating and nourishing a new ideology of citizen participation. The second probes a more specific area, really the residue of leftist tradition in community organizing: can the oppressed masses, having seen their oppression, throw it off by militant action? First we look at the core U.S. culture, then at a particularly important ideological perspective that influences current organizing practice.

The section on neighborhood ideology discusses whether contemporary organizing in Havenot communities can simultaneously effect the political education of the residents and channel their outrage into constructive action sustained over a lengthy period. Leftist tradition holds that it can, but there is new disagreement at every step, including even that neighborhood organizing must move beyond this tradition. The second part of this chapter seeks to resolve these differences and establish a coherent link between contemporary U.S. culture and the neighborhood movement. Although the investigation provides no final answers, it is valuable as a bridge to the future from the values of the present.

TOWARD A NEW POPULISM

Belief in People

At first blush, the literature on citizen participation seems to divide itself into pessimistic observations on the limitations of organizing and upbeat views by those who envision such work as the last best hope. Yet the division is really not between pessimists and optimists; virtually everyone who writes about community organization, citizen participation, grassroots coalition, or public interest groups, shares a deep-seated idealism, an assumption that each person reaches a fuller state of human existence as he or she participates in community life. This external community role is a political one. It includes the act of informed voting, but it views the participation of the person in political life as a regular activity, not limited to the ballot. We may choose our political leaders, they say, but we ourselves are the true leaders. "The Voice of the People is the Voice of God," inscribed over courthouse doors, reflects this concept. To believe in the people is to believe in their collective intelligence, their potential for right action, their perfectibility.

The debate over the validity of this belief has been raging in the United States since the time of John Adams and Thomas Jefferson. Jefferson repeatedly challenged Adams's protection of what he took to be a natural aristocracy of males with property and education. Jefferson railed against the idea that the people are not to be trusted, that if they gained control, they would be as tyrannical and cruel as any king. Their ordinary condition is not depravity, Jefferson said, although he admitted that they did not always do what was just and good. In commenting on this debate, sociologist Rodman Webb stated that Jefferson's view was that if human beings were organized properly, they were "capable of civic brotherhood, intelligence, justice, and kindly discourse." But Jefferson was no dreamy-eyed romantic, Webb continued,

Although far-reaching, Jefferson's faith in human nature was not unlimited. He understood that the moral sense of human beings could be stunted by deprivation and misuse. Just as a human limb will atrophy if not exercised, so will moral capacity be crippled if not put into action. If a people are poorly governed; if they are denied a voice in their own role; if they are deprived of the information and education needed for warranted judgments; if they are pushed around by tyrants, distrusted by those in power, or kept vulnerable by poverty, their moral sense will diminish. The social bonds of community will decay.[1]

Jefferson's perspective accounted for the imperfect humans we experience in our cities, while at the same time it placed the source of hope for improvement in these very people themselves. The Jeffersonian legacy is the central pillar of contemporary community organizing. Activists intuitively believe that organizing among Havenots is the most effective rehabilitation therapy for citizenship and fuller human life. They have seen what little change social service agencies have accomplished by "doing for" the poor.[2]

Community organizing relies on the belief that Havenots can be brought to understand and throw off their oppression through collective action. Alinsky stated that understanding and acting are mutually reinforcing:

It is when people have a genuine opportunity to act and to change conditions that they begin to think their problems through—then they show their competence, raise the right questions, seek special professional counsel and look for the answers. Then you begin to realize that believing in people is not just a romantic myth.[3]

For Alinsky, as for most activists, believing in people is justified by experience, even though this faith may be sorely tested at times. Oppressed and powerless people may know that they are oppressed, but they frequently cope with their condition in unproductive and self-defeating ways. Throughout his writings, Alinsky cites examples of people discovering the power they could exert through collective action. This kind of belief in people reflects a faith that the individual will grow (the current phrase is *become empowered*) precisely to the extent that he or she participates in collective action in the political arena. It is a trust founded on the social nature of humans: connect us to each other properly and we thrive; sever us through suppression and we wither. To throw off this bondage, we must unite.

While philosophers still disagree with each other on the precise boundaries of human perfectibility, there is some evidence that a new populist ideology is evolving, one in which both liberals and conservatives can find a place. But whether this ideology may be the basis for a new political platform depends on its acceptance by much more of society.

Ideology is imbedded in culture, that complexus of knowledge, beliefs, customs, laws, habits, and expressions that is the social world humans build. The core of U.S. culture consists of those beliefs and values that virtually all U.S citizens take for granted. Any generalizations about evolving ideology have to rest on a demonstration that some of these core cultural values are changing or at least becoming tolerant of such ideology.

What cultural changes are occurring, then, that would support an ideology of much broader citizen participation, a kind of New Populism? Since it may be easier to identify cultural elements that blunt or oppose such a perspective, I will address them first.

Cultural Obstacles to New Populism

Martin Carnoy and Derek Shearer explored in their recent book, *Economic Democracy*, the feasibility of greater citizen participation in the U.S. economic system.[4] The authors accepted as a well-established value that U.S. citizens have the right to participate in the political system by voting, although even current practice does not conform perfectly to the value, as demonstrated by the mild debate about extending the Voting Rights Act. The question for them is whether there is a developing awareness that citizens should be much more directly involved in the *economic* decision-making process. Are we as a people becoming desirous for a *democracy of production,* rather than merely a *democracy of consumption?* they ask. To be sure, individual competition, ambition, and striving for success are still sacred cows in the pastures of the meritocracy myth. The fatalism of Havenots is difficult to slough off, although the idea of a culture of poverty—patterns of behavior that keep people poor even if their environment is improved—has been largely debunked.[5] And the relative affluence of most Americans numbs the urge for social change and keeps warm the fantasy of superabundance, though, at the same time, we seem to be anxious about scarcity.[6]

Carnoy and Shearer do not provide survey data to answer their own questions; they assume that our capitalist tradition will continue to emphasize consumption and an aversion to government-oriented solutions to social problems. They suspect that hierarchical labor unions will continue to function schizophrenically: trying to protect their workers while simultaneously delivering them docilely to the bosses. The absence of a strong labor party in U.S. history bodes ill in their view for quickened democracy in the workplace. Yet their entire book is a collection of case studies in such democracy that now exist. The cases are not major movements, but they do provide evidence of nuclei for cultural change.

Harry Boyte outlines cultural obstacles in slightly different terms.[7] In his view, a new corporate or *technetronic* culture seems to be growing while the old democratic culture erodes. Career takes precedence over relationships; meritocracy over egalitarianism; the rights of property over the rights of persons; elite governance over direct participation. To be a worthwhile citizen in the cultural shift, one must be a consumer, a client helped by specialists and professionals, an object reducible to a computer card. Individual autonomy in the corporate culture withers away.

Boyte's is not a recent insight. One of Kurt Vonnegut's earliest novels, *Player Piano* (1952) is built entirely on this theme of the corporate culture. Webb supports Boyte's contentions with recent polls that indicate a *new privatism* is developing, whereby many individuals withdraw from public involvement because they are unable to cope with the public sphere.[8] According to Webb, they now seek satisfaction more in themselves than in their social roles within the community, the workplace, and the family. These social roles have become an increasing source of personal anxiety, and the mediating institutions that help people cope have also come upon bad times.

Despite the sad fact that neighborhood organizations can be and often are reactionary, racist, and anti-progressive as a result, many people in

neighborhoods across the country are resisting the powerful cultural
tides that threaten to drown their autonomy and overwhelm their uniqueness. Where this resistance is most effective, it binds them more closely
to their communities and forms the fertile soil for the growth of a true
democratic culture.

Seeds of Cultural Change

Sociologist Jessie Bernard contended that when consciousness of
cultural core values heightens, changes in them are already well under
way.[9] Economic forces have come into play that are making us reex-
amine the old nostrums. Economic growth based on cheap energy and
raw materials seems no longer viable. Inflation, rising taxes and interest
rates, and ever higher unemployment are undermining our real income.
Homeownership, that cornerstone of middle-class aspiration, now has
wealth as a prerequisite.

Dislocation in the old cultural core is evident in other ways. Increased
drug use among the young, corrosion of the work ethic, reduced inter-
generational commitment, the rise of the New Right, and a general
increase in worrying are all documented in recent polls.[10] A 1982 Harris
poll indicated heightened alienation across many sectors of American
society. In 1966, 45 percent of the people polled agreed with the statement, "The rich are getting richer and the poor are getting poorer"; in
1982, 72 percent agreed—a near record level. In 1966, 37 percent felt
that "What I think doesn't count anymore"; in 1982, the overall figure
was 65 percent, and it was even higher among blacks and people aged
18 to 30 years. Even the speedup in the pace of change itself due to
technological innovation underlies the transmutation of American values, as Alvin Toffler was at pains to show in his well-known *Future
Shock* (1971).

What is the evidence that the seeds of a democratic culture are growing? Boyte points to the following:

1. an increase in volunteerism among Americans over 14 years of age from
   24 million who averaged 5.3 hours every week in 1965 to 37 million who
   gave 9 hours per week in 1974.
2. a flourishing of neighborhood and grassroots newspapers.
3. an increase in urban gardening.
4. a social justice perspective beginning to show in even fundamentalist religions.

5. a 1977 *Christian Science Monitor* poll on neighborhood activism that indicated (a) that nearly three quarters of the population believed in antiredlining legislation, (b) that most respondents felt voluntary associations were more active in helping cities and neighborhoods than government or big business, and (c) that 85 percent took pride in their neighborhoods, often *because* they were racially diverse.[11]

Mother Jones magazine summarized a series of Louis Harris polls from 1966 to 1978 that suggested a liberalizing trend in race relations and a growing distrust of big business despite the media's touting of the rise of the political right at the same time.[12] A recent Daniel Yankelovich study concludes that the Me Decade is over, citing as evidence a shift to commitment (engaging in activities "to create closer bonds with neighbors, co-religionists, co-workers or others who form a community,")[13] by 50 percent of Americans surveyed. A bitter cultural struggle is being silently fought between *meism* or *privatism* on one side and commitment on the other, with signs that a new set of norms embodying greater social connectedness is emerging.

Stuart Langton underscores that fact that the presence of two quite different cultural trends in the same time period is not at all contradictory. "As evidence of citizen apathy mounts," he writes, "so does evidence indicating a democratic resurgence."[14] Meism, privatism, or social withdrawal is only one response to the growing political alienation in the U.S. The other is a return to the commitment of community roles. Bruce Stokes, a senior researcher at Worldwatch Institute in Washington, DC, documents a wide diversity of forms of this commitment in his recent book, *Helping Ourselves: Local Solutions to Global Problems.*[15] It is estimated that there are three-quarters of a million self-help groups in the U.S., with a total membership of 15 million. These groups constitute a much larger set than neighborhood organizations. The oldest, Alcoholics Anonymous, is the model for countless others formed to meet the medical, psychological, or physical needs of specific groups.[16]

Outlines of the New Ideology

There are signs that a new democratic culture is emerging in the U.S. Whether it will become embedded in the cultural core remains to be seen, although its adherents will press on under that assumption.

The potential for ideological innovation exists to the extent that there is support for it in the cultural core. Such support focuses on the mediating structures of our society: the family, the church, the voluntary association, and the neighborhood. These are the human (or smaller) scale institutions through which we learn to cope with the bureaucratic public sphere. The elements of the new ideology are principally an exhaustion or disillusionment with privatism and a desire for more control over one's life, control that has been arrogated by the great power structures of society. This neopopulism is different from the old middle-class conservative emphasis on private property rights,[17] although it is still rooted in a concern for the protection of one's turf. But the conservative emphasis on local autonomy, if not self-rule, continues to be present in a wide range of cries for community control, decentralization, and power to the people. The neighborhood organization as a voluntary association is a principal mediating institution through which these essentially conservative values are being reappraised.

Liberals, on the other hand, have traditionally sought a government activity that enhances the inherent capabilities of every citizen. This concern for the down-and-out found form in the social programs of the New Deal and the War on Poverty. Although faith remains that government can offset the forces of inequity built into capitalist society, frustration with the ways that government has gone about it is widespread. As a result, the Democratic coalition of the past 50 years has splintered, its guiding principles no longer clear. Big government has become a government of, by, and for the corporation, not the people. A return to control by the people is a common theme demonstrated somewhat by current political rhetoric but more by tax revolts across the land. There is a share of meanspiritedness in this trend because the U.S. is a low-tax nation, but many liberals have joined it without renouncing their concern for Havenots.

Despite the evidence of widespread concerns with local political control and the recapture of a greater degree of economic autonomy for the citizenry, we are far from the ideal of democratic culture with present-day neighborhood organizations.

Chiding even the strongest of existing community and public interest organizations for their political timidity, Carnoy and Shearer declare that citizen groups must come to grips with the fact that the large corporations have begun to consolidate their power further because they recognize that "the government—at all levels—is the key arena in the struggle for economic democracy."[18] In other words, grassroots associations must build upon the cultural groundswell a clear agenda that will institutionalize the yearnings of so many people for meaningful participation and control over decisions affecting their very survival. Boyte concurs: "Only a movement with the power sufficient to transform the structures of the corporate state could ultimately sustain a democratic alternative."[19]

POWER THROUGH ORGANIZATION: CHALLENGES TO LEFTIST TRADITION

Though there is evidence of cultural change favoring increased citizen participation, the harder question is whether neighborhood organizations can reach the point where they wield real power. For the most part, they do not now compete directly in the public sphere for political and economic leverage. Can they? Or, to put it in one activist's words, "Is there life after institutionalization?" The neighborhood association she coordinated had existed successfully for ten years, yet she felt the whole thing was in some sort of holding pattern. I interpret her question to be a concern about what could be done on a much larger political scale. Many activists are hungry for more meaningful involvement, while at the same time they grapple with doubts that it can change things. Two main objections to attempts to empower Havenots through local organizing have been raised by thoughtful observers: (1) that localist solutions to socioeconomic inequities are inadequate, like trying to mow a lawn with a fingernail clipper, and (2) that militancy and organization do not mix, that protest either cannot or should not be institutionalized. Careful assessment of these critiques may provide some insight into how neighborhood organizations can enter more effectively into the public area.

Overcoming Localism

The first objection holds that the very essence of localized control is turf-based and therefore somehow provincial or inward in perspective, so that the vision necessary to join battle with faroff powers is lacking in most of the residents.[20] Another variant of the localist objection contends that the small size of the neighborhood territory and its relative lack of capital *vis-a-vis* the wealthy downtown militates against its ability to compete for necessary goods and services. This latter view, presented by Milton Kotler in his classic book, *Neighborhood Government*, sketches the relationship between neighborhood and downtown as analogous to that between a poor colonized country and an imperial power.[21] Whether his solution, the formation of neighborhood corporations with powers similar to those of city government itself (e.g., the ability to levy taxes, to defend its territory, or to exert the right of eminent domain) is feasible is beside the point. Kotler has done the neighborhood movement a service by highlighting the fact that local control questions are *power* questions, that they challenge the very manner in which urban society is economically and politically arranged.

Those who would root societal change in local neighborhoods must therefore demonstrate how to overcome the twin hobbles of shallowness of political understanding and lack of capital resources. In response to the shallowness criticism, Curt Lamb's massive study of neighborhood groups in 100 U.S. cities showed that they have been nurseries of leadership and incubators of political awareness for several decades.[22] As residents gained sophistication through their leadership functions in these associations, they often moved out of the local group positions into organizations broader in scope, such as local, state, or federal public office or national coalitions with democratic agendas. This attrition of local leadership may present its own problems for the neighborhood organization, but it supports the contention that grassroots organizing is exactly the vehicle needed to overcome the political ignorance and subsequent apathy of many citizens. This process is what Alinsky meant by popular education.

A Havenot neighborhood's lack of capital resources stems from both the private and the public sectors. Chapter 1 alluded to some of the ways big business drains inner city neighborhoods, such as leaving the city and moving to the suburbs, the South, or out of the country altogether, for lower taxes and payrolls. A big bank can also siphon capital out of the central city by loaning these deposits elsewhere. Later sections of the book detail neighborhood organization efforts to address the lack of capital resources, many of which look to government as partner or big brother to force the issue.

But the relationship between the neighborhood and government, particularly City Hall, can itself be problematic. At bottom is the chasm between local government's control of resources and the neighborhood's lack of control. We see an example in John Fish's sympathetic analysis of The Woodlawn Organization (TWO), a grassroots group in the black ghetto of 120,000 bordering the south side of the University of Chicago campus. Despite TWO's stature in city politics and its accomplishments for its residents, Fish acknowledged that it never disturbed the power balances of the Daley machine: "As important as they were for the organization, these major achievements similarly did not threaten the established power of City Hall or the urban bureaucracies and did not draw massive opposition."[23] Thus, even though TWO did gain some resources (particularly in housing and manpower training) for its residents, it never by *itself* proved a match against the local establishment.

Focusing attention on a single prominent neighborhood organization up against City Hall is bound to lead one toward skepticism. The competition in most cases would indeed be unfair. Yet most case studies in the neighborhood literature do just this, concluding reluctantly that local organizations do not carry enough clout. The truth of the matter is that numerous neighborhood organizations have begun to demand attention and gotten it, have demanded improved services and gotten them, have demanded resources and gotten them. This very assertiveness has led at least to formal recognition of neighborhood councils in over a hundred cities and to fruitful working relationships in several of these, although few neighborhood organizations have sophistication in working together.[24] It is repeated actions from many organizations across the city, like raindrops drumming on a tin roof, that make the government constantly aware that neighborhoods are part of the city, that neighborhood needs are city needs, that the struggle is really win-win rather than win-lose.

Mixing Militancy and Organization

The last part of the previous sentence should not distract the reader from the basic fact of inequity that the neighborhood organization labors mightily to reduce. The phrase win-win in the urban context simply means that if neighborhoods become more livable, so does the city as a whole. But now the other reservation about organizing comes into play. This second objection addresses the paradox of militancy and organization. Strong protest against oppressive conditions is essential to bring Havenots into the mainstream and to empower the majority who are not now empowered. Yet even if that protest can be organized, can that organization be sustained? And should it? Some serious critics claim that self-help organizations have never empowered the poor.

One of Alinsky's most cherished dogmas was that organization was the key to power for Havenots. As long as the organization was vigorous, the poor had a lever to pull, a weapon to use, a last recourse. Most community-based groups share that assumption, but the very drive to institutionalize a movement has been derogated as an obstacle to progress for the poor. Frances Fox Piven and Richard Cloward examined the unemployed and industrial workers' movements during the depression, and the civil rights and welfare rights movements of the 1950s and 1960s.[25] Since they assumed that the disruptions characteristic of these movements were the driving forces for change, their criticism centered on the organizers' technique, which they said was preoccupied with internal leadership prerogatives in building the organizations.

Our main point, however, is not simply that efforts to build organizations are futile. The more important point is that by endeavoring to do what they cannot do, organizers fail to do what they can do. During these brief periods in which people are roused to indignation, when they are prepared to defy the authorities to whom they ordinarily defer, during those brief moments when lower-class groups exert some force against the state, those who call themselves leaders do not usually escalate the momentum of the people's protest. They do not because they are preoccupied with trying to build and sustain embryonic formal organizations in the sure conviction that these organizations will enlarge and become powerful. Thus, the studies that follow show that, all too often, when workers erupted in strikes, organizers collected dues cards; when tenants refused to pay rent and stood off marshals, organizers formed building committees; when people were burning and looting, organizers used that "moment of madness" to draft constitutions.[26]

Piven and Cloward's conclusions follow from their analysis of the social forces that define protest movements in the U.S. A protest movement entails both new consciousness and new behaviors. The system in question loses its legitimacy; the people stop fatalistically accepting the status quo and begin asserting their rights; there is a new feeling of power; and finally there is collective defiant action. But insurgency is short-lived and limited by several constraints. The poor usually blame themselves for their condition, particularly in the U.S. where "riches and power are ascribed to personal qualities of industry or talent."[27] In addition, if the poor are to rise up in anger, they must perceive the deprivation they experience as both unjust and able to be changed for the better. The scale of their distress influences the reevaluation of their circumstances. Some in power may also contribute to the reappraisal by speaking out, for example, against the injustice of not having the vote or jobs.

One must ask about the outcomes of protest in order to understand the limits that institutional structures place on it. What difference does protest against an institution make? First, "people cannot defy an institution to which they have no access and to which they make no contribution."[28] It follows, therefore, that protest takes on more meaning if the protesters play a central role in the institution or if other powerful groups have large stakes in the disrupted institution. The power elite, particularly the government, can respond by ignoring the defiance, repressing it, or seeking conciliation. When the above conditions are present, the powerful have to conciliate. Furthermore, the political impact of institutional disruptions depends on "electoral conditions." If powerful voting blocs are sympathetic, the outcomes of disruption stand a greater chance of stabilization, such as the right to vote or the right to join a union. In other words, "protesters win, if they win at all, what historical circumstances have already made ready to be conceded."[29]

And what of leadership and organization? Piven and Cloward conclude that leadership is effective if it rides the crest. The organizer then becomes a developer of strategies to escalate the momentum and impact of disruptive protest at each stage of its emergence until the desired social, political, or economic realignments are secured.

There is much insight in the Piven and Cloward analysis, particularly in their conclusion that protest gains what is, in some sense, ready to be conceded. But their contention that the imposition of organization itself helps hold the people in bondage is strangely discordant. At the very least, it does not seem to square with the experience of veteran organizers, such as Alinsky and Si Kahn.

Tolerance for social disruption varies from one context to another. Piven and Cloward point out that where one state was acquiescent in the face of industrial workers' strikes in the late 1930s, another would respond with hair-trigger quickness and massive force to squash them.[30] This tolerance, when it exists, corresponds to the *political slack* that exists within every community. Robert Dahl coined this phrase to describe the unused power resources that any organization could utilize without seriously challenging the community's existing power arrangements.[31]

We can now distinguish two types of disruptive protest: that which is revolutionary and threatens to topple power structures and that which is reformist and uses available political slack. Community-based organizations that have employed militancy as a basic tactic, and most of them have at one time or another, have been reformist in this sense. To acknowledge that there are institutional limits to protest is not to concede its uselessness. John Fish, for example, admitted that TWO's skillful organizing helped it extend its influence on behalf of its members:

TWO needed to stimulate conflict, but not too much. The "enemy" had to be defined in such a way that the issue corresponded to TWO's definition of the situation, but the issue had to be such that the full resources of the opposition were not unleashed. By defining the issues, TWO was, in a way, able to define its own "success." By mobilizing around issues which were deemed important by the residents of Woodlawn but did not pose a basic threat to Mayor Daley, the Machine, or the major governmental bureaucracies operating in Woodlawn, TWO could build the organization, pyramid resources, and extend influence without eliciting formidable resistance.[32]

Perhaps where the people's anguish is so deep-seated that it erupts uncontrollably, organization has had the net effect of damping the outburst. On the other hand, neighborhood organizations have demonstrated their capability to channel this misery into political ramrods, battering back the closed doors of the citadels of power. To agree to the former view is not to contradict the latter. The issue is whether neighborhood organization can use the medium of militancy even more effectively in the coming years to build a movement for greater political and economic equity.

Facing the two criticisms against localism and institutionalization of protest does not make them disappear, nor does it invalidate them. There is yet much narrowness of political understanding in neighborhood organizations and a subsequent reluctance to take action in the form of protest, even letter-writing. This immaturity is not remarkable. What is noteworthy is the recent growth in the number of such organizations, the sprouting of information networks represented by countless neighborhood newsletters, national journals, and organizer training centers, and the rise of many grassroots leaders to statewide and even national prominence. The implication of the movement of such individuals into influential positions is that their voices are affecting policy at all levels, which will in turn hasten the development of the new democratic culture.

Ultimately, the development of political perspective, which is the antidote to narrow inwardness, must merge with the creation of effective political strategies. Neighborhood organization members should know that they are engaging in interest group politics and that the institutionalization of protest is merely a stage representative of the interaction between powerless and powerful. Yet the culture of the movement must vibrate in sympathy with the larger culture. It must mature beyond the leftist tradition of sudden revolution.

Beyond Leftist Ideology

Thoughtful leftists may find the reformist quality of neighborhood organizations a sticking point. Although such grassroots groups have wrought some improvements in poor neighborhoods in the short span of their organizational existence, grossly skewed priorities in the allocation of U.S. wealth remain. For example, the 1981 cost *overrun* of the Army's VH–60A helicopter program was estimated to be $4.7 billion. This amount is equivalent to the annual capital investment needed to restore New York City's roads, bridges, aqueducts, subways and buses.[33]

Decentralization of power in the urban U.S. requires organization toward that end. It must be grounded in the locale of the neighborhood, but must transcend it through coalition network. It must employ militancy as part of its repertoire, but it should also be pragmatic, utilizing negotiation, cooperation, and compromise where necessary. But it has no chance at all unless it can educate the public to embrace a new participative agenda. The education process itself must be an active one that occurs through organizing. The great silent majority must become a myriad of vocal minorities, welded together, whatever their differences, under the banner of local autonomy, equity for all, and a government that empowers people rather than megastructures.

Leftist ideology is compatible with such educational goals, but it must come to grips with general concern over apparent disintegration of the mediating structures of the family, the local church, the school, and the neighborhood. Boyte's extensive critique of leftist dogmatism in the face of these political realities focuses on its unwillingness to account for *how* ordinary people can take action on their own behalf:

It is through experiences with institutions that are partly autonomous from dominant power, that have become activated in a new way, and that link up with similar structures into larger group-defining networks, that people develop the self-consciousness, skills, knowledge, and confidence to challenge those in control of their destinies.[34]

Although this brief statement glosses over the internal dissensions that inevitably arise between interest groups in coalition and the limits placed on each group when it enters a pact, it does highlight where the real power must come from. These semiautonomous institutions are voluntary associations of previously uninvolved citizens organized to demand more control over their lives. The new way of being organized is even now occurring, especially in the form of neighborhood organizations that are reaching for higher levels of command through "larger group-defining networks." The skills, knowledge, and confidence developing to make these challenges are forming the basis for a new democratic perspective.

NOTES

1. Rodman Webb, *School and Society* (New York: Houghton Mifflin, 1981), 352–53.

2. Saul D. Alinsky, "The War on Poverty—Political Pornography," *Journal of Social Issues* 21 (January 1965), 41–47.

3. Saul D. Alinsky, *Rules for Radicals* (New York: Vintage, 1972), 106.

4. Martin Carnoy and Derek Shearer, *Economic Democracy: The Challenge of the 1980s* (New York: M.E. Sharpe, 1980).

5. See, for example, discussion of the culture of poverty in Ulf Hannerz, *Soulside: Inquiries into Ghetto Culture and Community* (New York: Columbia University Press, 1969) or Carol Stack, *All Our Kin: Strategies for Survival in a Black Community* (New York: Harper Colophon, 1974).

6. Surveys are mentioned in Frances Moore Lappe, *Diet for a Small Planet*, Tenth Anniversary Edition (New York: Ballantine, 1982).

7. Harry C. Boyte, *The Backyard Revolution: Understanding the New Citizen Movement* (Philadelphia: Temple University Press, 1980).

8. Webb, chaps. 6 and 7.

9. Jessie Bernard, *The Future of Marriage* (New York: Bantam, 1973), 113.

10. Richard J. Cattani, "The 'Me Decade' Is Over," *Grand Rapids Press*, Sunday, December 13, 1984, 5c; Boyte, p. 181; Webb, p. 111.

11. Boyte, pp. 181–86.

12. Adam Hochschild, "The Mirage of the Rising Right," *Mother Jones*, August 1979, 5.

13. Cattani, p. 5.

14. Stuart Langton, "Citizen Participation in America: Reflections on the State of the Art," in *Citizen Participation in America: Essays on the State of the Art*, ed. Stuart Langton (Lexington, MA: D.C. Heath, 1978), 1.

15. Bruce Stokes, *Helping Ourselves: Local Solutions to Global Problems* (New York: Norton, 1981).

16. Stuart Langton and James Petersen, "What Is Self-Help?" *Citizen Participation*, January-February 1982, 3–4.

17. Joan Lancourt, *Confront or Concede: The Alinsky Citizen-Action Organizations* (Lexington, MA: D.C. Heath, 1979), 48.

18. Carnoy and Shearer, p. 402.

19. Boyte, p. 186.

20. Zane Miller, "The Role and Concept of Neighborhood in American Cities," in *Community Organization for Urban Social Change: A Historical Perspective*," ed. Robert Fisher and Peter Romanofsky (Westport, CT: Greenwood Press, 1981), 3–32.

21. Milton Kotler, *Neighborhood Government: The Local Foundations of Political Life* (Indianapolis: Bobbs-Merrill, 1969).

22. Curt Lamb, *Political Power in Poor Neighborhoods* (New York: Schenkman, 1975).

23. John Fish, *Black Power/White Control: The Struggle of the Woodlawn Organization in Chicago* (Princeton, NJ: Princeton University Press, 1973), 112.

24. Greta Kotler, "Organizing for Neighborhood Power: New Possibilities," *South Atlantic Urban Studies*, September 1979, 64–71.

25. Frances Fox Piven and Richard Cloward, *Poor People's Movements: Why They Succeed, How They Fail* (New York: Pantheon, 1977).

26. Piven and Cloward, pp. xi-xii.

27. Piven and Cloward, p. 6.

28. Piven and Cloward, 23.

29. Piven and Cloward, p. 36.

30. Piven and Cloward, pp. 142–46.

31. Robert Dahl, "The Analysis of Influence in Local Communities," in *Social Science and Community Action*, ed. Charles R. Adams (East Lansing: Michigan State University Press, 1960), 25–42.

32. Fish, p. 110.

33. *The Grantsmanship Center News*, November/December 1981, 11. Similar statistics are cited in a brochure from the Coalition for a New Foreign and Military Policy (120 Maryland Avenue, NE, Washington, DC 20002) prepared by Steve Sowle and Steve Daggett. They suggest, for example, that "The extra $13 billion spent on the XM–1 Tank program through 1981 due to cost escalations . . . would provide the funds needed to rehabilitate New York City's transit system ($6.8 billion) and sewer system ($5.1 billion)."

34. Boyte, p. 179.

PART II

The Dynamics of
Neighborhood Organization

4

HISTORICAL ANTECEDENTS AND PRESENT CHARACTERISTICS

A BRIEF HISTORICAL OVERVIEW

Change in organizing at the neighborhood level has paralleled the shifting conception of neighborhood itself over the past century. Robert Fisher and Peter Romanofsky group these activities and perspectives into four periods.[1]

1890–1920

This period marked the heyday of neighborhood organizing before 1960. Liberals and progressives sought to meet the challenge of industrialization—the bigness of cities and their chaotic social disorganization—by organizing immigrant neighborhoods into "efficient, democratic, and, of course, enlightened units within the metropolis" (p. xi). Since the emphasis of the reformers was mostly on building community through settlement houses and other service mechanisms, the dominant approach was *social work.*

1920–1940

During this time, *community organization* became a professional subdiscipline within the social work field. Little was written about decentralized neighborhood organizing efforts throughout the Great Depression. Most organizations had a national orientation because the economic problems the nation faced did not seem soluble at the neighborhood level. Mark Naison, however, investigated an exception: attempts by the American Communist Party to organize the unemployed in Harlem.[2] Party organizers did create a link between neighborhood and workplace strategies over a number of years, but their rigid adherence to internationalist policies and lack of internal democracy led to the ultimate dissolution of their organizations. This period, with its extensive organizing of the vast numbers of the newly impoverished into unions, forged a new political activism at the local level for the next two decades.

1940–1960

A new interest in community organizing from the social work perspective dovetailed with the emergence of the distinctive approach of Saul Alinsky.[3] Federal involvement in reshaping cities and their neighborhoods through the post–World War II urban renewal programs abetted this unique alignment. Since Alinsky spans the latter two periods, his work will be dealt with separately.

1960–1980

Neighborhood organizing became widespread: a revolution. Literature analyzing events at the grassroots during this period is extensive. Experience with federal anti-poverty programs and the upheavals in the cities produced a thoughtful response among activists and theorists in the early 1970s that has informed the movements of the present.

Note that this terse history has emphasized community organizing for social reform among urban Havenots. There were periods, however, of counter-progressive local organizing that flared with equal intensity. Fierce anti-black ''Neighborhood Improvement Associations'' formed in Detroit after 1915, as blacks poured into the city from the South to work in the auto plants.[4] These neighborhood organizations had only one purpose: to maintain their all-white areas against black encroachment. The Citizens' Council in New Orleans during the late 1950s opposed school integration orders.[5] This community organization was actually a citywide group that was localized only as it dealt with specific neighborhood schools. One might surmise that some of the present-day resistance of affluent neighborhoods to attempts by government to build low- and moderate-income housing in their open spaces echoes the sentiments of the anti-progressive organizations of the past.

THE EARLY ALINSKY TRADITION

Alinsky's work from 1938 to his death in 1972 is unique in the history of community organizing.

Community organizing had old roots in the United States. From nineteenth-century ethnic associations through Jane Addams and the Settlement House Movement, activists had long sought to organize communities in their own behalf. But community organizing as a distinct and developed method of insurgent struggle came into its own with the work of Alinsky.[6]

Although he was not the first to combine political activism with the emphasis on rebuilding a specific community, he was the first to do it in a number of neighborhoods across the nation by organizing each area's existing groups into a federated coalition. But he is the main bridge between the past and the future of organizing primarily because of the extent of his work and the number of his students currently influencing the movement. His work is central to a comprehensive understanding of current organizing.

Beginning in 1938, Saul Alinsky, a criminologist by training, wove together the Back of the Yards Council in Chicago. This group took its name from the depressed neighborhoods abutting the city's mammoth stockyards, an area that had gained earlier notoriety through publication of Upton Sinclair's novel *The Jungle* in 1906. Alinsky employed the insights he had gained as a union organizer during the depression to create a neighborhood bloc led by parish priests and labor leaders to exert pressure on the local meatpacking, landowning, business, and political establishments. His style was confrontational utilizing picketing, rent strikes, and boycotts.

Three general principles of organizing stood out for him as the Back of the Yards Council gained strength. First, the poor neighborhood gets only what it is strong enough to get through organization. Second, the organizer proves to people that they can act effectively and then gets out of their way. Third, the organizer has to believe in people if they are to believe in themselves. Later, when Alinsky began organizing in Woodlawn, adjacent to his alma mater, the University of Chicago, he made two additions to these principles: (1) self-interest, not altruism, moves people, and (2) when the neighborhood organization wants something, it should cut through official bureaucracy. Or, as he put it, ''Go to the man who can give you what you want and make him hurt until he gives in.''[7]

Although Alinsky's writings eschew specific how-to-do-it advice because he understood that context means everything, they contain many examples of how he put his general principles into practice. He sometimes casts these examples into hypothetical form to make his points more lucid. One such case, summarized below from his 1946 manifesto, *Reveille for Radicals*, conveys the flavor of the Alinsky strategy.

A mammoth department store, fictitiously named Tycoon's, dominated business in the Across-the-Tracks community. It would not contribute to the support of the neighborhood organization, which upset people. But worse, it was blocking the efforts of its employees to organize a union. It was secretly paying outside organizers to try to form a rival union so the store could claim neutrality.

The leaders of the neighborhood organization (Alinsky called it a *People's Organization*) got fed up when they found out about this chicanery. They sent a telegram to the store's president demanding that he answer to them at a community hearing the next day. Predictably, he refused, saying only that they should consult his attorney. The attorney, when contacted, demanded that the organization's representatives meet him in his office. When these representatives, most of whom were priests, ministers, or labor leaders, arrived, he blustered at them and took their names. The following day, paid thugs from Tycoon's visited each of these activists and threatened to kill them if they did not back off from Tycoon's.

The trap had sprung. The neighborhood organization telephoned the attorney that they were seeking a court injunction to stop Tycoon's from murdering priests and ministers of the area. They were to hold a press conference that afternoon to announce this plan. Panic-stricken, Tycoon's caved in to the organization's demand that the store support the neighborhood organization and let the authentic union organize.

This was an application of power through community organization to get what the poor neighborhood needed: money for its own organization and a union for some of its residents. Alinksy leaves us in the dark about how the organization came about in the first place, how the organizer got the leadership together, whether everybody agreed on the goals and the strategy, whether the organization went on to win other victories, and especially what limitations it encountered. No matter. For the younger Alinsky, the key was the application of the conflict tactics he had learned as a union organizer to the kaleidoscope of problems poor neighborhood people faced in their everyday lives. His capacity for abrasiveness, his uncanny sense for the twitchings of the human ego, and his deep belief in the dignity of those he was organizing, formed a perfect balance. He was his own model community organizer.

THE LATER ALINSKY TRADITION

By the time his second book, *Rules for Radicals*, appeared in 1972, he had begun to shift his attention from exclusive concern with the powerless Havenots of the slums to inclusion of the middle class as his constituency. This broadening of perspective resulted from his growing awareness of the concentration of economic and political power in the hands of the large corporations. From organizing marches on City Hall, he had come to proposing a new strategy, called a *proxy tactic*, in which dissidents use stockholders' meetings to raise issues of company responsibility in order to hold corporations accountable for their behavior.

The late 1960s and early 1970s saw similar changes in the perspectives of those Alinskyites who had worked by his side and had begun to organize in other cities from New York to Los Angeles. They had seen how homogeneous action groups of poor people had been isolated and gotten clobbered, so they designed what they called a majority strategy, utilizing coalitions of black and white, men and women, poor and middle class to fight the rich and powerful.[8]

The Alinsky tradition was thus growing two new branches of emphasis: (1) a broadening of the meaning of *Havenot* to include middle-class *Have-a-little-want-mores* in a coalition of the disenfranchised and (2) a focus on large corporations as the target of citizen action. For example, Chicago's Citizens Action Program, formed in 1970 and formerly named Campaign Against Pollution (CAP), conducted successful fights against Commonwealth Edison and U.S. Steel as huge polluters of the area.[9] CAP represented a coalition of both the poor and the middle class, and turf-consciousness was in the background; coalition members came from many neighborhoods.

Despite the tensions inherent in organizing across class and neighborhood boundaries, Alinsky's work is being carried on by his training school for organizers, the Industrial Areas Foundation (IAF), which began in Chicago in 1969 and is now located in Long Island, New York. Headed by Ed Chambers, one of Alinsky's longtime associates,

IAF trains organizers for 11 community groups, from New York's Queens Community Organization (QCO) to East Los Angeles' United Neighborhood Organization (UNO), and a statewide coalition in Wisconsin.[10]

Although still true to the combative style of its founder, the IAF has made some changes in his modes of operation. For example, organizers now build almost exclusively on the social networks already existing in church groups. This approach gives immediate respectability to their activity and provides the added advantage of financial support from within the church structures themselves. Most of these organizations operate on annual budgets of between $150,000 and $300,000, and the organizers themselves are paid between $20,000 and $40,000 a year. Organizing has become a profession, according to Chambers, who adds that Alinsky was wrong in expecting his organizers to wear hair shirts. They are skilled strategists orchestrating the same sort of abrasive campaigns as the one Alinsky related about Tycoon's almost four decades ago.

BEYOND ALINSKY: TOWARD SOME GENERAL CHARACTERISTICS OF TODAY'S NEIGHBORHOOD ASSOCIATIONS

Although the Alinsky legacy is central to understanding urban organizing, time, reflection, and new crises have wrought their transformations. While the more sophisticated among the movement's leaders look to the national arena for their battles, little People's Organizations are blossoming in every city. Perlman wrote that in 1976 New York City alone had ten thousand block and neighborhood associations.[11] In 1978, Langton cited a National Commission on Neighborhoods study that put the figure at eight thousand nationally.[12] Boyte claimed in 1980 that 60,000 existed across the land.[13] Although the discrepancies appear to be considerable, all are probably right according to their own definitions. In any given city, one would expect to find many more informal block clubs than formal organizations with paid staff members. Small organizations must exist before they can coalesce with each other into federations.

This new crop of young neighborhood organizations—meaning less than five years old—owes much to the experience of the mature organizations in the large cities. Many organizers of the recent past have left these older organizations and formed national support networks and training centers that provide technical assistance and information to neighborhood groups and train their organizers. In 1981, there were two dozen such national centers and associations.[14] Another evidence of the mushrooming neighborhood movement is the number of newsletters and periodicals that focus extensively on this phenomenon for a national audience. A recent estimate puts the figure at 300.[15]

Although contemporary neighborhood organizations differ as markedly as the neighborhoods they are in, the size of the surrounding city, the residents' agenda, and the resources available to act on that agenda, they share similarities in both structure and function, and they are distinguishable from other kinds of voluntary groups. A neighborhood organization occupies just one shelf in the whole cupboard of citizen participation. There are four general ways that people participate in U.S. society as citizens.[16] First, there are citizen *obligations* (such as paying taxes and doing jury duty or military service). Then there is the opportunity to participate as an *elector*. Third, citizen *involvement*, which springs from government administrative needs and is initiated by government, differs from citizen *action*, which refers to activities initiated and controlled by citizens for the main purpose of influencing decisions of government officials, institutions, or voters. A neighborhood organization is a form of citizen action group.

This classification needs further refinement. Citizen action or voluntary associations are still of many varieties. How is the neighborhood organization unique among these groups, even though it may share some of their qualities? The answer lies in comparison and contrast: how is it like other groups? how is it different and thus unique?

First, comparison. The neighborhood organization has the political thrust and concern of public interest research and consumer groups, the best known of which is Ralph Nader's Public Citizen. It has democratic openness of structure in much the same way as do self-help associations, such as Alcoholics Anonymous and consumer or producer cooperatives. It focuses on issues and may include those most important to women and minority groups. It often pursues the same economic and commercial priorities that grassroots community development corporations do. It promotes local pride just as traditional chambers of commerce do for their cities. It establishes and supports networks of local residents helping one another, as do the Scouts, Foster Grandparents, or even parents trading babysitting chores with each other. It likes a party or a social event just as do the parish, the union local, and the community recreation center.

But the neighborhood organization is different from all of these. Any confusion about its nature in the minds of its members is probably due to their simultaneous membership in some of these other groups. Its current uniqueness lies in its distinct way of amalgamating these characteristics. The following distinguishing marks of the neighborhood organization are drawn from a number of data sources and are subject to considerable variance with context:

1. The urban neighborhood organization is geographically localized and takes its strength from resident identification with place.

2. It is a citizen action group that seeks greater voice in decisions that affect the neighborhood.

3. Its internal structure aims to be democratic, allowing for accountability to its members and opportunity for membership open to all residents.

4. Although it avoids the overt trappings of ideology, it tends to be populist and reformist in its perspective. (History shows numerous examples of very reactionary groups, however.)

5. It usually operates in older, economically depressed urban areas, although there is considerable activity in middle-class areas as well.

6. Its organizational size and structure tend to be commensurate with its goals for neighborhood improvement and the resources available to it.

7. It addresses several issues at a time in order to maintain its mass base. A neighborhood organization may persist over a long period of time, however, while focused on only one major issue.

8. It uses multiple strategies to achieve its ends. There are three general strategic categories, all requiring widespread dissemination of information: (a) making demands on existing institutions; (b) using conventional electoral politics; (c) developing alternative economic or service institutions.

9. Where such organizations employ staff, their funding comes from a variety of sources, ranging from individual members to churches or the federal goverment.

What most distinguishes the neighborhood organization, it seems, is the residents' interest in exerting some degree of control over their common living space. Yet many factors complicate this process. Since the neighborhood is a mosaic of wants, needs, and ideologies, the structure of the neighborhood organization must allow for the pursuit of several goals simultaneously. Furthermore, underlying the concept of *issue* is conflict over scarce resources for the community. Either the neighborhood must obtain capital for home maintenance, small business revitalization, and public services, or it must retain what resources it already has. How a localized organization effectively encompasses several goals under the aegis of conflict is a complex phenomenon.

More reflection brings more questions. For example, what modes of conflict have neighborhood organizations found useful? Is the Alinsky model of organizing organizations outmoded? What organizing strategies seem appropriate to which issues and circumstances? How does the organization itself function? That is, who are its leaders and members and why? How do they interact effectively? What are the organization's goals and norms? How are resources obtained to keep it operating? What is its potential? What are its limits? What is its future?

One way to begin answering these questions, although the remainder of the book is devoted to that task, is to extend the general characteristics theme to attributes of those organizations that work and of those that have failed.

Janice Perlman listed attributes of the *successful* neighborhood organization:

1. Full-time, paid, professional staff

2. Well developed fund-raising capacity

3. Sophisticated mode of operation, including:
   a. Neighborhood street organizing
   b. Advanced issue-research capacity
   c. Information dissemination and expose techniques
   d. Negotiation and confrontation skills
   e. Management capability in the service delivery and economic development areas
   f. Policy and planning skills
   g. Lobbying skills
   h. Experience in monitoring and evaluating government programs

4. Issue growth from the neighborhood to the nation

5. A support network of umbrella groups, technical assistants, action-research projects, organizer-training schools

6. Expanding coalition building with one another, with public interest groups, and with labor.[17]

Although Perlman placed paid, professional staff as the single most important factor in success, Joan Flanagan, who has written extensively on the operations of voluntary groups, places *clear goals* at the head of the list.[18] Perlman seems to have in mind the mature, federated, Alinsky-type organization, a number of which formed in Chicago up to two decades ago. The Woodlawn Organization (TWO), the Organization for a Better Austin (OBA), and the Northwest Community Organization (NCO) at their peak each represented tens of thousands of citizens, employed several staff, and expended many thousands of dollars annually in their struggles to rebuild and defend their parts of that city. Typically, they engaged in a range of activities that included militant direct action, delivery of various social services, and development of alternative institutions, such as food stores and housing programs.

As these organizations gained success, they had a tendency to attract large funding (especially from the federal government) for service programs such as youth employment training, housing rehabilitation, and day care.[19] Even those groups steadfastly committed to protest as their principal mode of advocacy for the poor, however, found their staff personnel spending inordinate amounts of time providing individual advocacy services for desperate constituents.[20] The solution to this dilemma of meeting the service needs of the poor while paying strict attention to issue-organizing has often been to focus protest on the agencies that have themselves been delivering these services inadequately.

The Chicago neighborhood organizations described may be mature, but they are not strictly prototypical. Organizations in smaller cities have adapted to their own environments in diverse ways. Yet it is safe to say that there is no substitute for leadership sophistication about organization, management, and the issues, if a neighborhood association is to be successful.

What this sophistication means becomes a little clearer when it is absent. Joan Lancourt's study of eight Alinsky organizations found several reasons why three of them failed.[21] They became isolated from prevailing social movements; their constituencies got out of focus; their internal disputes could not be resolved; they made few appeals to third parties who could help them; their issue selection was poor; they could not slough off their own members who opposed the organization's goals; and, precisely as a result of all this, they experienced funding difficulties.

Listing the attributes of success and failure, particularly of Alinsky organizations, is a way of paying homage to the man's contributions while at the same time acknowledging that the movement has of necessity had to transcend him. Lively debate within neighborhood organizing circles signals this passage. The questions raised earlier are still being answered in all the ways different neighborhoods can address them. If the image of *neighborhood organization* is yet fuzzy to the reader, it ought to be. The neighborhood organization is a new form of organization struggling to comprehend itself. This book is an attempt to draw together the works of many students of neighborhood organizing under the discipline of organizational theory in order to gain clarity of vision and unity of purpose for those unknown thousands toiling through their neighborhood organizations to make cities more livable The following chapters begin to apply organizational theory to the inner dynamics of these groups.

NOTES

1. Robert Fisher and Peter Romanofsky, Introduction to *Community Organization for Urban Social Change*, ed. Robert Fisher and Peter Romanofsky (Westport, CT: Greenwood Press, 1981), xi-xviii.

2. Mark Naison, "Harlem Communists and the Politics of Black Protest," in Fisher and Romanofsky, pp. 89–126.

3. Sidney Dillick, *Community Organization for Neighborhood Development—Past and Present* (New York: William Morrow, 1953), 146–49.

4. B.J. Widick, *Detroit: City of Race and Class Violence*, (Chicago: Quandrangle Books, 1972), 3–22.

5. Neil McMillen, "The Citizens' Council in New Orleans: Organized Resistance to Social Change in a Deep South City," in Fisher and Romanofsky, pp. 157–85.

6. Harry C. Boyte, *The Backyard Revolution: Understanding the New Citizen Movement* (Philadelphia: Temple University Press, 1980), 49–50.

7. *Current Biography*, 1968, 16.

8. Boyte, p. 53.

9. Derek Shearer, "CAP: New Breeze in the Windy City," *Ramparts*, October 1973, 12–16.

10. Laural Leff, "Community Spirit: Local Groups That Aid Poor Flourish by Using Confrontation Tactics," *Wall Street Journal*, May 13, 1981.

11. Janice Perlman, "Grassrooting the System," *Social Policy*, 9 (September-October 1976), 8.

12. Stuart Langton, "Citizen Participation in America: Reflections on the State of the Art," in *Citizen Participation in America: Essays on the State of the Art*, ed. Stuart Langton (Lexington, MA: D.C. Heath, 1978), 3.

13. Boyte, p.3, extends the evidence of neighborhood organizing to intercity alliances and renters' coalitions.

14. Boyte, pp. 210–11.

15. *Community Jobs*, March 1982.

16. Langton, pp. 1–12.

17. Janice Perlman, "Grassroots Participation from Neighborhood to Nation," in Langton, pp. 71.

18. Joan Flanagan, *Community Jobs*, May 1982, 7.

19. Joan Lancourt, *Confront or Concede: The Alinsky Citizen-Action Organizations* (Lexington, MA: D.C. Heath, 1979), chap. 7.

20. See, for example, Paul Wellstone, *How the Rural Poor Got Power: Narrative of a Grassroots Organizer* (Amherst, MA: University of Massachusetts Press, 1978), 179; and William Ellis, *White Ethnics and Black Power: The Emergence of the West Side Organization* (Chicago: Aldine, 1969), chap. 5.

21. Lancourt, p. 159.

5

LEADERSHIP: THE DRIVING GEAR IN THE NEIGHBORHOOD ORGANIZATION

> If we strip away all the chromium trimmings of high-sounding metaphor and idealism which conceal the motor and gears of a democratic society, one basic element is revealed—the people are the motor, the organizations of the people are the gears. The power of the people is transmitted through the gears of their own organizations, and democracy moves forward.
>
> —Saul Alinsky[1]

If a neighborhood organization is a machine, then leadership is the main cog. But human organization exhibits a crucial difference: its parts are aware of themselves and their interrelationships and, for this reason, vary widely in the efficiency of their operation. Good organizational leaders, then, are not only the central components of the mechanism; they are also master mechanics in that they know how the organizational gears mesh and how to keep them functioning efficiently.

Alinsky wrote anecdotally about the dynamics of relatively small groups, the cadre of activists who handled the organization's day-to-day operations. Formal studies of leadership in neighborhood organizations acknowledge the applicability of small group theory to such associations, even though their memberships may be quite large.[2] An understanding of the internal structure and process of any neighborhood organization should begin, therefore, with its central variable, leadership. Issues of representation and democracy raised by critics of neighborhood organizing will become clearer as a solid conceptual foundation is laid.

Si Kahn, a veteran of many organizing campaigns, defined a leader simply as ''someone who helps show us the directions we want to go and who helps us to go in those directions.''[3] Yet the reality of neighborhood leadership is hardly a simple one. In order to unravel the complexity, this chapter first explores some general research findings about leadership. It then presents a typology of urban leaders and concludes with a review of studies of leadership in poor neighborhoods and a discussion about leader-organizer differences.

GENERAL RESEARCH ON LEADERSHIP

Conventional wisdom and early research held that effective leadership was the result of the leader's special qualities or traits; later studies found little overlap of these traits as situations changed. In other words, these special traits could not be universally identified.[4] A military leader, for example, might excel in the exercise of authority, whereas an industrial manager might bring the best out in subordinates by treating them as equals. A 15–year research program that covered more than 35 studies and 1,600 groups concluded that leadership effectiveness is conditioned by context and group response:

1. The effectiveness of a group is contingent upon the appropriateness of the leader's style to the specific situation in which he operates. Most people are effective leaders in some situations and ineffective in others.

2. The type of leadership style that will be most effective depends upon the degree to which the group situation enables the leader to exert influence.[5]

People move into positions of leadership in one of two ways: (1) they emerge, take charge, or show a willingness to take responsibility, or (2) they are appointed by someone else. One experiment found that, although emergent leaders tended to exhibit more authoritarian behavior than did the appointed ones, both demonstrated two unique behaviors in the group.[6] They took the lead both in analyzing situations and in initiating required action.

Once in the leadership role, the effectiveness of the leader depends heavily on situational, member response, and task variables. The leader's overall pattern of analysis and initiating action can include within it a range of behaviors from outright authoritarianism to a *laissez-faire* approach that facilitates the group's definition of and commitment to a decision. Figure 5.1 displays this range of leadership styles. The successful neighborhood organization leader must be able to behave across this range, since some situations call for the authoritarian response, others for the democratic, still others for the *laissez-faire*.

Another way of thinking about the leader's job is to realize that he or she must attend to the tasks of the group while at the same time encouraging the personal commitment of each group member to carrying out these tasks. The decision-making grid shown in figure 5.2 has become a familiar symbol in the literature of group dynamics. Its principal value lies in its depiction of the different proportions of attention to task and maintenance, or product and process, functions that correspond to different leadership styles. The autocratic leader, for example, is high on attention to task (9/1) and low on focus toward maintaining commitment (1/9). *Laissez-faire* is the reverse. Democratic stands somewhere in between (5/5 or ideally 9/9).

This grid is limited in its usefulness, however, because it fails to acknowledge the importance of context. A leader committed to only one style is bound to experience frustration when the context changes. Relatively few people possess this range and flexibility, and most probably cannot be trained to achieve it. Several studies, in fact, have not been able to produce evidence that leadership training promotes productivity or group effectiveness, probably because such training tends to indoctrinate individuals into adopting one predominant leadership style.[7] The folklore of street organizing, which requires that the organizer listen to people's grievances and help them to plan redress, highlights the democratic and *laissez-faire* styles. Such lore masks the reality that the organization is the one doing the analysis and initiating action, which are autocratic behaviors. No one listening to Saul Alinsky address an audience could miss his authoritative, even intimidating, personality quality. In another life, he might well have been the four-star general he wrote about. In fact, one of the chief criticisms of militant neighborhood groups is that they are steered by a small core of like-minded individuals who do not wait for a neighborhood vote before acting.[8] When these groups are effective, however, it is because they are representative of the residents and have their backing, a point to be reinforced later in this chapter.

The need for flexibility in leadership style is heightened in the neighborhood organization because it addresses several different goals (tasks) simultaneously. By implication, then, occupants of leadership roles in

Figure 5.1

The Leadership Continuum

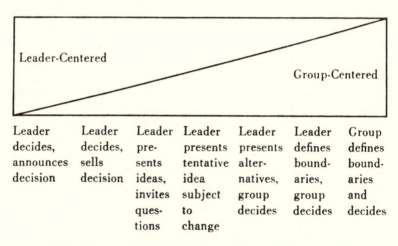

Leader decides, announces decision	Leader decides, sells decision	Leader pre- sents ideas, invites ques- tions	Leader presents tentative idea subject to change	Leader presents alter- natives, group decides	Leader defines bound- aries, group decides	Group defines bound- aries and decides

Source: Rodney Napier and Matti K. Gershenfeld, *Groups: Theory and Experience,* Copyright © 1973 Houghton Mifflin Company. Used with permission.

Figure 5.2
The Decision-Making Grid

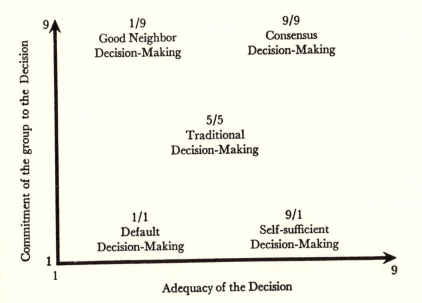

Source: William Bergquist and Steven Phillips, A *Handbook for Faculty Development, Volume I* (Washington, D.C.: Council for the Advancement of Small Colleges, now the Council of Independent Colleges, 1976), 158. Used with permission.

this sort of group may change repeatedly over time. The latter part of this chapter provides some examples of how various members of the organization can fulfill leadership roles even where there is a strong central figure.

A classic investigation by Ralph White and Ronald Lippitt demonstrated differences among autocratic, democratic, and *laissez-faire* leadership behaviors and their effects on members' behaviors.[9] Although they studied adult leadership effects on ten-year-old boys during recreational club activities, much of what they learned is transferrable to adult groups.

In the autocratic group setting, the dominant leader behaviors were giving orders, issuing disruptive commands, and offering nonconstructive criticism. The democratic leader emphasized giving suggestions and stimulating members' self-confidence. The only predominant behavior of the *laissez-faire* leader was extending knowledge or giving information.

Members of the democratic group completed their tasks as efficiently as did those subject to autocratic control and more efficiently than those in the *laissez-faire* setting. In addition, autocratic leadership created much more member hostility and aggression, including aggression against scapegoats, than was evident in the other groups. Also under autocracy group members exhibited more dependent behavior, less individuality, and a lowering of spontaneous work interest. Finally, democracy promoted more group-mindedness and friendliness than did other leader styles.

General leadership research suggests points to bear in mind when we turn toward the neighborhood organization as a particular group form. First, there are several leadership styles or patterns of behavior that range from autocratic, in which the leader determines the course of action and urges that it be carried out, to *laissez-faire*, in which the group itself is in effect the leader, giving direction and enacting it by consensus. Second, to be effective the leader's style must match the situation, both the task at hand, as the group perceives it, and the members' degree of responsiveness. Effectiveness means only that the group achieves the goals it sets for itself. Hence, no one style is inherently better than any other. Third, meeting group goals implies two functions, (1) that the group get down to the business of working on the task and (2) that it continue to work on it. Some leaders are adroit at getting down to business, while others are better at keeping the group together. The most effective leaders must do both. Fourth, people who can adapt their leadership behaviors to situations along the continuum from autocratic to *laissez-faire* are the exception. This fact implies that, in a successful multipurpose organization, the diverse leadership styles required will probably be filled by several people, each in his or her own way. Finally, the context for leadership is critical. The neighborhood territory, in which the seedling organization takes root, is the context for the leadership we are discussing. It contains a montage of interests and concerns, of personalities, dreams, and expectations. By no stretch of the imagination could all these neighbors be called a group. Yet what we have learned thus far about leadership applies here. Let us now distinguish the kinds of leaders likely to exist in a neighborhood, those people who will create the neighborhood group. Before we do this, however, we should type urban leaders more broadly.

TYPOLOGIES OF URBAN LEADERS

The city can be viewed as a social system that manages the competition and conflict arising from the common need to exchange goods and services.[10] From this perspective, a city is a complex collection of groups that produce and consume. These groups are interdependent because of the division of labor in a technological society and the relative scarcity of each good and service. Thus, competition, and sometimes even open conflict, over who gets which goods and services is ever present. These private interest groups may include a family, a hardware store, an elementary school, a church, or a workers' union.

Our first typology of leadership recognizes two very broad categories of leadership behavior: authoritative and coordinative. Each economic cell has a leader or leaders whose control within the group is based on position. In such situations, leadership behavior is grounded in the right of authority. Formal authority to hold these specialized interests together exists in government leadership as well.

Another kind of leadership behavior is also necessary to glue this complexus of groups together. This less formal category of leadership, Harold Nix terms *interstitial*. He distinguishes two kinds. The first type of interstitial leadership behaviors are *exchange*, typified by merchant-customer and professional-client relationships. The small businessperson, the dentist, and the schoolteacher provide a kind of leadership that adjudicates economic competition at the individual level. The second kind of interstitial leadership behaviors, more important in Nix's view, is the "coordinative leadership within interstitial groups" (p. 315). Such groups help manage the competition between organizations and are exemplified by chambers of commerce, community development councils, or informal decision-making cliques. Coordinative leaders have influence rather than authority; their control is based on their personal abilities or their access to scarce resources rather than on their formal authority. Coordinative leaders may also be authoritative leaders within their own special interest groups; many of the original members of the Back of the Yards Council, for example, were priests, ministers, or labor chiefs.

There is no necessary dichotomy between authoritative leaders and interstitial leaders. *Authoritative* and *interstitial* refer to categories of behavior that are highly situational. All acts of leadership rely on some basis of power, the ability to influence other people, which is itself situational. There are at least five types of power.[11] *Legitimate* power is an authority relationship in which one person by virtue of his or her position holds the right to make decisions for others. *Reward* and *coercive* power may or may not flow from legitimacy, depending on the context. *Referent* power, a subtle form of influence over those who respect the opinion or the status of the powerful one, and *expert* power, which flows from knowledge and may exist independent of position, may overlap with each other and with the other three. The possible permutations of these forms of power imply a continuum of leadership activities between the authoritative and interstitial polarities. This continuum of leadership behaviors helps to locate neighborhood leaders. As we might suspect, their leadership functions are largely interstitial.

Nix named four kinds of urban leader: *legitimizers, effectors, activists*, and the *general public*. *Legitimizers* are policymakers in the public and private sectors, those whose authority rests on their position. They are mayors, police chiefs, bank presidents, or large landowners. *Effectors* are the managers of our society, the technocrats whose power is so ably explored by John Kenneth Galbraith in *The New Industrial State*.[12] These bureaucrats are trained professionals who form the mind and sinews of any large corporation or institution; their power flows from their technical knowledge and their ability to manipulate financial and material resources. Together these two types of leaders exert the lion's share of influence in any city.

Activists are those doers and joiners at the lower levels in the hierarchy of power who have traditionally lacked technical skills and a power base. The fourth category is the *general public*. Although we do not ordinarily think of them as leaders, many members of this category exert a passive sort of leadership through their voting patterns and their influences on their peers at work or in the neighborhood.

There is a broad gulf between the first two kinds of leaders and the latter two. It is the power gap Alinsky describes between Haves and Havenots. His genius lay in his ability to create a new kind of coordinative interstitial group, a People's Organization, that bonded diverse private interest groups among the poor into a larger coalition that could compete more successfully with established urban power structures for scarce goods and services. He accomplished this feat by balancing the leadership equation in the community. His organizing practicum, the action, sent activists into the fray armed with carefully culled information and the power base of numbers of fellow residents—the general public—who accompanied them.

Thus, the twin underpinnings of neighborhood leadership development were (1) a higher level of technical understanding among the activists and the general public (for example, an understanding of the facts outlining why it was profitable for slumlords to let their properties deteriorate) and (2) the creation of a power base (the tenants who to this point had no recourse). What Alinsky means when he writes, "power and organization are one and the same,"[13] is that the Havenots emulate the Haves by building their organization on better technical knowledge and a power base of human resources.

In the Alinsky model, the Havenots gain legitimacy, though not formal authoritative power, in the urban system by developing their expertise and using their massed strength to coerce change within legal limits. The neighborhood organization's leaders come from the ranks of the activists and the general public, particularly from those organizations already existing in the area, such as parishes, social service agencies, school groups, and voluntary associations of all kinds. The new People's Organization is an umbrella group with a different agenda. It seeks to effect institutional change: better housing, more jobs, improved goods and services. The emphasis is on localizing political and economic power in the neighborhood.

The Alinsky model might not work in all neighborhoods. Some of the established social agencies or churches may resent the new organization as an indictment of their previous work in the community or as another mouth to feed in the struggle for scarce social program dollars. Alinsky experienced this opposition and warned of it.[14] The fledgling organization may be able to draw on the existing leadership of preexisting groups, but often it cannot. The next section examines the origins of leadership in Havenot neighborhoods more closely and suggests that only those with more radical attitudes, especially alienation from government, are likely to become leaders in a Havenot neighborhood organization. Furthermore, individuals living in the neighborhood may emerge to form their own group in irate response to a specific problem on the block, such as speeding traffic or street crime. There may be no intent to create a coalition or an umbrella organization. The stereotypical example of such a person is Lois Gibbs, a previously passive and politically unaware housewife, who rose to lead a two-year fight against the government when she discovered her neighborhood rested on a toxic chemical dump—Love Canal. More frequently, however, leaders come from the activist ranks, people with a history of involvement in social issues and generally higher political awareness. Alinsky-style organizations especially look for involvement of experienced neighborhood leaders.[15]

THE DIFFERENTIATION OF NEIGHBORHOOD LEADERSHIP

Simply distinguishing between activists and general public at the grassroots level of urban leadership does not provide much insight into the wide variety and effectiveness of leadership in poor communities. Curt Lamb reanalyzes the data gathered for a million-dollar government study that sought to determine what changes had occurred between 1964 and 1969 in inner city neighborhoods as a result of the War on Poverty.[16] The original study, entitled the *Local Change Survey*, involved over 8,000 interviews with residents and leaders in low-income neighborhoods of 100 U.S. cities of population greater than 50,000. The procedure was to designate target areas of poverty, interview 40 residents per neighborhood, and during the interview have them identify grassroots leaders. The 630 leaders, not heads of institutions or large established organizations, who were thus identified were interviewed a minimum of an hour and a half each. In addition, five cities, Atlanta, Detroit, Hamilton (Ohio), Philadelphia, and San Jose, were chosen for intensive analysis. An extended series of questions concerning their socioeconomic status, community involvement, political values and activities, and racial attitudes was asked of 1,114 residents of these cities. About half the interviewees were white, because the study sought to correct the heavy emphasis of previous research on studying black communities only. Worth noting as well was the fact that the neighborhoods studied were among urban America's most economically depressed.

Lamb's analysis of the original data seeks to answer questions such as these:

—What is the group life of the poor and what groups do leaders belong to?

—What *kinds* of leaders are there among the poor?

—What is the relation between racial or ethnic self-awareness and leadership effectiveness?

—How do leaders in poor neighborhoods differ from the residents at large?

—What groups among the poor are most likely to bring about revitalization in declining or deteriorated urban areas?

The Group Life of Havenots

Three general conclusions arise. First, only about one poor person in four (25%) belongs to *any* formal group at all, even church groups, as opposed to one in two (50%) among the middle class. Second, membership in various kinds of groups depends on socioeconomic status. Poor residents in the study, when they do belong to groups, are much more likely to emphasize membership in civic-political or service organizations (78% total) than Americans at large (15%). Leaders of the poor follow this pattern. As Lamb puts it, "there is a remarkable *political cast* to all forms of association in poor neighborhoods."[17] Third, the race or ethnicity of leaders of the poor distinguishes their membership in neighborhood groups. Black leaders are more likely than white leaders to belong to militant ethnic, civil rights, and other community-action groups. Mexican-American leaders are even more likely than blacks to belong to these sorts of groups, as Figure 5.3 indicates.

Kinds of Leaders Among Havenots

Lamb differentiates five general types of leaders in poor urban communities: neighborhood radicals, respectable militants, the uninvolved,

Figure 5.3
Varieties of Group Membership Among Leaders by Race

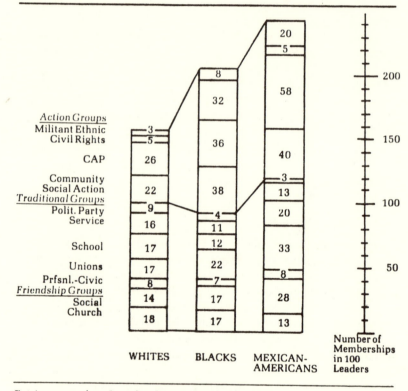

Entries are number of memberships per hundred leaders.

Source: *Political Power in Poor Neighborhoods* by Curt Lamb. Copyright © 1975
Schenkman Publishing Co. Cambridge, MA, p. 109. Reprinted by permission of the publisher.

elder elites, and the neighborhood establishment. Each of these requires explanation.

Neighborhood radicals belong primarily to action groups, such as block, tenant, welfare, or civil rights organizations; and they entirely avoid traditional groups, such as PTAs, political parties, and civic and professional groups. They are intensely angry at their local neighborhood conditions and are alienated from both local and national government. Among all leadership types, they have the highest propensity to disruptive political activity, although they are also active in conventional politics. They are more interested in exerting their leadership through community organization, however, than simply getting people angry. Finally, they are younger (average age: 35 years) by an average of six years than other leaders, come from a slightly higher socioeconomic level than other residents, and have lived in their neighborhoods an average of 14 years, making them distinctly local. They constitute one third of the neighborhood leadership (33%).

According to Lamb, 20 percent of the leaders among the urban poor are *respectable militants*. Although they are active in protest and local action groups, they differ from their radical counterparts in that they belong to traditional community organizations and have little hostility toward government. They perceive local problems very acutely, but they do not translate this perception into vocal political demands. They are five years older (41 years) and four years longer in residence (18 years) than the neighborhood radicals.

The *uninvolved*, a curious term for a small (9%) leadership group, belong to action groups, but they are not politically active. The name is meant to convey the current neutrality they exhibit toward government and local problems. At an average age of 43, they are interpreted by Lamb as being "on the verge of greater involvement" because 83 percent of them said there were political activities they would agree to participate in but had not yet. "Evidently," says Lamb, "their involvement with a local action group was the first tentative step on a path that remains to be followed."[18] So far 62 percent of the leadership has been typed. For purposes of organizing the community to bring about change, neighborhood radicals form the most potent leadership pool of the three, but the other two may be thought of as supporting the radicals' thrust, at least potentially. The next two categories of local leaders are more problematic from the community organization's perspective.

Lamb calls his second largest category (27%) the *elder elite*. Averaging 50 years of age, with little education and the lowest leader incomes of all, these people represent the end result of a process that sees the most effective leadership leave the local area. Elder elite members belong neither to traditional nor action groups, nor do they participate very much in politics. They do not contribute to community-building in the social sphere either. Although they are unusually cynical about local government, their lack of current involvement and consequent tenuous hold on local influence allows us to bypass them as potential activists. Recall that they are called leaders only because one or more residents nominated them as such.

The fifth category of leaders, the *neighborhood establishment*, is not so easily dismissed. Although it numbers only 11 percent of all leaders in the study, its members have the unusual combination of relatively low education and yet very high income. About half are housewives, the other half white-collar or professional. They belong exclusively to traditional community groups—the exact antithesis of the neighborhood radicals. They are not angry and tend to see poverty as the result of personal inadequacies. On the one hand their perception of local problems is superficial and their political demands feeble; on the other hand they report much more contact with influential officials than any other group, a dangerous obstacle to changes that would distribute influence or resources more broadly throughout the neighborhood. The neighborhood establishment, in fact, is likely to aggressively oppose efforts at such change, as Robert Bailey reports in his study on the formation of the Organization for a Better Austin (OBA) in the Chicago area.[19] Town Hall Assembly and Black Concerned Parents are two organizations in Austin that, led by the neighborhood establishment, actively opposed OBA on several issues.

Lamb concludes his comments on neighborhood leaders by making two points. First, the study finds that effective leaders of the poor stand conventional political science theory on its head. It is precisely their alienation from, not their support of, the political system that enables them to mobilize the poor to political involvement. The second point follows from the first: a keen awareness of how little government and social service agencies do for the poor is a prerequisite for political involvement of the leaders of the poor. In general, the study indicates that the new leadership in poor neighborhoods is made up of people even more alienated from government than are most residents. The balance between progressive and status quo forces is not the same across neighborhoods, however. For instance, white leaders outnumber black leaders in the status quo neighborhood establishment by five to one.

Representativeness and Ethnic Pride

Lamb's study of these intertwined topics focuses primarily on the black percentages of the survey. Race pride correlates with being more politicized or sensitive to local problems and with a greater knowledge of efforts to solve these problems. Racial pride also correlates with a higher probability of belonging to local membership groups, of engaging in political activity, and of being hostile to national institutions. Poor blacks perceive racial antagonism by whites but are willing to approach each problem on its own terms, and they demonstrate an ability to recognize and accept racial good will when it occurs. All this adds up to a *militant pragmatism* that characterizes black neighborhood leaders. Where positive racial values and feeling exist among poor blacks, they play a role in fostering political involvement. The same is doubly true for leaders among these poor; their racial pride greatly adds to their commitment as community leaders.

Lamb investigates three aspects of representativeness among leaders of the poor. The socioeconomic status of leaders was essentially the same as that of the residents, although on the average, the leaders' age, income, education, and length of residence were all slightly higher than residents at large. Second, the leaders lived among the poor and were daily accessible to them. Third, the political beliefs of leaders were highly congruent with those of the neighborhood population. Precisely this alignment enables the neighborhood radicals to achieve maximum effectiveness in involving their neighbors politically. This statement also implies, however, that status quo leaders, those of the establishment, also find community support. It should also be noted that a depressing 59 percent of all residents interviewed in the 100 cities could not name even one leader of any type.

Black neighborhood leaders have taken the lead in using their sense of outrage, shifting tactics toward more confrontation and showing a willingness to recognize and grapple with poverty problems as neighborhood realities. But white and Hispanic leaders have also followed this pattern. We now have evidence in poor black neighborhoods of "a stratification favoring low-status (i.e., poor), anti-establishment persons in positions of power."[20]

Bailey's study of leadership in the predominantly black neighborhoods of South Austin at the west edge of Chicago's expanding ghetto
corroborates many of Lamb's much broader generalizations.[21] For example, in line with Lamb's findings, OBA's leaders (activists) tended
to be among what Bailey called the socioeconomic elite of South Austin,
mostly middle-class blacks (although there were some whites), with
personal resources such as higher incomes, more education, and good
health and stamina (some attended as many as 200 meetings a year).
Middle-class meant that activists were more than twice as likely to have
incomes over $13,000 (59% to 23%) and some college or a degree
(52% to 23%) in 1970.[22] Few of them, however, were already leaders
of local organizations, such as church pastors, before their affiliation
with OBA. Within the Lamb typology, they fit both the respectable
militant and the neighborhood radical categories, the former because
their civic participation was greater in all respects than that of other
residents, including belonging to traditional organizations; the latter
because they shared and even surpassed the residents' alienation from
local and national government. Since OBA was an Alinsky organization,
these activists were quite comfortable with the tactic of disruptive protest, a characteristic of neighborhood radicals. OBA leaders were of
longer residence, were more than twice as likely to own houses, and
knew much more about the local community than other residents. They
also shared their local issue orientation, a finding that parallels Lamb's
conclusion that leaders in poor neighborhoods share the political ori-
entations of the residents at large.

Bailey concludes, as does Lamb, that the major difference between
radical leaders (those comfortable with disruptive protest as a tactic)
and conventional leaders is their stance toward government. Strong
evidence indicates that radical leaders feel strongly that government at
all levels is neither interested in nor effective in dealing with neighborhood problems, a sentiment widespread throughout the communities
studied. William Ellis's 1969 study of Chicago's black Westside Organization also substantiated these findings about the political alienation
of effective leaders of the poor.[23]

Groups That Best Aid Revitalization in Poor
Neighborhoods

Based on the previous analysis of leadership, Lamb looks at the
potential of five kinds of neighborhood groups to bring about local

social change. He dismisses most *churches* in poor communities because of their promotion of a sense of fatalism; besides, only 35 of the 631 neighborhood leaders in the *Local Change Survey* are clergy. *Political parties* in these neighborhoods are effectively moribund, he contends, because their leaders do not see poverty as a political problem. These leaders tend to fall into the elder elite category, the most effete of the leadership types. *Civil rights* groups as such claim few of the effective leaders in the ghettos and barrios. Insofar as *community social action* groups provide organizational support for the poor, they are effective. But *militant ethnic* groups present the greatest promise of efficacy because of the large number of neighborhood radicals in their ranks. One Mexican-American activist in five, one black in 13, and one white in 30, among all the 631 leaders said they belonged to a militant ethnic group. This dispersion of radical leadership indicates that "the influence of these groups over policy and popular values is undoubtedly even larger than the figures suggest."[24]

COMMUNITY ORGANIZER AS LEADER

There is a distinction to be made between community organizer and neighborhood leader although the research literature is practically silent on the leadership characteristics of the effective organizer. Lamb's study makes no such distinction and Bailey investigates only those leaders who are not paid staff of the OBA organization. Organizers themselves, however, write about their experience and offer advice for those who would take on the organizing role. In most of his writing, in fact, Alinsky speaks more to this group than to other would-be neighborhood leaders. He puts the difference between organizer and leader succinctly:

This is the basic difference between the leader and the organizer. The leader goes on to build power for purposes both social and personal. He wants power himself. The organizer finds his goal in creation of power for others to use.[25]

But organizers exert leadership nonetheless, even though they do not thrust themselves to the front of the organization as its spokesperson or figurehead: "In the beginning the organizer is the general, he knows where, what and how, but he never wears his four stars, never is addressed as nor acts as a general—he is an organizer."[26] Thus the distinction between leader and organizer among the Havenots parallels somewhat that between legitimizers and effectors among the Haves. In practice, however, the differentiation of leader roles in the neighborhood organization is important only because some organizers themselves fret about their roles when they are looked to for answers by the members. Alinsky makes no bones about their role. He sees the organizer initially as a Socrates leading the members to accept his vision of what's to be done. Then the role begins to change:

As time goes on and education proceeds, the leadership becomes increasingly sophisticated. The organizer recedes from the local circle of decision-makers. His response to questions about what he thinks becomes a non-directive counter-question, "What do you think?" His job becomes one of weaning the group away from any dependency upon him. Then his job is done.[27]

The point at which the organization has no further need of the organizer-leader is a mythical one. If the tasks of the organization require full-time attention, by one or several individuals, it is inevitable that these jobs will come to be paid positions or the work will not get done.

In many cases, organizer positions are entry-level openings. Individuals move from the unpaid leader or activist roles in the young organization into more formalized, paid (though the pay is usually quite low), and semiadministrative responsibilities. As the neighborhood movement has matured and broadened in scope, a cadre of professional organizers has grown, many of whom come from Alinsky organizations.[28] Where neighborhood organizations have been large and staffs have included from five to 20 paid workers, there has been opportunity not only for some upward mobility within the organization but also horizontal movement from one organization to another.

One can answer the question about whether a community organizer is really a leader by checking how well the characteristics of low-income neighborhood leadership fit the person. Does the organizer work among people who feel powerless to some degree? Does she bring analysis and perspective to the issues and initiate action on them? Is she at least skeptical about the efficacy and concern local and national government and institutions show toward the people's problems? Is he a resident of the neighborhood or at least committed to its people, a possessor of interpersonal skills, and motivated by race or ethnic pride where appropriate? Since the answers to these questions are usually *yes*, there is a strong argument for blurring the psychological distinction between leader and organizer. The main difference seems to be whether one is paid for one's time and efforts or not.

Those leaders of a neighborhood organization who work full-time at organizing and are paid for their labor do exert considerable influence. Relationships between organizers and leaders must remain flexible as the organization changes. Seymour Sarason has portrayed this need for flexibility in clear strokes.[29] Every new setting—a network of organized relationships—is at first the work of one person with an idea who gathers a small coterie of like-minded individuals. It is the nature of successful organization, however, that as work on the task proceeds, members of the group come to see the task differently due to their increasing competence and self-confidence. They begin to assert their own leadership.

The function of the originator then shifts from primarily an orientation to the task. There is now a growing concern for maintaining the members' commitment to the task, which requires that the task (the goals, objectives, or issues of the group) be redefined to include the members' changed perceptions. The leader must accommodate the emerging leadership of the group. A crisis is at hand. Too rigid a response on the one hand, or too much accommodation on the other, could put the entire enterprise in jeopardy.

So the organizer must change with the organization but remain the organizer. Seemingly contradicting his earlier statement about the organizer's job being done, Alinsky indicates the continued reliance of the organization on the organizer:

While the organizer proceeds on the basis of questions, the community leaders always regard his judgment above their own. They believe that he knows his job, he knows the right tactics, that's why he is their organizer.[30]

The staff-leadership relationship changes over time. For Alinsky that change should not diminish the organizer's status within the organization, but it often can. Bob Vondrasek, an organizer for Chicago's South Austin Coalition Community Council, calls this psychological demotion the "staff/leadership hang up."[31] In such a case, the leaders who work at other jobs during the day announce that the staff are hired to do the research and followup, or that "organizers don't talk at meetings." But no organization will be successful where the organizer is seen as a lackey who must do all the gruntwork. Unless the leaders are also activists, cooperating with the organizers in every way, organizers risk becoming disillusioned, frustrated, and burned out.

This important digression on the leadership tensions involved in being an organizer should not obscure the obvious but frequently overlooked fact that leadership in the organization can take many forms. Therefore many quite different individuals can function as leaders at one time or another. They might work on tasks related to the main goals of the organization, such as fundraising, block work, writing, or telephoning. But many other little tasks need doing, too, which left undone might make the difference between success or failure. Support for this multilevel concept of neighborhood organization leadership can be found in Bailey's study of OBA. First team leaders, who devote a great deal of time to many issues in the organization, differ from specialized leaders who focus on only one issue while ignoring others. Both are important in the neighborhood organization.

Since the other major leadership function is maintaining the group's commitment to working together, there will be individuals who show ability at resolving personality conflicts, keeping the group on course, or countering the multitude of self-serving behaviors that occur at any neighborhood meeting. Such people have just as much claim to be called leaders as those so designated officially. It is a wise organizer who is aware of their worth. What Alinsky meant by believing in people is clear; it is believing in their potential for leadership. And that leader is said to be democratic who can balance the dual concerns for getting the job done and keeping the people sold on doing it.

THE CONTEXT FOR NEIGHBORHOOD LEADERSHIP

The phenomenon of leadership in the neighborhood organization can be understood only within a web of interconnected variables: the context, the behavioral style of the leader, group member response, and the tasks at hand. The context is a principal variable influencing who will become leaders. Chapter 2 explores the meanings of neighborhood as a preparation for understanding how grassroots leaders are fashioned by the soil that grows them. Furthermore, we are now aware that, even though we are addressing the central question of restoring blighted neighborhoods, there are degrees and types of blight. According to the Warren and Warren typology of neighborhoods, described in chapter 2, transitory or transitional neighborhoods are those most often mentioned as locales of impending decline, wherein middle-class residents feel invaded by the lower class. Racism often, though not always, accompanies this process. The Warrens' other five types of neighborhood are also subject to deterioration, which is popularly defined as spot physical delapidation accompanied by the increasing appearance of undesirable people. Other neighborhoods are far more advanced in their deterioration. Typically described as slums, they are characterized by high incidences of abandoned property, street crime, and multiproblem families and individuals. Our discussion encompasses the spectrum of blight.

The second important feature of the Havenot neighborhood is psychological: resident alienation. Thus the context for organization will also be a neighborhood in which most people feel a sense of powerlessness about affecting the condition of their community through established channels. Residents of affluent neighborhoods may approximate this feeling, for example in the face of government decisions to build low-income housing nearby or bus their children for purposes of desegregation, but their sense of powerlessness is a mere shadow of that weighing on Havenots in inner city areas.

Bailey's study of the Organization for a Better Austin provides a link between context and leadership. After comparing four Alinsky-style organizations in Chicago, he concluded that such groups will emerge and flourish only under certain narrow conditions. First, the area must be experiencing serious economic and social problems not being addressed by local politicians. Second, most of the residents must feel alienated and powerless to resolve these problems through conventional channels. Third, among these residents there should be a substantial number with an orientation toward social participation and the personal resources to attack community problems. These limits generally correspond with Janice Perlman's assessment of the characteristics of successful neighborhood organizations in chapter 4. However, Perlman does not mention neighborhoods with serious socioeconomic problems, nor did OBA demonstrate "issue growth from neighborhood to nation," one of Perlman's marks of the mature neighborhood organization.

Although leadership is a function of the interaction between the person and the context, this chapter has focused on describing the characteristics of the leader and the style that he or she regularly displays in the organizational setting. Research suggests that the successful leader analyzes the issues and tasks at hand, initiates action on them, and remains flexible in the face of different follower responses, providing direction where it seems required and letting the group go once they have set their course. Effective leaders in poor neighborhoods are activists and coordinators, but also are motivated by an alienation from government and institutions, both local and national, a disaffection they share with many of their fellow residents. Although they have lived in these areas a long time, they have more personal resources in terms of time, social and neighborhood commitment, stamina, years of schooling, and interpersonal skills, than their neighbors. They have often been previously active in grassroots activities although they are rarely established community leaders, such as clergy. In black, Hispanic, or white ethnic neighborhoods, race or ethnic pride typifies the effective neighborhood organization leader.

Organizers are a special kind of leader among community activists. Other members of the organization may also show leadership behaviors, depending on the task to be done and the response of the group. This potential for broadened leadership draws our attention from the organization's core to its fullblown structure, from its members to its norms, goals, issues, and life cycle. The following chapter investigates these variables.

NOTES

1. Saul D. Alinsky, *Reveille for Radicals* (New York: Vintage, 1965), 46.

2. Richard Rich, "The Dynamics of Leadership in Neighborhood Organizations," *Social Science Quarterly* 60 (March 1980), 570–87.

3. Si Kahn, *Organizing: A Guide for Grassroots Leaders* (New York: McGraw-Hill, 1982), 21.

4. Launor Carter, William Haythorn, Beatrice Shriver, and John Lanzetta, "The Behavior of Leaders and Other Group Members," in *Group Dynamics: Research and Theory*, 3rd ed., ed. Dorwin Cartwright and Alvin Zander (New York: Harper and Row, 1968), 381–88.

5. Fred E. Fiedler, "Personality and Situational Determinants of Leadership Effectiveness," in *Group Dynamics: Research and Theory*, 3rd ed., ed. Cartwright and Zander (New York: Harper and Row, 1968), 362.

6. Carter et al., p. 387.

7. Fiedler, p. 378.

8. Clarence J. Davies, *Neighborhood Groups and Urban Renewal* (New York: Columbia University Press, 1966), 218.

9. Ralph White and Ronald Lippitt, "Leader Behavior and Member Reaction in Three 'Social Climates,' " in *Group Dynamics: Research and Theory*, 3rd ed., ed. Cartwright and Zander (New York: Harper and Row, 1968), 318–35.

10. Harold Nix, "Community Leadership," in *Leadership and Social Change*,

ed. William Lassey and Richard Fernandez (LaJolla, CA: University Associates, 1976), 313–24.

11. Napier and Gershenfeld, pp. 154–57.

12. John Kenneth Galbraith, *The New Industrial State*, 2nd ed. revised (New York: New American Library, 1971).

13. Saul Alinsky, *Rules for Radicals* (New York: Vintage, 1972), 113.

14. Alinsky, *Reveille for Radicals* p. 84.

15. Robert Bailey, *Radicals in Urban Politics: The Alinsky Approach* (Chicago: University of Chicago Press, 1972).

16. Curt Lamb, *Political Power in Poor Neighborhoods* (New York: Schenkman, 1975).

17. Lamb, pp. 106–7.

18. Lamb, p. 92.

19. Bailey, p. 102.

20. Lamb, p. 87.

21. Bailey, p. 105.

22. Bailey, p. 123.

23. William Ellis, *White Ethnics and Black Power: The Emergence of the West Side Organization* (Chicago: Aldine, 1969).

24. Lamb, p. 129.

25. Alinsky, *Rules for Radicals*, p. 80.

26. Alinsky, *Rules for Radicals*, p. 93.

27. Alinsky, *Rules for Radicals*, p. 92.

28. Laurel Leff, "Local Groups That Aid Poor Flourish by Using Confrontation Tactics," *Wall Street Journal*, May 13, 1981; Harry Boyte, *The Backyard Revolution* (Philadelphia: Temple University Press, 1980).

29. Seymour Sarason, *The Creation of Settings and the Future Societies* (San Francisco: Jossey-Bass, 1972).

30. Alinsky, *Rules for Radicals*, p. 93.

31. Bob Vondrasek, "Working the Streets," *Disclosure* 63 (June 1981), 4.

6

OTHER GROUP PROCESS VARIABLES IN THE NEIGHBORHOOD ORGANIZATION

Leadership is by no means the only gear in the organizational mechanism, though it is a key one. Motivation to become and remain a member is linked to the group's goals and norms. The organization itself also undergoes change; how it does so has been the subject of research on the life cycle (or evolution) of working groups. This chapter investigates these other important variables in the neighborhood organization.

MEMBERSHIP MOTIVATION

No clear line separates the motives of leader and member. Leaders are members and members might be leaders. What differentiates the two may be the mix of reasons why they joined and remain in the neighborhood organization. Four broad motives for initiating and continuing membership are as follows:[1]

1. *Altruism*, or caring for the issue the group is working on, whether or not there is a direct personal outcome for the individual
2. *Self-interest*, when there is a direct personal benefit, sometimes triggered by fear and defensiveness about potential or actual changes in the neighborhood
3. *Transaction*, related to self-interest but much weaker as a motivator, in which a person expects a tangible commodity, such as a newsletter or a front door decal announcing ''I support this organization,'' in return for joining
4. *Social needs*, in which a person seeks to be with friendly and interesting people, to feel a sense of belonging and involvement, to conform (often in

response to peer pressure), or to reduce personal feelings of responsibility for the problem

Social needs should also include a striving for *status* within the organization, which is closely related to power needs. Alinsky distinguishes between organizers, who seek to build power for the organization, and leaders, who seek power for themselves. Nonetheless, status and power are not quite the same. Listen to Alinsky describe status in the organization as a motivator for a poor ghetto resident:

It is a desperate search for personal identity—to let other people know that at least you are alive. Let's take a common case in the ghetto. A man is living in a slum tenement. He doesn't know anybody and nobody knows him. He doesn't care for anyone because no one cares for him. On the corner newsstand are newspapers with pictures of people like Mayor Daley and other people from a different world—a world that he doesn't know, a world that doesn't know that he is even alive.

When the organizer approaches him part of what begins to be communicated is that through the organization and its power he will get his birth certificate for life, that he will become known, that things will change from the drabness of a life where all that changes is the calendar. This same man, in a demonstration at City Hall, might find himself confronting the mayor and saying, "Mr. Mayor, we have had it up to here and we are not going to take it anymore." Television cameramen put their microphones in front of him and ask, "What is your name, sir?" "John Smith." Nobody ever asked what his name was before. And then, "What do you think about this, Mr. Smith?" Nobody ever asked him what he thought about anything before. Suddenly he's alive![2]

The achievement of status in a neighborhood organization may lead to a desire to consolidate and formalize what power it provides. Richard C. Rich's study of leadership in 11 Indianapolis neighborhood organizations indicated that altruism, or devotion to the community, was a much stronger motivator than any other, such as a personal share of collective goods (i.e., money) or deference to the leadership position.[3] The collective goods they generated were minimal, as was the recognition they received in the community for their work. Ethical commitment was the cause of their job satisfaction, and what power they had achieved was mainly an instrument for continuing that commitment. Although those with long experience in neighborhood organizing would view Rich's findings with no surprise, the electronic media rarely depict altruism as a motive, preferring instead to portray poverty leaders as scrambling for dollars and power. Neoconservative writings about the failure of the neighborhood movement also ignore altruism as a motivator.

Roger Ahlbrandt and James Cunningham corroborate the hypothesis that the most involved members of neighborhood organizations show active commitment to the area, rather than a more passive satisfaction with it.[4] The authors' surveys do indicate a difference in concerns between leaders and residents at large, however. For example, the latter focused on dog and garbage issues, the former on blockbusting, housing, and drugs. Thus, neighborhood organization leaders are both like and unlike their neighbors. In poor neighborhoods, they share the residents' characteristics, especially in their alienation from government and other institutions. We would expect them to have a deeper understanding of the problems plaguing the neighborhood, however, for ultimately this perception is the source of their leadership power. Therefore, the most active members of a neighborhood organization represent their neighbors' characteristics, but their alienation and their understanding of their collective problems are much sharper.

This distinction between leader motives and member motives, founded on differences in awareness and commitment, is a prelude to understanding how activists draw members into the organization. The process of involving citizens really means persuading them to pay whatever costs are necessary to achieve the organization's goals. These costs may be financial, such as dues or contributions, but in an impoverished community they are more likely to be social: attending meetings, communicating with fellow residents in various ways, fundraising, or engaging in conflict with institutions.

A psychological model of resident-activist contact that draws on the classification scheme of motivations just presented explains the process of interaction with reasonable accuracy.[5] In a sample situation, the organizer approaches a resident to sign a petition, to get a new program in the local school or to stop a proposed major street widening that will result in considerable commercial demolition. This initial requested behavior is often an easy one to elicit.

A behavioral mechanism then swings into play on the assumption that *first* we behave, then we look for reasons to justify that behavior. The petition signers realize that they do not know much about the issue, but they have just made a subtle public commitment. So they seek information that buttresses their action, in order to reduce this dissonance they feel between acting publicly without much knowledge and their need to justify that action with reasons. The organizer can employ this need for self-justification to invite signers to a meeting to find out more about the issue and what further they can do about it. If this "Behavioral Commitment Model" is correct, a cycle of public behaviors followed by reinforcing information can begin that will lead to the individual's developing consistent and reflective political attitudes.

Although this model ignores prior internal commitments as relevant to the involvement process, we often rationalize our behavior after the fact. Alinsky did it himself.

I remember that when I organized the Back of the Yards in Chicago I made many moves almost intuitively. But when I was asked to explain what I had done and why, I had to come up with *reasons*. Reasons that were not present at the time. What I did at the time, I did because that was the thing to do; it was the best thing to do, or it was the only thing to do. However, when pressed for reasons I had to start considering an intellectual scaffolding for my past actions—really, rationalizations. I can remember the "reasons" being so convincing even to myself that I thought, "Why, of course, I did it for those reasons—I should have known that was why I did it."[6]

The model also implies the need for a neighborhood organization to constantly balance action and education. Action may well mean confrontation, but it may also include social events, fundraising, or cooperative institution building, such as a day care center or a food-buying club. These are all *involvement behaviors* and as such they will lead to the participants' learning more about the organization's goals and strategies. Alinsky taught that when people had genuine opportunities to change conditions through their own actions, they began to think in a new way.[7] They raised the right questions, and showed competence in looking for the answers. They educated themselves when they had a reason for seeking knowledge. The effective neighborhood organization is literally an educational instrument.

The attraction and subsequent binding of residents to the neighborhood organization as members is a never-ending process. It involves appeals to their sense of altruism as well as to their self-interest. Their social needs, for belonging and involvement, for achieving status, and for solving social problems, must be met in diverse ways. Out of this growing pool of members come future leaders, and perhaps these leaders later will become organizers themselves. It has often happened.

THE NEIGHBORHOOD ORGANIZATION'S GOALS

Without clarity of purpose, communicated to and understood by even the most marginal member, the neighborhood organization risks irrelevance and dissolution. At least one commentator thinks that clear goals are more important than paid staff to the success of a grassroots organization.[8] Although the tasks of each association are specific to its unique characteristics and context, there are larger purposes that encompass these works and are common to neighborhood organizations across the nation. They answer the question, "What are neighborhood organizations for?"

Joan Lancourt, a former Alinsky organizer, in her analysis of eight Alinsky-style organizations, categorized their goals into three groups of long-, intermediate-, and short-range.[9] Despite differences in structure between Alinsky-modeled associations and others, her taxonomy of goals is applicable on a broader scale than she may have intended.

First among the long-range (or *terminal*) goals was accountability to the residents. Remember that the structure of the Alinsky organization was the umbrella, in which the members of the central group were representatives from other organizations in the community, including churches, recreation centers, PTAs, unions, and political parties. The membership and governance was completely representational, whereas in smaller neighborhood groups anyone residing in the area can become a member. Nonetheless the Alinsky structure sought a representation more accountable to all the inhabitants than their politicians or other powerbrokers were.

The goal of accountability to the people is paramount whether the membership is representative or direct. Even those neighborhood organizations with direct membership structures inevitably witness the emergence of a leadership cadre that makes many organizational decisions without taking a poll of the residents beforehand. Leaders of neighborhood organizations must take care to balance this natural tendency to centralize decision making by regular and honest public notice about the organization's activities and financial condition and by constantly replenishing the membership.

Lancourt identified four other long-range goals: (1) *Stabilizing the community*, that is, preventing its further decline; (2) Encouraging more residents to *participate* in decisions that shape their neighborhood, so as to alter a fatalistic psychology endemic to those in poverty; (3)

Promoting *social justice* and civil rights; and (4) Disseminating as widely as possible *information* about events and conditions important to the well-being of the neighborhood. Literature about neighborhood organizations and the newsletters they themselves produce verify that these goals are indeed operative. Yet stabilization of the community may clash with promotion of social justice, depending on the type of neighborhood. For example, a parochial neighborhood might oppose the inmigration of racially or ethnically different individuals. An affluent neighborhood might resist proposed zoning changes allowing the building of multifamily dwellings. In the poor inner city neighborhood, on the other hand, organization might occur to stop displacement of low-income people due to gentrification by high-income people. In this latter case, however, there are isolated instances in which the new arrivals become sensitized to the plight of the potential displacees and organize to achieve stability through incumbent upgrading for those low-income residents who remain.[10]

Neighborhood organizations, regardless of the income of their constituents, share a single overriding goal: defense of their turf. Information sharing and stabilization are implied in this objective. Accountability as a goal is a function of the residents' alienation from the political establishment. It is thus more likely to be found in low-income organizations. Promotion of civil rights and social justice is also more likely to be a goal of the Havenot organization.

Lancourt then outlined four *intermediate process* goals for the Alinsky groups she studied: (1) the development of an organization, (2) the steady acquisition of power, (3) community control, and (4) the halting of neighborhood deterioration. At first glance these may seem to be a continuation of long-term goals, and in some sense they are. Neighborhood organization is never completely developed because it is sensitive both to changes in its internal leadership/membership interaction and to larger forces outside the neighborhood that may demand severe organizational adaptations over time.[11] The second and third goals are essentially the same, though rhetorically different. Control and power over local affairs will always have to be shared—albeit grudgingly—with the larger powers of government and business. How much control is enough? The answer is wholly dependent on local context and personalities. Traditionally, the halting of neighborhood deterioration has come about through decisions made outside of neighborhoods by captains of public and private capital. Whether the neighborhood organization can become a significant new voice in that discussion remains to be seen, although cases of its effectiveness are cropping up with increasing frequency.[12]

Although there may not be a real distinction between the long-range and the intermediate goals of the neighborhood organization, the intermediate process goals do provide further insight into its workings. The development of an organization that seeks to halt neighborhood deterioration by taking matters into its own hands to some degree is a recent phenomenon. Even in areas with mature neighborhood organizations, many residents are still unaware of the existence of these groups; and after they do become aware, they do not comprehend their purposes except in the vaguest ways. This ignorance is not a denial of the broad understanding of self-help—people know what that means. Often they just do not know what it means in the neighborhood organization form.

Lancourt finally distinguishes all these larger goals from one she calls *short-term: victory*. When the Alinsky People's Organization goes into battle with the forces arrayed against the neighborhood, it wants to win the fights it picks. Although most neighborhood organizations are not in the Alinsky style, they cannot avoid occasional skirmishes. Anger and frustration at local conditions of neglect and poverty, and the residents' own feelings of pain, are the fuel driving the organization's thrust for change. These are the emotions of conflict and confrontation. They must have a constructive outlet, *victory*, a simple word for an extremely difficult accomplishment, particularly as the organization builds a victorious track record. In fact, it is fair to say that every neighborhood organization has as its more immediate objectives the gaining of some tangible benefits for the neighborhood as a result of its activity. Taking credit for a good outcome, whether it be a street newly paved or an anti-redlining battle won, is essential for the continued health of the neighborhood organization. Success develops members' confidence in the organization and themselves, the organization's credibility to outsiders, and its ability to continue as the sole voice of the residents.

Thus residents organize their neighborhood in the face of threats to its stability or to bring it back to such a point. The organizational machinery they build for this defense effort seeks to embody accountability to and participation by all residents so as to reassert local control over neighborhood living conditions. The organization publishes its effectiveness through its victories, by which tangible benefits accrue to the neighborhood. This latter objective is really the successful prose-cution of issues. In other words, defining and resolving issues is the main short- to intermediate-range goal of the neighborhood organization. Now what is an issue?

ISSUES

The mere presence of a bad condition or a threat does not of itself constitute an issue. Issues are the result of the following process within the organization: (1) selection of a specific bad condition or threat, (2) research into its immediate causes and consequences, (3) publication of this information to residents, (4) creation of strategies to attack the sources of the problem, (5) proposal of desired outcomes gauging expected resistance to the organization's attack. This entire process is called *defining the issue*. John Fish admitted that The Woodlawn Organization (TWO) in Chicago pursued only those issues in which the opposition was not so aroused, entrenched, or powerful as to make the desired outcome impossible.[13]

A main function of the neighborhood organization is defining or redefining the issues of local importance. *Redefining* implies that City Hall, for instance, may have defined the issue previously in terms unfavorable to the residents. In Woodlawn, the University of Chicago defined the issue of slum housing adjacent to its campus by attempting to buy it, raze it, and build new student housing in its place. They said, in effect, "There is bad housing. What can we do about it? Get rid of it and use the land for our purposes." The black community answered the what-to-do-about-the-bad-condition question with a completely different response: this is *our* housing, help *us* rehabilitate it or build new housing for ourselves. TWO redefined the issue by restructuring the discussion about strategies and outcomes. It simply brought local self-interest to compete with the interests of established institutional powers in the area.

Issues harbor unique qualities, as Alinsky pointed out: they are controversial,[14] they must be created out of preexisting bad conditions,[15] they must be multiple in order to meet the different value hierarchies of the members,[16] and they are "specific, immediate, and realizable."[17] Issues are controversial because when they are redefined by the neighborhood association, as in the Woodlawn-University of Chicago example, neighborhood and institutional interests clash. In almost all cases, they represent competition for scarce goods. As we have seen, issues are created out of the bad condition; the organizers make an issue of housing deterioration or poor services by drawing public attention to it and by showing those who suffer from it ways to collectively demand change for the better. The organization has to include several issues on its current agenda simply because differences in need must be met to insure greater participation. For instance, attending to Mr. Jones's concerns about getting a loan to fix up his house while simultaneously helping Mrs. Smith combat street crime may result in Mr. Jones and Mrs. Smith getting interested in each other's issues. Finally, requiring that issues must be specific, immediate, and realizable underscores the point that the successful organizer touches people's felt, personal concerns about their neighborhood and aids them in planning feasible solutions to these problems. As solutions (victories) come into being, residents gain confidence to confront larger local issues.

There are fallow periods in the life of each community organization when little seems to be happening, but the pursuit of issues, even if the strategies used are not confrontational, is its lifeblood. Inequities and injustices are particularly acute in economically depressed urban neighborhoods. Tea and social clubs are not the stuff of neighborhood organizations. There may be social events, fairs, raffles, bazaars, and other manifestations of community building, but the issues of the neighborhood organization are politically and economically localized in nature, ranging from public order on the streets to higher employment, adequate housing, and sufficient social services. Chapters 7, 8, 9, and 10 provide examples of organizations acting on these issues.

Thus far in this chapter we have explored membership and goals, including issues, as principal explanatory variables in the neighborhood organization. Two other variables remain: group norms and a description of expected organizational cycles (sometimes called the evolution of the working group).

ORGANIZATIONAL NORMS

Group norms are rules or standards that govern the behavior of the organization's leaders and members; these behaviors decide to a great degree whether the organization meets its tasks and survives as an organization. In distinguishing formal and informal norms, we should note that many of the most important norms are unspoken or not actually written in the bylaws. For example, organization bylaws may state clearly that membership is open to all interested residents and that greater participation by diverse individuals is to be desired. Yet when someone new comes to a meeting and constantly gets discussion off track, the more fundamental norm, smooth cooperation in conducting business, may collide with and overrule the formal democratic standard. Again, the formal norm may be that since this is a people's organization, the *people* will make the decisions about the issues and strategies to be pursued or the expenditure of funds. The informal norm, that it is often more efficient for the dedicated core to make these decisions, sometimes overrides the formal norm. Because norms are the bones of an organization's body, unseen but essential in supporting the entire structural mass, the organization's leaders and members should reflect often on what the operative norms are and whether they are conducive to group maintenance and the productivity of group efforts.

Many norms for proper behavior in the neighborhood group are common to other types of organizations, often quite different in purpose. For example, norms for conducting meetings, publication of information, and other forms of communication, such as thank-you notes for contributions or favors done, are almost universal. But groups that engage in militant protest behaviors require special rules for the successful prosecution of their aims. These norms include not only the dos and don'ts of confrontation itself, but also the pitfalls that leaders and organizers should avoid if they are to be productive. Alinsky's aphorisms of effective militancy are well known in the organizing field. They include, for example,

—Power is not only what you have but what the enemy thinks you have.

—Never go outside the experience of your people.

—Wherever possible go outside the experience of the enemy.

—Make the enemy live up to their book of rules.

—Ridicule is man's most potent weapon.

—A good tactic is one that your people enjoy.

—A tactic that drags on too long becomes a drag.

—Keep the pressure on.

—The threat is usually more terrifying than the thing itself.

—Pick the target, freeze it, personalize it, and polarize it.[18]

Since the implications of these generalizations are situation-specific, Alinsky exemplifies them in some detail for would-be organizers. In their skeletal splendor, however, they function as norms of conducting conflict through the neighborhood organization. More recent books on community organizing expand on these prescriptions and recognize that militancy, while remaining a basic ingredient in the mix of strategies, is not always necessary or effective in gaining the desired objective.[19]

People who organize to demand their rights, however, quickly discover that it is a stressful enterprise, not only for institutions they are hassling, but for themselves as well. All leaders and organizers need to examine their behaviors in the organization in order to achieve some balance between stress and productivity. William Bryan, founder of the Northern Rockies Action Group, summarizes problems that every organizer has come to experience at one time or another, and how to avoid them.[20] These conditions can easily be translated into how-tos for everyone working hard for the neighborhood organization.

It is natural to be preoccupied with and worried about the sometimes intense pressures the neighborhood organization is creating, Bryan says. Other factors magnify this stress. Within the group, lack of clear direction in the work environment, of ways to say no to more demands on one's energy, of clear rewards (especially adequate salary), of security in the form of supportive friends, and of success itself (since it is hard to win on many issues), can turn the screws on the organizer. Add to these the intensity of the workplace itself and one's own undisciplined work habits (the Ralph Nader syndrome or workaholism), and one has the recipe for quick burnout. Bryan suggests revising the norms for the organization so as to skirt these pitfalls. Positive changes might include requiring realistic planning, periodic evaluation, and effective rewards. In addition, the organizer needs to develop a personal support group, hold a realistic view of the job to be done, and have a little fun besides. Alinsky, the tough-skinned general, always made sure he and his people had fun!

Norms are standards or behavioral criteria by which the organization acts to achieve its goals of self-maintenance and improvement of neighborhood conditions. The rules of its operation are both conscious and unconscious, formal and informal. Successful neighborhood organizations have achieved enough cohesiveness among members and leaders to identify threatening or self-defeating norms and replace them with more practical yet still ethical ones. This process of self-evaluation is a mark of the mature neighborhood organization and correlates positively with reasonably low leadership turnover and high rates of success in bettering neighborhood conditions.

THE LIFE CYCLE OF THE ORGANIZATION

Mention of organizational maturity brings to mind the fact that to fully understand organization, one must look at it over a period of time. If cities change, if neighborhoods change, then certainly neighborhood organizations themselves change. The forces for change are both internal and external. An analogy could be made between the neighborhood organization and a growing human organism. Defining the sources of organizational change parallels the nature-nurture and heredity-environment controversies of psychology and sociology. Most investigations of organizational life cycles have focused on change *within* the organization, while less work has concentrated directly on how the larger environment affects it.

Rodney Napier and Matti Gershenfeld suggest a typical set of stages in the internal dynamic of a group from its beginning to its maturity.[21] There is first, of course, the *beginning*, in which the members test their expectations of one another and seek to divine where they belong in the group setting. Then, as patterns of power and leadership begin to gel, members of the group *confront* one another, seeking to fulfill their own personal aims. This hostile movement is countered in the third stage by *compromise* and harmony as personal issues submit to the group's agenda. A fourth phase of *task reassessment* eventually promotes tolerance, shared leadership, accountability, and other characteristics of independent maturity. This fullness of organizational function leads finally to *resolution* and recycling, by which the group deals effectively with new crises from outside and problems arising later among its members.

From this point of view, group process is essentially a continual adaptation to stress and tension. Recall Seymour Sarason's requirement that organizational leaders retain flexibility, as mentioned in Chapter 5. A major crisis in any organization occurs when the members begin to seek their own goals. At this point the leader must adapt to their changing needs by compromising, reassessing, and resolving this basic internal conflict. To be a leader, then, is to be a facilitator, an adjustor, one who keeps it all together.

This perspective on the internal dynamics of the group is necessary but insufficient to explain organizational change. The external environment of the organization profoundly affects it. Henig, in his study of gentrification in the Adams-Morgan neighborhood of Washington, DC, argues that events transcending individual neighborhoods can squeeze the neighborhood organization beyond its limits of adaptability.[22] He traces how two older, previously dormant organizations (the Kalorama Citizens Association, formed in 1919, and the 18th and Columbia Road Business Association, formed about 1920) and a new government-initiated association (the Advisory Neighborhood Council) have absorbed as members most of the new professional class coming to reside in the area. Subsequently, the previous claimant to being the voice of the people, the Adams-Morgan Organization, a multiracial, multiethnic neighborhood organization, has undergone decline in membership, some change in issue-focus toward historic preservation, and a marked shift in style toward the pragmatic and away from the radicalism of its heyday in 1974–76. Thus, although vigilant respect for proper organization maintenance is a large part of the price of effectiveness, it is only part of the price. Leaders and organizers must constantly monitor the environment of the neighborhood as well, because as it changes, the organization cannot but be affected.

This need to be aware of demographic, political, and cultural trends is so important that this book began with such an analysis. Nonetheless, most observers of change in neighborhood organizations emphasize the predictability of stages based largely on organizational theory, or the *internal* perspective. Linda Easley, Rick Cohen, Sarason, and Alinsky exemplify this inward emphasis, although they do include environmental elements in their models.[23]

Easley's analysis of stages in the development in the Eastown Community Association of Grand Rapids, Michigan, attempts to bridge the two perspectives. Her first stage is *Identity Development*, in which a core group forms around such issues as the need for physical cleanup and fixup. The identity aspect is internal to the group (i.e., it is building its own identity). It has only a superficial understanding of the community's problems at this point; its solutions address only unpleasant symptoms of blight.

Easley's second stage is the creation of a public image through actions. Implied is a shift in goals toward more militant purposes. It usually involves a change to new leaders. The organization bursts onto the scene. Having gone through some internal conflicts, the association does battle with more formidable forces at the city level. This is a phase of *Militant Reaction*.

In Easley's stage three, *Structural Development*, the organization stabilizes itself and seeks to broaden its participative base. (Reasonable expectations for active membership in an effective people's organization range between 1 and 5 percent of the total population of the neighborhood.) Funding becomes more important, and the organization may begin to offer alternative services, such as a food coop, printing shop, or day care. Oddly, it is then ripe for stagnation and decline. The major need is to maintain its original enthusiasm and sense of community. Organizers do this by retaining some militancy in the organization's activities, since the question of power underlies all else. The association was effective in mobilizing against inequities because the people could see that they were making a difference in what City Hall or Big Business was doing to them. Their organization was their lever of power, their weapon against the Establishment. Without this exercise of power, the injustices, never completely rooted out, grow back rapidly. Recall Curt Lamb's conclusion that those organizations are perceived to be most effective that combine militancy and cooperation in their repertoire of activities.

The developmental approach to organizational change assumes that organizations are analogous to living organisms, especially humans. On the one hand, the analogy with growing children is apt. At times they are in sheer pain due to expansion, at other times contradictory elements war within them, and still other periods show an almost apathetic calm. Yet the comparison is invalid for two reasons: organisms necessarily die, and they go through clear and predictable developmental stages. Organizations do neither of these. Studies of a variety of institutions have suggested that their vulnerability to decline may depend on their rate of growth, their access to outside resources, and their resistance to innovation. It is also possible for an organization to fail, yet not die.[24]

Whether there are stages of development in neighborhood organizations is debatable, but there seems to be agreement on some points regarding their evolution. Neighborhood organizations usually begin with issues; over time they tend to shift from protest to program emphasis, especially in the poorest areas; and if organizations die, they do so for common reasons. Recall Lancourt's analysis in Chapter 4 of three Alinsky organizations that dissolved because they violated good organizational practice. Compare her list (following) with the principles just mentioned that correlate with organizational decline:

1. They became isolated from prevailing social movements.
2. Their constituencies got "out of focus."
3. They suffered internal disputes which their organizational structure could not handle.
4. They made few appeals to "third parties."
5. Their issue selection was poor.
6. They did not unburden themselves of members who opposed the organization's objectives, and partially as a result of all of this,
7. They experienced funding difficulties.[25]

Planning for the future of the organization, keeping it alive, useful, and vibrant when victories seem harder to come by, is a central problem for the neighborhood organization. So far we have engaged in a relatively abstract analysis. Alinsky used a mechanical image, in which the people were the engine and the organization the gears to move democracy forward. Understanding how the engine and the gears work in relation to each other is essential if forward motion is to be initiated and even more so if it breaks down and needs repair.

NOTES

1. Bruce Ballenger, "Why People Join," *Community Jobs*, April 1981, 3–6.

2. Saul Alinsky, *Rules for Radicals* (New York: Vintage Books, 1972), 121.

3. Richard C. Rich, "The Dynamics of Leadership in Neighborhood Organizations," *Social Science Quarterly* 60 (March 1980), 570–87.

4. Roger S. Ahlbrandt and James V. Cunningham, *A New Public Policy for Neighborhood Preservation* (New York: Praeger, 1979), 43.

5. Ballenger, p. 6.

6. Alinsky, pp. 169–70.

7. Alinsky, p. 106.

8. Joan Flanagan, *The Grassroots Fundraising Book*, 2nd ed., (Chicago: Contemporary Books, 1982).

9. Joan Lancourt, *Confront or Concede: The Alinsky Citizen-Action Organizations* (Lexington, MA: D.C. Heath, 1979), 34–46.

10. Sandra Schoenberg and Patricia L. Rosenbaum, *Neighborhoods That Work: Sources for Viability in the Inner City* (New Brunswick, NJ: Rutgers University Press, 1980).

11. Jeffrey R. Henig, "Community Organizations in Gentrifying Neighborhoods," *Journal of Community Action* 1 (November-December 1981), 45–55.

12. The entire issue of *Citizen Participation* 3 (January-February 1982) is devoted to the matter of self-help. See especially Ginsburg, "Prospects of Economic Self-Help" and St. George and Thompson on cooperatives, both articles in this newsprint issue.

13. John Fish, *Black Power/White Control: The Struggle of The Woodlawn Organization in Chicago* (Princeton, NJ: Princeton University Press, 1973), 110.

14. Alinsky, p. 117.

15. Alinsky, p. 119.

16. Alinsky, pp. 76–77.

17. Alinsky, p. 120.

18. Alinsky, pp. 127–31.

19. For two recent books on organizing strategies, see Si Kahn, *Organizing: A Guide for Grassroots Leaders* (New York: McGraw-Hill, 1982) and Douglas Biklen, *Community Organizing: Theory and Practice* (Englewood Cliffs, NJ: Prentice-Hall, 1983). See also Steve Burghardt, *The Other Side of Organizing: Resolving the Personal Dilemmas and Political Demands of Daily Practice* (Cambridge, MA: Schenkman, 1982) for insights into how an organizer might cope successfully with the stresses of the job. Another recent book by William Berkowitz, *Community Impact: Creating Grassroots Change in Hard Times* (Cambridge, MA: Schenkman, 1982) is particularly useful for those creating alternative programs or institutions.

20. William L. Bryan, "Preventing Burnout in the Public Interest Community," *The Grantsmanship Center News*, March/April 1981, 15–77.

21. Rodney Napier and Matti K. Gershenfeld, *Groups: Theory and Experience* (Boston: Houghton Mifflin, 1973), 247–55.

22. Henig, pp. 49–55.

23. Linda Easley, "The Development of a Neighborhood Organization," unpublished Ph.D. dissertation, Michigan State University, Department of Anthropology, East Lansing, 1982; Rick Cohen, "Neighborhood Planning and Political Capacity," *Urban Affairs Quarterly* 14 (March 1979), 337–62; Seymour Sarason, *The Creation of Settings and the Future Societies* (San Francisco: Jossey-Bass, 1972); Saul Alinsky, "The War on Poverty—Political Pornography," *Journal of Social Issues* 21 (January 1965), 41–47.

24. John R. Kimberly and Robert H. Miles, *The Organizational Life-Cycle* (San Francisco: Jossey-Bass, 1980).

25. Lancourt, p. 159.

PART III

The Tasks of Neighborhood Organizations

7

NEIGHBORHOOD REINVESTMENT STRATEGIES

People with options don't just buy a house. They buy a neighborhood.
—Robert Cassidy[1]

Havenot neighborhoods represent the desertion of capital. Deteriorating homes, vacant businesses, unkempt public spaces all shout silently that they are starved for capital. Reinvestment means feeding them the rehabilitative funds they need, and it means building new homes and attracting new businesses as well. This chapter explores the twin issues of housing and commercial revitalization and how neighborhood organizations are wrestling with them.

HOUSING

Housing is a natural theater for community organizing. The physical face of a residential area is the first image denizens conjure when they speak of their locale. The units they dwell in are like a second skin to them. Inadequate housing is a source of emotional stress and unhappiness, and the condition of a neighborhood's housing largely defines the value of living there. Housing is the major feature of the *place*.

The Problem

The availability of adequate housing has always been of particular concern for low- and moderate-income persons, even though the American dream of single family home ownership became a reality for many after World War II. Government policies, including FHA guaranteed mortgages, highway construction projects to facilitate suburban commuting, and income tax laws making interest and property tax payments deductible, boosted home ownership rates from 44 percent in 1940 to a high of 65 percent in 1977. Renters continued to be largely those who could not afford to buy: the poor, the elderly, the urban minorities.

The public and private sectors have not built enough good housing for these latter groups. When housing squeezes occur, these are the people who feel the pinch most painfully. And most cities are in a housing crisis. In November 1979, the Government Accounting Office estimated the country's vacancy rate at 4.8 percent, the lowest on record.[2] Just how bad is this?

Though the Federal Government defines any vacancy rate of less than 5 percent as an emergency, rates in many American cities are far worse: 2 percent in Baltimore, less than 1 percent in San Francisco and Newark, and 2.6 percent in Washington. In Los Angeles, where the rate plummets to .5 percent in Hispanic and .4 percent in black ghettos, more and more of the poor are living in autos and paying between $20 and $30 a month for bathroom or kitchen privileges in nearby apartments.[3]

How can cities be in a housing crisis while at the same time they are losing population to the suburbs? The answer is that while the absolute numbers of people in the city are declining (with the exception of some sunbelt cities), the number of *people per household* is declining faster, so that the total number of households is actually increasing.[4] This paradoxical state of affairs is easier to understand when we realize that as the age of the population increases there are more and more elderly people living alone in oversized houses. They are seeking smaller, more efficient, and less expensive apartment units. At the other end of the age spectrum, young married couples are priced out of the housing market and forced to settle for more cramped quarters—also in multiunit housing. Between 1970 and 1977 *small* urban households increased by 19 percent, while all other urban households *decreased* by 4 percent.[5]

The fact that housing is tight, especially for the poor, is not lost on certain landlords. They know that low-income tenants have few options and that City Hall is keenly aware of this. So an unspoken bargain is struck: tenants don't complain about bad conditions, landlords agree not to raise rents dramatically or to evict them, and the city occasionally slaps a landlord's wrist for flagrant code violations. Though not all rental property owners are slumlords, rapidly changing economic conditions in recent years have increased the numbers of investor-owners who exploit the low- or moderate-income tenant.

There are at least seven types of investor-owners for multiunit housing:[6]

1. Sophisticated *established owners* with integrity who are in business a long time for steady returns and to whom tenants are important

2. Unsophisticated *blue-collar investors*, also with integrity but who are easily overwhelmed by changes in the neighborhood

3. *Traders* who speculate in rising markets and whose chief interest is quickly increasing resale price by increasing gross rents or making cosmetic improvements

4. *Operators*, stereotyped as the slumlords, whose shortsightedness includes providing housing almost solely to high-risk tenants, avoiding taxes and repairs, and maximizing short-term profits

5. *Shareholders*, professionals who invest as limited partners often without a grasp of housing issues and responsibilities

6. *Rehabbers and developers*, who are not concerned about ownership but only with making money at the front end and who shape market trends

7. *Special forces* (distressed property handlers), who specialize in the newest gimmicks, such as conversion to condominiums. Rehabbers may also be a subset of this group.

In uncertain and fluctuating markets, where market values may rapidly inflate or deflate, interest rates move ever upward, taxes on rent income balloon, and operating expenses soar, the first two types of investor-owners cannot survive, and they are not replaced by their own kind. Enter the traders, operators, and shareholders, each lured by the expectation of large short-term returns on investment. As the housing deteriorates rapidly, the last two types are in a position to completely reshape the face of the housing market, razing and rebuilding or rehabbing and converting for an entirely new class market (the gentry). Another ominous possibility, and growing more frequent in occurrence, is that the property may be deliberately torched to recoup losses through inflated insurance policies.

So far landlords (or at least five kinds of them) have been painted as the bad guys, but bankers, government officials, insurance executives, and a host of other legitimizers and effectors have contributed to the mess, either overtly or unwittingly. Neighborhood organizations have battled for better housing in a number of ways and with some success, although some critics maintain that little headway has been made as long as a third of all renters live in substandard housing in such cities as Detroit, Baltimore, and Chicago.[7] The tactics neighborhood-based organizations have used fall into two very broad categories that require some detailed explanation: direct action against the power brokers or cooperation with them.

Direct Action Strategies

Since housing is a natural issue, it is to be expected that the first fights for many community organizations were over housing. Alinsky's organizing in Chicago's Back of the Yards in the late 1930s included rent strikes by tenants living in substandard apartment buildings. They would collectively withhold their rent until the landlord made needed repairs. Rent strikes, to be effective, however, require strong support from the appropriate areas of government. They need legislation allowing the establishment of escrow accounts for the deposit of the rent money pending arbitration, and protection from sanctions by landlords against their upstart tenants. Housing inspectors need to place the dwelling high on their list of priorities, and judges need to be stern with the miscreant owners when they are brought in. In most cases, these many factors have not operated in synchrony, and tenants have been evicted or gotten no redress in the form of improved living quarters. The rent strike may be relatively easy to organize, but in the long run it is very difficult to win. One of the most successful tenant organizations of this century, New York's Citywide Tenants' Council (CWTC), operated across several large neighborhoods between 1936 and 1943.[8] Although it helped low-income tenants and predicted today's housing problems, CWTC was not effective at the policy level and was unable to solve the problem of tenants dropping out of the organization once their own crisis was resolved.

Another direct action taken by neighborhood organizations is *squatting*, patterned after a long-standing British tradition in which the displaced and homeless simply move into abandoned units and take up housekeeping. Milton Street claims to have moved several hundred Philadelphia families into abandoned residential buildings. Some of these families have done considerable rehabilitation to make their new nests livable.[9] ACORN, a multistate organization, has been organizing the same types of actions in Detroit and Lansing, Michigan.

The media attention that accompanies squatting actions is intended by organizers to rouse officialdom to the plight of the homeless. Since it is a basic sort of self-help project by obviously needy individuals, city bureaucrats have been prone to look the other way while trying to untangle the legal and procedural snarls that it creates. But squatting can also create disruption in the very neighborhood itself, if the nearby residents oppose the squatting process because they would rather that occupancy occur through normal channels.

A third form of action engaged in by neighborhood organizations over the past decade has sought to push lending institutions and insurance companies to increase their investments (loans and policies) in economically depressed neighborhoods. In either case, the institutions have refused to grant an improvement loan, a mortgage, or an insurance policy on a home simply because of its location. All of these actions fall under the generic term of *redlining*. Consider lender redlining first.

Studies of redlining since the early 1970s are nearly unanimous in pointing out that lending institutions functioned as siphons for urban deposits, turning them into suburban mortgages at the cost of inner-city decline.[10] In other words, the *effects* of lender practice were discriminatory against cities. Bankers and loan officers retort that such studies are out of date and so much hogwash. In fact, redlining has never been proved to their satisfaction because lending criteria, other than location, have not been met by applicants. These criteria generally seek to reduce the higher risk in depressed areas by, for example, demanding a higher than usual down payment, setting interest rates and closing costs higher, or granting shorter-term mortgages. The net effect of such higher standards is to price housing out of the reach of the low- or moderate-income people who would buy there. Lenders defend themselves further by saying that neighborhoods deteriorate first and then lenders are hesitant to loan. The lenders also contend that they have no ill will, that there is no real demand for loan money in poor areas, that they have been singled out for blame, or that in fairness to their depositors they have no right to unduly risk their deposits.

The studies of financial segregation are reminiscent of those finding *de facto* racial segregation, upon which massive court-ordered busing plans for integration were based. They pointed out the *fact* of segregation. So too did the redlining studies, even though the lenders would not call it redlining. As noted in chapter 1, however, without a steady flow of capital into a neighborhood, it will decline and die. Capital is its lifeblood. The hemorrhage of its deposit capital has to be stopped.

To add to the problem, insurance companies appeared to be imposing their version of redlining, deterring reinvestment in lower income neighborhoods. Exorbitant premium rates, inadequate coverage, or outright refusal to insure based on location characterized this practice. Although insurance redlining has proved to be harder to grapple with because most insurers do not have localized service areas as do lending institutions, Michigan's statewide Coalition on Redlining and Neighborhoods pushed for an insurance law with teeth. It came into effect January 1981. This insurance anti-redlining law, however, required that the complainant assume the burden of proof by showing that comparable houses in a different neighborhood have lower rates or were not denied insurance. Although a few cases were prosecuted at the outset, none have been brought recently. Michigan had passed a law several years earlier against lender redlining. The first anti-redlining regulations were passed by the state of Illinois in the early 1970s under pressure from a strident coalition of neighborhood associations in Chicago.[11] Michigan's law was modeled after Illinois' and its passage was also aided by pressure from various neighborhood groups. On a national scale, neighborhood-based pressure led to the enactment of the Home Mortgage Disclosure Act (HMDA) of 1975.

The new weapons of legal access to lending information and laws against redlining, though flawed, have helped win some skirmishes in the battle to bring investment dollars back into the urban neighborhood. For example, a study in the Eastown neighborhood of Grand Rapids showed evidence that the Michigan law has encouraged reinvestment there in areas with working class homeowners.[12] A more complex example utilizes a strategy originally devised by Chicago's National Training and Information Center. Two different groups, Citizens for Community Improvement (CCI) of Des Moines and Group 14621 of Rochester, working independently, won battles that solved problems of lender and insurer redlining and high interest rates—all without federal subsidy. Here is how they did it.[13]

First each group targeted one local financial lending institution that held deposits from the neighborhood but that also chose to redline. The federal Home Mortgage Disclosure Act, which requires documentation of lending patterns although it does not actually outlaw redlining, gave clout to researching the targets, which, in Des Moines, became the Scandia Savings and Loan Association and, in Rochester, the Dime Savings and Loan. Another federal law, the Community Reinvestment Act (CRA), requires a reinvestment plan of all lending institutions for their service areas in exchange for the privilege of conducting certain of its activities, such as branching, merging with other lenders, or acquiring stock. After CCI threatened a suit against Scandia when they sought a merger with two smaller savings and loans, and Group 14621 picketed Dime in Rochester, both lenders increased the number of their loans in blighted areas fivefold. But bloated interest rates still kept loan money from many low-income people.

As they tell it, activists armed with HMDA and CRA and pressure tactics from the grassroots, sought a large pool of money that the two savings and loans could dip into at much lower rates of interest. They found just such a pool as a result of their assault on the redlining by the richest U.S. property and casualty insurer, State Farm Fire and Casualty. Edward Rust, State Farm's president, as a result of local direct actions and of sit-down negotiations with National People's Action, a Chicago-based national coalition of neighborhood groups, signed and distributed an anti-redlining directive to all his offices. He also ordered the development of a new, more affordable homeowner's policy and an affirmative advertising program that announced State Farm's intention to return to inner city neighborhoods. But the most important result had to do with making loans more affordable.

State Farm agreed to deposit $100,000 annually in each of the two savings and loans at a low interest rate of return, 6 percent in Des Moines and 5 percent in Rochester. The lenders' profit and service fees would bring the rate to 8 percent, a full 10 percent below market. In Des Moines, the loans, up to $5,000 for rehabilitation, are targeted for low-income owner-occupants in selected inner city neighborhoods. In Rochester, the loans, up to $6,000 and matched by the city, go for improvements in small businesses in inner city residential areas. Although the loan ceiling is low because the initial pool of money is small, the potential for increasing the funds is good. There are many other insurance companies, and their funds could be matched by Community Development Block Grant Program (CDBG) money through city government.

This strategy is instructive in several ways. It exemplifies the need for thorough knowledge of how the system works, how data is vital to support action, the necessity for federal regulations to pressure the private sector, and the requirement that activists be imaginative in constructing alternative solutions.

The direct action strategies of neighborhood organizations have demonstrated that owners, lending institutions, and government agencies charged with regulating them can be sensitized by the application of public pressure. But reliance on militant measures alone often falls short. As the evidence shows throughout this book, engaging in battle is just the front end of a long struggle for recognized access to the levers of power. Even if the neighborhood organization succeeds in getting the city government to create a whole new machinery to correct the problem of inadequate housing for renters, this tool may not be big enough for the job. Take the case of Baltimore's model approach to code enforcement:

Touted nationally as a city responsive to its poor, Baltimore has a Department of Housing and Community Development (HCD) that is armed with standards, teams of inspectors, repair crews, a computerized system for recording complaints and two state's attorneys who do nothing but handle court cases involving code violations. The city also has a Housing Court that hears an average of 1,000 cases a year and a Rent Court, which, though established as a tool for landlords, is now also used by tenants to establish escrow accounts and sue negligent owners.[14]

Baltimore is a city of powerful neighborhood organizations and coalitions, among them the Southeast Community Organization (SECO), Citizens for Fair Housing (CFH), and the Coalition Against Displacement (CAD). They have had much to do with the establishment of this government machinery to enforce the housing code. Yet some of their leaders are discouraged. Code violations are still criminal offenses. Slumlords cannot be ordered to make repairs, judges can only fine them or send them to jail. And they fine them small fines and *never* send them to jail. In addition, landowners know how to use the law to delay; the model Housing Court is drowning under an impossible caseload. For every inspector there are approximately 1,200 substandard units, and even when a violation is found, getting it corrected is far from easy. The head of the Inspection Division complains, ''whom do you serve when the owner of 100 dilapidated houses is a Panamanian corporation, managed by a German national living in Venezuela?''[15]

The Baltimore case is meant to illustrate that old adage about winning battles and losing wars. The battles don't end; they change as the neighborhood organization gains legitimacy and its immediate goals are realized. Activists from neighborhoods discover among the enemy, bureaucrats of good will and competence. There are also landlords, bankers, and federal and state officials sympathetic to the cause of revitalizing decaying neighborhoods. The effective organizer finds these people and builds their efforts into cooperative ventures. Cooperation is the other edge of the double blade; militant action is the first. In the State Farm example, depositing the pool of money in the savings and loans was a cooperative act, not coerced (despite activist rhetoric to the contrary) by recourse to any government regulation or court sanction. Certainly State Farm stood to gain some favorable publicity, but it was clearly a contribution of the interest differential between market rate and 6 percent. Some observers think successful neighborhood change strategies require that activists include the interests of *all* parties in devising their solutions.[16] Although complete polarization is sometimes necessary, savvy organizers take the opposition's needs into account instinctively. Healthy skepticism and wariness must always be there, but sooner or later, protest overlaps into program.

The move to program carries considerable risk. The neighborhood organization leadership, always more attuned to the technical points of the organization's agenda, can become technocrats, skilled in the legal and financial intricacies of developing revitalization plans, cooperative business ventures, or needed neighborhood services. While expertise is essential, it can at the same time divide those becoming skilled from those not yet skilled who had heretofore participated regularly. These citizens can be left behind. And they had better not be, because they are the sinews of the militant neighborhood organization. Such a group should never lose its grassroots connection or its nerve; for if it does, it cannot compete with other forces shaping the neighborhood.

Cooperative and Partnership Strategies

Having made this caveat, we should discuss the other side of the coin, cooperative ventures. These programs are much more variable and complex, and they almost always involve government in its regulatory or funding capacities or both. Where laws against redlining exhibit flaws—and they do in most states—relying strictly on pressure tactics may not be enough to bring about change. Michigan's law, for example, forbids class action suits by neighborhood coalitions against a lender affecting them collectively. Illinois may require disclosure of loans, but not deposits, making it hard for the neighborhood organization to build a complete case that money is draining away from the neighborhood. Although a 1976 California law sidesteps these difficulties and places the burden of proof and practice on the lender and/or insurer, often government must catalyze working partnerships and keep them together. This section explores the concepts of *greenlining*, housing cooperatives, the Neighborhood Housing Services (NHS) program, and miscellaneous other programs that employ the neighborhood organization as a partner in the rehabilitation process.

Greenlining is the attempt to reinvest capital in the form of home loans and mortgages in a previously redlined area, a neighborhood that has not had such activity and is dying as a result. The capital is primarily from the private sector. Banks can greenline in high-risk areas in several ways.[17] First, they can *improve their services* by advertising more in the neighborhood or providing special loan counseling and other educative services. Second, they can *target neighborhood deposits*, which means using local deposits for local loans. Third, banks can *establish loan review boards* that will review cases in which loan applicants feel they have been denied unjustifiably. Fourth, they can *establish a savings and loan service corporation*, a separate corporation that could receive up to 1 percent of their assets for high-risk investment that they themselves might be prohibited from loaning.

More radical approaches to greenlining include setting up a community credit union to give relatively small loans, or a community bank, only two examples of which currently exist in the U.S. They are the State Bank of North Dakota (hardly a neighborhood bank) and the South Shore National Bank in Chicago, owned by the Illinois Neighborhood Development Corporation, a bank holding company that will eventually be owned by the community. None of these strategies can occur unless the banks and savings and loans can be persuaded to act, whether alone or *in consortia*. There are a few cases where neighborhood organizations have brought about such collaboration without the hand of government becoming involved. The cases of insurance company investment, as outlined in the State Farm example, are even fewer. This fact, however, should not discourage neighborhood organizations from aggressively pursuing such avenues with lenders open to enlightenment. Much of what has been accomplished thus far started with neighborhood assertiveness.

A broader type of partnership that got its start in 1968 in Pittsburgh is the Neighborhood Housing Services (NHS) program. The federal partner is the National Neighborhood Reinvestment Corporation (NNRC), which represents jointly the federal financial regulatory agencies. The local partners include four distinct groups. The *neighborhood organization* serves as watchdog of the process and promoter in the neighborhood of the need for stricter code enforcement. The *city* provides improvements and better services in the area and a more complete housing inspection program. The *lending institutions* fund the operating costs of the NHS program ($20,000 to $50,000), participate in planning, and agree to reinvest by making loans in the area to homeowners meeting normal criteria. The *local foundations and corporations* contribute funds to a revolving fund that makes loans at rates from 0 to 6 percent to high-risk homeowners. The NNRC also makes a one-time grant of up to $100,000 to this same fund on a matching basis. Once launched, the NHS local is run by a private nonprofit tax-exempt corporation whose board of directors must include a majority of neighborhood representatives. The NHS is set up under the guidance of a representative of the federal corporation.

Robert Cassidy calls NHS "one of the hottest housing games in town."[18] Citing a nationwide study of NHS programs (87 neighborhoods in 74 cities by March 1979), he points out that NHS is working because it is not strictly a bureaucratic federal program. It is flexible because it is locally targeted and controlled. And it enables the community to help itself; it is not just another giveaway program. Seventy-five million dollars in investments and 7,500 homes brought up to code are directly attributable to NHS activity. But there is a multiplier effect. Many homeowners go directly to local lenders rather than to NHS because the neighborhood is looking up. Public infrastructure investments and sweat equity also add to the total.

But what about neighborhoods where the percentage of homeowners is less than 50 percent (NHS requires more) and decline is more serious? A variety of *land banking* and other cooperative experiments have sprouted up in the past decade, specific to each area's unique context of need, resources, and legislation. The Saint Ambrose Housing Aid Center (SAHAC) in Baltimore is one of the better-known examples of a grassroots group devoted to helping low-income tenants secure ownership of the homes they inhabit. Begun in 1972, by 1980 the organization had helped about 1,000 families purchase modest homes in Baltimore. The median price of these houses rose from $13,000 in 1976 to $17,690 in 1980. The median income of the purchasing families rose in those years from $10,500 to $12,600. About 70 percent of the families were black and 30 percent were single parent families.[19]

Although originally a citywide organization in scope, SAHAC's efforts began to focus intensively on the Harwood neighborhood, a pocket of small row houses near Johns Hopkins University. There was pressure by white middle-income families to displace the black tenants. Three SAHAC staff canvassed tenants, encouraged them to buy, negotiated prices with landlords, drew up contracts, and secured mortgage loans from local lenders. Progress was slow, although 35 houses were converted from tenant to owner occupancy. The staff also organized block clubs to foster expertise in repair and develop a reserve of tools. The former tenants resurrected the Harwood Community Association and took on these practical tasks.

The experience in Harwood pointed to other opportunities to convert absentee-owned properties to owner occupancy. Some landlords would welcome an opportunity to quickly unload some of their recently vacated and deteriorated homes. SAHAC purchased these homes and held them until former tenants could buy them. Where did SAHAC's money come from? A large donation of $30,000 was augmented by local bank lines of credit backed by sympathetic guarantors, such as the Associated Catholic Charities, the Maryland Jesuits, and two local contractors. In addition, the city contributed $125,000 in CDBG funds for repair grants.

Barclay, an apartment-dominated neighborhood south of Harwood, became the next target for displacement of poor blacks. SAHAC's reaction is instructive because three-story multifamily dwellings did not lend themselves to owner occupancy strategies as did the single-family units of Harwood. For one thing, the apartment dwellers were even poorer than those in Barclay. SAHAC's 1978 annual report admits, ''we are finding that many Harwood and Barclay tenant families are too old or too poor to become homeowners.[20] SAHAC shifted its strategy from promoting owner occupancy to trying to establish tenant cooperatives, whereby tenants could enjoy secure residency in housing that received regular maintenance at rents they could afford.

By 1981, the cooperative venture was well under way, but as interest rates hit new highs every month, SAHAC was faced with a new phe-nomenon, according to Vincent Quayle, SAHAC's executive director. What SAHAC buys, it is no longer able to resell. The tenants just don't have enough money to pay back the revolving 6 percent fund that the religious groups and local corporations invested in SAHAC, the total of which now stands at about $700,000. The organization owns 70 units, 50 of which are coop. Quayle describes the coop further.

Our tenants work as a cooperative, collecting the rents and managing the houses as a group. They choose new houses for the coop, screen new tenants, etc. Hopefully, in a few years, as the properties appreciate, they will be able to buy out our interest and assume total control. (I'm not sure how realistic this last point is, but we aim to find out.)[21]

In a housing cooperative, each family owns a share of the whole complex. In a low-equity housing cooperative the amount of a share is kept low, say $500, to accommodate the low income of the shareholder. Coop members who sell their shares get back only what they put into it, without the increase in value that normally accompanies conventional homeownership. The rest of the capital necessary to purchase the build-ing must come from somewhere else.

The Jubilee Housing Development Group, Inc., of Washington, DC, has spun off several apartment rehabilitation projects in low-income neighborhoods of Maryland, Kentucky, and the District of Columbia. Their goal also is conversion of the buildings to tenant cooperative ownership. Salaried resident managers and volunteers train tenants with this end in mind. In addition their model includes in-house child care, food service and health programs, an arts program with dramatic pro-ductions and photography classes, and a thrift (second-hand) shop. Their literature emphasizes the organization's religious context and orienta-tion, and although it is not made explicit, it is reasonable to assume that much of their capital and many volunteers come from church groups who see this work as a ministry to the poor. The original group from Washington's Church of the Saviour had worked in conjunction with the Adams-Morgan Organization.

A similar, more grassroots-based housing strategy that one neigh-borhood group in Grand Rapids has begun is patterned on successful housing cooperatives in England. The Madison Square (Tenant) Co-operative, a group of renters, in effect rents to themselves. A financial package pieced together from numerous federal and private grant and loan sources is used to buy the houses they live in and rehabilitate them. Where the tenants might not qualify individually for loans because they are out of work, on Aid to Families with Dependent Children (AFDC), or otherwise indigent, the cooperative itself does qualify. Functioning as manager, it oversees the finances, construction, and rehabilitation. Representatives from the ten tenant families sit on the coop's board and help set policy, and their monthly payments provide for maintenance of the buildings and the salaries of the office workers. It is a tactic designed to give low-income renters a sense of real control of their own housing and a pride in their neighborhood.

These selected cases of housing conversion and rehabilitation projects under significant control of a neighborhood organization are not enough evidence to warrant blanket support of these strategies for all deteriorating neighborhoods. The existence of a strong organization with capital connections is a must. Then the type of housing dictates the strategy, as we saw in the SAHAC case.

Two further considerations must be made in applying these models for rehabilitation and conversion from tenant to homeowner in low-income neighborhoods. First, where single-family homes are being converted from low-income tenancy to owner occupancy, default and delinquency can become problematic. SAHAC has run an extensive delinquency and default counseling service for new low-income owners facing foreclosure. Sometimes these people have brought misery upon themselves by not heeding budgeting advice. More often the misery has come uninvited: a key household member is laid off or falls ill. Most of the time there is a way out if all parties show good will. Another program that builds on the advocacy theme without directly purchasing property itself is the Eastside Housing Action Committee (ESHAC) in Milwaukee. It has established its own real estate marketing program to locate housing for local lower-income seekers and to steer upper-income reinvestors into other areas. ESHAC also provides prepurchase counseling, home management training, and default and delinquency counseling.

Tenant coops, if they are small, have a good chance for solid participation from each member in operating the organization. But the British experience, in which vast tracts of inner London housing, for example, are publicly subsidized, prompts us to be cautious in advocating the creation of huge tenant cooperatives. The Holloway Tenant Cooperative has existed for ten years in Islington, a borough of 700,000 people in London's north end. This grassroots group buys the extraordinarily expensive rowhouses with government funds and uses the rent collections from the low-income tenants to support maintenance and organizational expenses.[22] Financially the 200–unit cooperative is in good shape. Its trouble is that with such a large operation, participation slips. Tenant leaders then may have to act like landlords and evict other delinquent tenants, although like SAHAC every effort is made to work things out.

The second consideration concerns the effectiveness of government funding for conversion, rehabilitation, or cooperative ventures. The U.S. government has a long but certainly not endless list of programs that are tapped by grassroots groups, but the U.S. commitment is far below that of the British government. Some of the current major programs have come under recent fire.[23] The Community Development Block Grant Program (CDBG) funds a wide range of financing techniques for programs that lower the cost of repairing and in some instances buying housing and small businesses.[24] It also includes money for public improvements, such as street and curb repair, and has supported citizen participation activities including paying organizers' salaries. The Urban Development Action Grant Program (UDAG) is similar to CDBG but differs primarily in that it has provided far more *mortgage* subsidies on *new* housing and *new* small businesses than has CDBG. UDAG requires in addition the stimulation and leveraging of private investment. The Low Interest Loan Rehabilitation Program (Section 312) provides rehabilitation loans at 3 percent for up to 20 years, to owners of small residential and commercial properties in blighted areas. The Homeownership Assistance for Low and Moderate Income Families Program (Section 235) provides mortgage insurance and monthly interest rate reduction payments on mortgage loans for eligible low- and moderate-income families.

Though these and other more limited programs have achieved some success, anti-government sentiment, culminating in the Reagan victory, has attacked them like a logger felling trees. What will remain is certain to be less than before. Strategies relying heavily on government funding have already begun to fall to the axe, particularly the Section 312 program. Private lenders, whose interests are on the upswing in federal circles, resent the "unfair competition" they face when government lends money to the poor. They also decry such subsidization as inflationary.

A principal conclusion of this presentation on housing reinvestment is that reliance on private investment of a profit-seeking kind alone is unlikely to ever do much for the housing needs of the urban poor. Flawed though it may have been, government support has been an essential weapon in the battle to rebuild declining U.S. neighborhoods.

This section has limited itself to partnership strategies in which the neighborhood organization plays a principal role in defining housing goals, planning, implementing strategies, and thereby controlling the outcome. The following section, on commercial revitalization, gives examples of types of partnerships with business and government that allow much less neighborhood control. This section on housing should not end, however, without discussing displacement, a cultural invasion that results in the affluent buying the rehabbed housing of the poor and pushing them out.

Displacement

It was inevitable as neighborhood organizing succeeded, as people felt better about where they lived, as housing was rehabilitated and new commercial ventures appeared, that low-income residents would be pushed aside by higher-income people rushing to live in these revitalized areas. This *Catch–22* is called displacement, and many veteran community organizers have only recently become aware of and alarmed about it. In order to understand the driving forces behind this problem, it is useful to picture the neighborhood as a teeter-totter. When the factors that contribute to decline pile up on one end, the neighborhood goes down. Revitalizing elements, however, can push toward upsurge and new vigor in the area. Rolf Goetze lists the symptoms of both declining and rising neighborhoods and some general suggestions for correcting imbalances.[25] The crux of his analysis of neighborhood change is that the media image and residents' own perceptions of their area are like self-fulfilling prophecies. If they think an area is not worth investing or reinvesting in, they will not do so, and decline will be accelerated. On the other hand, positive perceptions of desirability can lead to excess demand for space, price inflation, and speculation. If neighborhoods are akin to teeter-totters in the market, achieving stability, the ideal or golden mean, becomes a constant concern for the community association. The model of comprehensive neighborhood change, proposed in chapter 2 of this book, incorporates this aspect of perception. Goetze outlines his dynamic in two schematic diagrams.

Figure 7.1, the Golden Mean Diagram, lists the indicators of rising or declining neighborhoods and some suggested remedies to bring the community back into a stable balance. Figure 7.2, the Matrix of Housing Dynamics, is a flowchart that illustrates how neighborhood housing market perceptions can rise rapidly from weak to strong, before the condition of the housing improves to warrant these heated perceptions. When this lag occurs, wealthy people buy into the neighborhood at inflated prices, forcing out the lower-income inhabitants, and rehabilitate the housing to their taste.

One hopes that the goal of the community association is to improve the neighborhood for those already living in it. *Incumbent upgrading* is the jargon term coined in the recent flood of literature on displacement. Its opposite is the British-coined *gentrification*, the movement into older, declining neighborhoods by high-income professionals (not really aristocrats), couples who usually have no children. As they settle in the territory, the poorer residents must move on. The mechanism of this process may involve conversion of low-rent apartments into higher-priced condominiums, the sale of rented houses by landlords to speculators, who in turn sell them to high-income owner-occupants, or direct sale by landlords to the next occupants. Such displacement requires a heated market, in which demand for housing in the area is high and is spurred on by perceptions that it's ''in'' to live there. Not all urban movement is displacement, however. Before a neighborhood organization can conduct research on the phenomenon in its own areas, it needs a comprehensive definition that covers all the possible conditions under which displacement can occur. Such a definition includes the following:

Displacement occurs when any household is forced to move from its residence by conditions which affect the dwelling or its immediate surroundings, and which:

1. are beyond the household's reasonable ability to control or prevent;
2. occur despite the household's having met all previously imposed conditions of occupancy; and
3. make continued occupancy by that household impossible, hazardous, or unaffordable.

One condition which fulfills this definition is a formal notice to vacate. But it also covers conditions which can force a household to move without such a notice. These conditions include, among others:

Figure 7.1
The Golden Mean Diagram

Neighborhood Market Types	Rising (Gentrifying) ++	Stable Or Ideal	Declining (Disinvesting) –
Symptoms Indicators (or Causes?)	• Excess demand • Price inflation (real or anticipated) • Speculation • Strong press image • Inmigration of higher class • Investment purchases • Conversion of marginal space into more dwellings	G O L D E N	• Excess supply • Uncertainty in property values • "Red-lining" • Negative press image • Departure of the able • Discretionary sales • Increase in low down payment and/or government insured lending • Increase in absentee ownership • Rising tax delinquency • Property abandonment
Corrective Remedies	• Dampen outside demand • Assist disadvantaged to remain • Enforce code • Prevent illegal conversions • Reassess only upon sale • Control rents if necessary • Construct additional housing	M E A N	• Boost neighborhood image • Value insurance for resident owners • Improve jobs and income without stigma • Support NHS if requested • Demolish excess housing (or mothball) • Land bank vacant lots until stable

Source: Reprinted with permission from Rolf Goetze, *Understanding Neighborhood Change: The Role of Expectations in Urban Revitalization*, Copyright 1979, Ballinger Publishing Company, p. 35.

Figure 7.2
The Matrix of Housing Dynamics

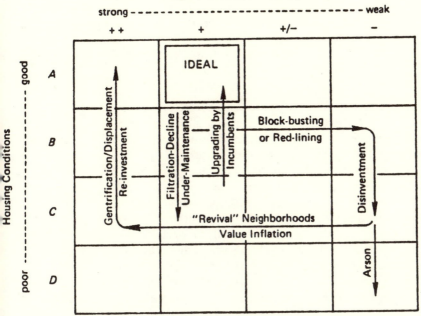

Source: Reprinted with permission from Rolf Goetze, *Understanding Neighborhood Change: The Role of Expectations in Urban Revitalization,* Copyright 1979, Ballinger Publishing Company, p. 38.

* failure of the landlord to provide heat or other vital services;
* lack of maintenance or partial abandonment of the building, bringing about conditions hazardous to health and safety;
* withdrawal of essential services from the neighborhood; and
* sudden large increases in taxes or rents, which raise them beyond the occupants' ability to pay.

On the other hand, this definition excludes:

* default on rent, mortgage, or taxes—except in cases of unaffordable increases;
* occupant behavior that violates the previously imposed conditions;
* voluntary moves to acquire more suitable housing, where the previous housing was still habitable; and
* job-related moves, since these do not involve conditions affecting the dwelling or its immediate sur oundings.[26]

How extensive is displacement nationally? Washington, DC, has seen more displacement occur than any other large U.S. city, although a 1975 survey by the Urban Land Institute showed that 70 percent of U.S. cities over 250,000 are experiencing "significant" private market housing renovation in deteriorated areas. In addition, 60 separate neighborhoods in 20 major cities were identified as undergoing "major" revitalization.[27] A 1982 U.S. Department of Housing and Urban Development (HUD) report indicates that nationally only 1 percent of urban households were displaced annually between 1970 and 1977.[28] But the effects are concentrated disproportionately. The HUD report cites San Francisco's Hayes Valley neighborhood in which displacees represented 25 percent of all movers between 1975 and 1978. In some revitalizing neighborhoods, the figure jumped as high as 57 percent. Displacement is most likely to hurt minorities, low-income households, and female-headed families. Also susceptible to displacement are those burdened with high housing costs, with short durations of occupancy, with low levels of education, or having a younger than average household head.

Once displacement has occurred, nothing can be done about it, so the neighborhood association must be vigilant for early warning signs of it. One of the most comprehensive treatments of the problem of displacement is the National Urban Coalition's book, *Neighborhood Transition Without Displacement: A Citizen's Handbook*.[29] Its long list of suggested strategies and references to neighborhood groups that have used them includes the following:

1. Use federal housing programs to propose funding an anti-displacement program, for example, buying out landlords and selling to tenants. Saint Ambrose Housing Aid Center in Baltimore has done this with 1,000 homes in the inner city.
2. Make the city focus financial priorities on housing.
3. Work with financial institutions to create demonstration loan and grant programs.
4. Work with local universities to research investment patterns.
5. Work with local legal services in bringing suits that buy time to search for upgrading (vs. displacing) investments.
6. Monitor lending and property value trends, using as indicators, building permits, property transfers, real estate publications, sales sections in newspapers, banking and Home Mortgage Disclosure information, vacancy rates and commercial activity, zoning proposals, the city planning department's land-use forecasts, and general city services for the neighborhood.
7. Work for anti-speculation or tenants' right-of-first-refusal ordinances.
8. Make the city enforce the housing code.

An even greater array of federal, state, and local government programs that aim to provide housing for low and moderate income persons can be employed in the anti-displacement battle. Some of these we have already described. In addition, local governments may adopt marketing strategies designed to spread housing demand to as many neighborhoods as possible. Boston and Seattle, two cities doing this, supplement their efforts with loan and grant programs to residents to fix up their homes. *Circuit breaker* tax rebates are provided in Baltimore, for example, whenever the property tax exceeds a certain percentage of income for elderly and low-income homeowners. The City of Denver has promoted low-income homeownership by approving a $50 million Housing Development Bond Issue to provide 8 percent interest rates to families earning less than $20,000 for the purchase of houses. The down payment requirements are as little as 5 percent.

Our emphasis has been on how to help the low-income potential victims of revitalization. This is as it should be. Anthony Downs of the Brookings Institution cautions against shortsightedness:

Completely opposing gentrification until enough federal subsidies are available to avoid all involuntary displacement amounts to indefinitely postponing most revitalization. In effect such a policy blocks the single most powerful housing upgrading force now operating within central cities.[30]

The problem with such a view is that it fails to take into account the shortage of housing that was documented at the beginning of this chapter. Where markets are loose, displacees have their choice of relocation sites. But where markets are tight—seemingly everywhere now—displacees are squeezed unmercifully. Downs outlines three options left for government: (1) stop gentrification by local means, (2) expand the housing markets, which requires a suburban growth strategy, or (3) give big subsidies to incumbent upgraders. Neighborhood organizations acutely aware of housing pressures are pushing all three options. City governments, on the other hand, see difficulty with each. The first two might well shrink the tax base even further. The last requires financial commitment that cities can't make politically.

Under a fourth strategy, many cities with available land inside their lines try to develop new multiunit housing. Cooperative planning with neighborhood groups is the only way to effectively accomplish this goal and it has been done. The difficulty here concerns retaining the original atmosphere of the neighborhood. Packing high density development, with its attendant lifestyle differences, into a predominantly single-family area is a sure formula for disruption, conflict, and neighborhood decline. An extreme example of how *not* to blend multiunit housing in with existing single-family use can be found in the Concordia neighborhood on Milwaukee's near west side. Here and there, stately old homes gave way to the wrecker's ball, and in their stead rose four-story cubes of 60 to 80 apartments each. It was a boon for the developers but a mess for everyone else. Although one consequence has been that the homeowners have begun to unite, they are digging in against the transient tenants. There are enough conflicts within neighborhoods without creating more.

Historic preservation strategies have usually led to gentrification and displacement where they have been tried. But in a study of five St. Louis neighborhoods, one, the Soulard area, provided an example of historic preservation that promoted incumbent upgrading for the lower-income working class as well as new housing for the middle class professional urbanites.[31] The key to this coexistence was that the Soulard Neighborhood Improvement Association, established in the 1960s as a channel for anti-poverty funds and activities, has become a progressive grassroots organization. It placed the housing needs of the poorer residents first, yet it welcomed the affluent newcomers interested in restoration. It encouraged these latter, more skilled people to join the overall revitalization effort. The tradeoff seems to be working, although displacement has not vanished as a problem.

Neighborhood organizations have begun to meet the challenges of maintaining the good housing they have, upgrading the bad, and coping with the demographic changes in the contemporary city. The list of their successes, whether they were the result of militancy or cooperation or a mix of both, is not endless. The issue is complex, and the national will to grapple with it is still weak. But vigilance and agitation at the grassroots level is building, where the organized neighborhood remains best equipped to diagnose and prescribe for itself. This awareness, though necessary, is not a sufficient condition for revitalization. Rhetorical stances, such as the use of "Not for Sale" signs by the Coalition of Peninsular Organizations (COPO) in South Baltimore, may be good public image–builders. But only high rates of homeownership, or at least psychological ownership, and low vacancy rates will be real buffers against traumatic neighborhood decline. Where the housing has begun to deteriorate, these must become overriding goals.

Public policy, according to Paul Levy, must support the neighborhood organization as it seeks to develop an internal sense of trust among residents. The neighborhood organization's other main task is the development of an advanced level of knowledge, participation skills, and organizational abilities within the community. These human resources, Levy posits, are the bedrock on which any other strategy must rest.[32]

EXTENDING THE NEIGHBORHOOD PARTNERSHIP TO COMMERCIAL REVITALIZATION

Entrepreneurs and profit-seeking organizations have long been the primary shapers of our cities' faces. Manufacturers, merchants, banks, bondholders, real estate developers, transportation enterprises, and even the media control much of the property and wealth that make up a city's economic base. If a city has areas of poverty and neglect, the decisions of these Have organizations—intentional or otherwise—have had a great deal to do with their existence. If rundown areas are to regain their vitality, these powerful nongovernmental actors will have to play a central role.

From the local community's perspective, economic development normally means *re*development of commercial strips, by either upgrading and retaining shops and stores or bringing in new ones to serve the needs of neighborhood consumers. At the same time, this revitalization seeks to employ local residents, who are subject to even higher unemployment rates than the city as a whole. Sometimes, economic development may include attracting light industry to a particular neighborhood, but for the most part, City Hall concentrates on bringing new industries to town and keeping the ones who are there happy. Housing redevelopment is usually a separate issue as well.

In the past two decades, neighborhood organizations have used two general strategies with entrepreneurial organizations in their communities: confrontation and cooperation. Much of the lore of urban grassroots groups has grown out of militant conflict with lending institutions, manufacturers, and other institutions that have sought to carve up neighborhoods for their own purposes or leave them high and dry. Partnership strategies, though quieter, have also been tried in virtually every city. The rest of this section explores some of the positive and negative aspects of such partnerships, fully aware that militance will continue to be a necessary counterpart in many cases. A third approach, establishing cooperatives, has been limited mostly to housing and food projects and constitutes a minute portion of overall retail business.

At least five groups that have a stake in the area have to become partners: (1) neighborhood residents, (2) existing merchants and commercial property owners, (3) local government, (4) new entrepreneurs attracted to the area, and (5) lenders.[33] Hartford, Connecticut, provides an example of such a partnership on a large scale. The Upper Albany Community Organization (UACO) is an umbrella organization of residents and business owners in the Upper Albany neighborhood. UACO teamed with the city to plan the revitalization of the neighborhood, including the one hundred storefront commercial strip. Since 1974, CDBG funds have paid for new sidewalks and trees. Other federal and private funds have supported new facades, interior refurbishment, and offstreet parking facilities. UACO guarantees low-interest bank loans for local businesses and processes Small Business Administration (SBA) low-interest loans. The organization is now trying to establish a factory to build solar energy hardware. It has already succeeded in developing a shopping center in the area, with a minority-owned supermarket as the anchor.[34]

Admittedly this sort of organization does not resemble most neighborhood associations. It is more like the community development corporations (CDC) that held such promise 20 years ago. An immediate question about these partnerships arises: how can the need for technical expertise be balanced against citizen participation? Lawyers, bankers, planners, and others necessary to put together the financial and legal packages to fit the detailed plans will most likely dominate any proceedings involving the rest of us. Many decisions may have to be made without even this meager consultation by citizens. But if a strong neighborhood organization has been involved in the planning from the start, it can maintain that input throughout the process.

A cynic might take the position that no organization can be "grassrooted" and technically sophisticated at the same time. Such naysayers imagine that grassroots people fear responsibility and are not to be trusted. In fact, where such organizations exist (and they do in many cities) the control remains grassroots and democratic, and the expertise is often exerted through a development arm of the organization. In any successful community organization leadership normally is somewhat centralized and limited to a proportionately few people. What makes these groups democratic is that the leadership is representative of the residents and positions of power are relatively open to any local resident who joins, stays with the organization, and demonstrates some degree of competence. That local leaders can develop the expertise to engage in technical planning and execution is demonstrated by the number of individuals who have found careers in local government as a result of their community activism. Others have developed and managed successful alternative institutions, such as food coops, schools, retail establishments, and even restaurants, laundromats, and bars.

If neighborhood organizations have potential to be partners, what else is necessary for them to be actual partners? Hans Spiegel, who analyzed seven successful housing partnership programs in New York City, suggests three preconditions.[35] First, the neighborhood group has to be involved at the start as the agenda is thought through and the project focus narrowed. Second, there should be an "intermediate organization" that acts as an advocate for the neighborhood association with city government. This intermediary provides technical assistance and training as well as the ombudsman function. Technical assistance in this case refers to both the substantive issues (such as zoning regulations and financial alternatives) and to the procedural questions (such as the best way to yoke the partners together for special tasks). The third precondition is money. Each partner ought to have secured funding before the venture is launched, so that leader and staff energy will not be diverted to the fundraising task. Front-end capital is also basic to success. These funds, mostly from the federal government in recent times, will have to come increasingly from church and foundation grants, special fundraisers, dues structures, or users fees.

This third precondition makes Spiegel somewhat pessimistic about the immediate future of these economic development partnerships. Where government support withdraws, the tripod of the partnership totters. Corporations and community groups left on their own cannot and should not be expected to reverse local poverty conditions. Where the corporation and the community lie down together, the community may not get up again. This last case underscores the need for neighborhood and City Hall vigilance in the community's interest.

Control Data Corporation, a Twin Cities–based multinational firm, used federal and other funds earmarked for urban reinvestment to support their City Venture Corporation, an organization that promised to create jobs, new and rehabbed housing, and a host of auxiliary commercial, education, and health services. Its centerpiece was to be a plant that made components for Control Data products, using the unskilled and semiskilled labor of the Elliot Park area.

Something went wrong on the way to the grand vision. City Venture was sucking up more and more public money without making good on its promises. Finally, a group of residents formed Elliot Park Neighborhood, Inc., to fight City Venture as a ripoff of funds their area desperately needed.

They succeeded in getting an $8.6 million UDAG proposal withdrawn from Minneapolis City Council consideration because it was so vague and requested so much public money without the necessary ratio of private money to match. The Mayor and City Council have told Control Data President William Norris they will sign no further contracts with City Venture until its plans have been approved by the neighborhoods.[36]

Not all corporations are colonizers, seeking to exploit the poverty of the natives. The story is told to highlight the need for governmental involvement in the process of redevelopment. Local government can insure public improvements in the district, uniform design standards, equitable financing, and overall management once the strip has been redone.

The neighborhood organization has been the missing partner until now. Most revitalization projects that have been packaged by government and the private sector and parachuted into the neighborhood have operated without linkages to that neighborhood. At best they risk inefficiency; more often they die of neglect after a time. Revitalization is not merely a bricks-and-mortar proposition; it is a rebuilding of spirit and will as well. The neighborhood organization must be a credible partner in the venture, if economic revitalization is to spur psychological satisfaction with and commitment to the neighborhood.

To be fair, there are veteran organizers who are highly skeptical of *any* neighborhood organization involvement in development programs. Gerson Green, of the National Center for Voluntary Action, holds that development and organizing are incompatible because the former not only requires time, expertise, and secretiveness, but also contains potential for considerable conflict over development issues because City Hall holds most of the cards.[37] James V. Cunningham, a former organizer and now professor at the University of Pittsburgh's School of Social Work, echoes this view, seriously doubting whether the weak forces of the community can ever achieve a balance with the powerful economic forces refereed by local government.[38]

Despite these caveats, neighborhood groups across the nation have begun to assert themselves in development matters. They often have little choice if they are to fulfill their role as vehicles for self-determination for residents. The Reagan administration, in applying the brakes to the U.S. "welfare state," has introduced its own proposal to resuscitate declining urban areas by relying on the private sector and the spirit of self-help. Commonly known as the Enterprise Zone concept, it deserves mention because of its potential impact on the neighborhood organization's efforts in redevelopment.

The Enterprise Zone bill passed the Senate during the 98th Congress but failed in the House. Indications are that it could be included in future budget proposals. Whatever its ultimate fate, the Enterprize Zone concept is notable as a conservative perpective on inner city revitalization. Given the conservative tenor of the era, it is likely to resurface in modified form in future years.

A Note on Enterprise Zones

In order to create jobs and encourage revitalization in distressed urban areas, Enterprise Zone legislation would invite private business, by means of tax incentives and regulatory relief, to provide needed jobs and services for local residents. *Service* may also include housing. Although successive versions of this experimental program have undergone moderate changes, the idea remains oriented toward attracting into the zone new small businesses that would benefit the local people both by employing them and bringing them services and goods. The prospective employer beginning operations in the designated zone would be granted investment and income tax credits, with extra income tax credits going to those employers who hire the disadvantaged from the zone. The employees could claim certain income tax credits themselves. Zone businesses would be granted continued access to industrial revenue bonds, even if the use of such bonds ended elsewhere in the city.[39]

The objective of an Enterprise Zone would be to stimulate employment and spur capital investment in declining urban areas, to spike economic growth under the assumption that where the engine of free enterprise is given full throttle, *all* will benefit by the increased economic activity. The localist flavor of this approach is said to appeal to both conservatives and liberals.[40] It is only fair, then, to examine these and other assumptions underlying the proposal and to suggest adaptations where they seem appropriate.

How reasonable is the claim that new types of small business will emerge in the zones as a result of the tax and regulatory breaks? George Humberger, of the Community Development Collaborative, a Washington group that works with low-income community organizations, cites studies indicating that business relocation decisions are not influenced at all by tax incentives.[41] He suspects that most existing small businesses would be unlikely to move into the Enterprise Zone. High technology and warehousing operations might do so, however, but the problem with these is that they do not need unskilled labor. Brand-new businesses are less likely to start up in a zone because they need capital to get going, not tax help with profits. There is nothing in the zone proposal that supplies federal funds for startup costs. Local revenue bonds as a capital source appear to be politically untenable, since many local governments are already stretched beyond their means.

Furthermore, as a businessperson contemplating investment in a zone, one would have several basic concerns: Is the infrastructure (roads, sewers, lighting, etc.) of good quality? Is there adequate police and fire protection? Will there be a dependable, trained labor force in the zone ready to go to work? To answer these questions affirmatively means considerable public investment. The most politically feasible way of attracting public funds for such redistribution is by federal grant. Yet there is nothing in the proposals for these purposes, although more liberal supporters of the zone idea are demanding inclusion of job training and citizen participation components.

Proponents of Enterprise Zones fail to make some larger distinctions in their zeal to devolve urban revitalization efforts from federal to local levels.[42] They ignore the fact that the federal government has never had an adequately funded, coherent urban policy. Cries about getting government off our backs are premature. Second, as Chapter 1 pointed out, urban problems are vast and complex, the result of systemic contradictions; they are not due merely to government tax and regulatory burdens. Third, we should distinguish between economic growth and economic development. Jobs and investment capital, the staples of economic growth, are indeed important to zone revitalization. But their effects can be short-lived if there is not a corresponding enhancement of neighborhood social fabric and self-reliance, rooted in the development of local leadership, entrepreneurial capacity, and diversification of enterprises. This comprehensive rebuilding for the long-term future is the essence of an overall development strategy.

This last consideration is the crux of the Enterprise Zone issue from the neighborhood organization's perspective. Infusions of investment capital aimed primarily at short-term growth and big profits can leave the last state of the neighborhood worse than the first. The poverty of Puerto Rico, the U.S.'s first Enterprise Zone (beginning in 1950), gives eloquent testimony to the folly of simply allowing free enterprise to have its way.[43] Sugar plantations, then textile, petrochemical, pharmaceutical, and mining multinationals in turn took their profits without helping the economy become self-reliant or diversified. Puerto Rico is now dependent on U.S. investment and welfare. Though there are differences, the similarities between this territory and U.S inner cities are striking. Neighborhood organizations, therefore, want a strong voice in the process of reinvestment in their community under the Enterprise Zone proposal.

Humberger suggests a model whereby this input might occur.[44] Presuming the necessary public and private capital can be obtained, elected neighborhood people would constitute one third of the Zone Development Board, the group that would set investment policy for the particular zone. The city and the private sector would each fill their third of the board membership by appointment. A Zone Authority would be a semiautonomous city agency, accountable to the Zone Development Board. This executive arm would broker public services, provide technical assistance in developing business investment applications, and help locate private financing.

The Enterprise Zone debate is important because it brings home to us that *how* reinvestment is to occur is just as crucial as *whether* it will occur. Neighborhood groups seeking to light the fires of reinvestment in their communities are still faced with the ancient problem of getting warm without getting burned.

In the final analysis, however, neighborhood organizations appear capable of doing a number of things to promote reinvestment in their community. They can demand increased housing and commercial improvement activity. They can organize partnership programs. They can develop their own cooperatives. But they cannot do it alone. They need government and institutional support, and they need capital.

NOTES

1. Robert Cassidy, *Livable Cities: A Grass-Roots Guide to Rebuilding Urban America* (New York: Holt, Rinehart, and Winston, 1980), 25.

2. Peter Drier and John Atlas, "Condomania," *The Progressive*, March 1981, 19.

3. Barbara Koeppel, "For Rent, Cheap, No Heat," *The Progressive*, March 1981, 23.

4. Anthony Downs, *Neighborhoods and Urban Development* (Washington, DC: The Brookings Institution, 1981), 76.

5. Downs, p. 77.

6. Rolf Goetze, *Understanding Neighborhood Change: The Role of Expectations in Urban Revitalization* (Cambridge, MA: Ballinger, 1979), 81–82.

7. Koeppel, p. 25.

8. Joseph A. Spencer, "Tenant Organization and Housing Reform in New York City: The Citywide Tenants' Council, 1936–1943," in *Community Organization for Urban Social Change*, ed. Robert Fisher and Peter Romanofsky (Westport, CT: Greenwood Press, 1981), 127–56.

9. Cassidy, chap. 2.

10. Cassidy, pp. 40–41. The best description I have read of redlining and effective neighborhood action against it can be found in Jane Jacobs' influential work from the beginning of the 1960s, *The Death and Life of Great American Cities* (New York: Random House, 1961), pp. 297–309. She provides a careful

and colorful historical analysis of the Back of the Yards Council's actions against lenders who blacklisted the area.

11. John Conroy, "Blackjacking the City Redliners," *Mother Jones*, November 1978, 11–12.

12. James Johnson, "Incumbent Upgrading and Gentrification in the Inner City: A Case Study of Neighborhood Revitalization Activities in Eastown, Grand Rapids," unpublished Ph.D. dissertation, Michigan State University Department of Geography, East Lansing, 1980.

13. "High Interest Rates—Organizing to Win!," *Disclosure* 63 (June 1981), 8.

14. Koeppel, p. 23.

15. Koeppel, p. 25.

16. Goetze, passim.

17. Cassidy, pp. 202–16.

18. Cassidy, p. 238.

19. Reports of St. Ambrose Housing Aid Center (Baltimore, MD: 1978, 1980).

20. St. Ambrose Report, 1978, p. 20.

21. Vincent Quayle, private correspondence with author, August 4, 1981.

22. Michael Williams, "A Neighborhood with Clout," *Grand Rapids Press*, August 26, 1979, 38.

23. "Public Sector Could Spell Relief," *Disclosure* 63 (June 1981), 7.

24. As a requirement for participation in the CDBG program, each municipality must submit a Housing Assistance Plan (HAP) every three years. This plan uses estimates of the number of people in the city who are ill-housed and the number of substandard units as a basis for setting housing objectives. The Housing Opportunity Program (HOP) was an idealistic strategy designed to establish a regional affirmative action in housing, using data from the HAP from each city and suburb in the area. It was to have enabled Havenots to move into the more affluent neighborhoods by subsidizing their movement, including subsidies to the municipalities themselves. Under the Reagan administration, HOP became defunct, though it was never a popular or effective program.

25. Goetze, chap. 3.

26. George Grier and Eunice Grier, "Urban Displacement: A Reconnaissance," in *Back to the City: Issues in Neighborhood Renovation*, ed. Shirley Laska and Daphne Spain (New York: Pergamon, 1980), 256.

27. "The Displacement Problem in Revitalized Urban Neighborhoods" (Washington, DC: Urban Consortium, 1977).

28. *Regionnotes*, West Michigan Regional Planning Commission Newsletter, May 1982.

29. Sandra Solomon, *Neighborhood Transition Without Diaplacement: A Citizen's Handbook* (Washington, DC: National Urban Coalition, 1979).

30. Downs, p. 149.

31. Sandra Schoenberg and Patricia Rosenbaum, *Neighborhoods That Work: Sources for Viability in the Inner City* (New Brunswick, NJ: Rutgers University Press, 1980), 99.

32. Paul Levy, "Neighborhoods in a Race with Time: Local Strategies for Countering Displacement," in Laska and Spain, 302–17.

33. Partnerships quickly become complicated, however, when some of the potential partners are sources of the problem, such as landlords who neglect their buildings in the commercial strip and operators of questionable businesses, such as liquor stores, bars attracting and not policing rowdy patrons, adult bookstores, or late-night convenience stores catering to very young consumers beyond curfew.

34. *Neighborhood Self-Help Case Studies: Abstracts of Reports on Revitalization Projects Funded by the Office of Neighborhood Self-Help Development* (Washington, DC: U.S. Department of Housing and Urban Development, October 1980), 26–27.

35. Hans Spiegel, "The Neighborhood Partnership: Who's in It? Why?," *National Civic Review*, November 1981, 513–20.

36. "City Venture Is Coming!", *Disclosure* 60 (January-February 1981), 5.

37. Gerson Green, *Who's Organizing the Neighborhood?* (Washington, DC: U.S. Department of Justice, 1979), 38–39.

38. James V. Cunningham, "Assessing the Urban Partnership: Do Community Forces Fit?," *National Civic Review*, November 1981, 521–26.

39. Clint Page, "President Unveils His Enterprise Zone Plan," *Nation's Cities Weekly*, March 29, 1982, 7.

40. Stuart Butler, "The Enterprise Zone as an Urban Frontier," *Journal of Community Action*, September-October 1981, 13.

41. George Humberger, "The Enterprise Zone Fallacy," *Journal of Community Action*, September-October 1981, 24.

42. Humberger, p. 22.

43. Humberger, p. 20.

44. Humberger, pp. 27–28.

8

THE ENERGY CRISIS

> The new resource realities force us to look to our local governments, our small businesses, our neighborhoods and households for leadership. Where, after all, do we turn in moments of crisis?
>
> —David Morris[1]

Most of us reach a painful point of awareness about energy when we are paying the energy companies: the gas or oil company for our home heat, the electric company that provides our light, refrigeration, and power for our labor-saving electrical devices, the attendant at the gasoline station when we fill up the car. Periodic leaps in these prices since 1973 have awakened us as a nation to our fundamental dependence on fossil fuels.

The ballooning cost of energy has hurt almost everyone in some fashion, but it has positively gouged the low-income population. For example, reports of elderly people freezing to death in their homes because they could not pay their winter heating bills are still infrequent enough to shock, but they keep recurring. Complaints about monthly heating and electric bills are plaintive and commonplace and have become the basis for widespread organizing tactics in recent years. The energy crisis has hit the neighborhood with full force.

This chapter has four objectives. First, the energy situation needs to be placed in an understandable framework. Second, examples are provided of organizing in much larger arenas than the neighborhood. Third, the chapter will present cases of neighborhood-level activity that deal with energy issues. Fourth, it will outline a program to create a Municipal Solar Utility in which neighborhood organizations play a key role.

UNDERSTANDING THE ROLE OF THE ENERGY CRISIS IN NEIGHBORHOOD DECLINE

How much fuel energy does the U.S. use? What sorts of fuels are used? What is this energy used for? In 1975, the U.S. used the equivalent of about two billion barrels of oil; the amount of energy we consumed equaled the amount that many barrels could provide. Our overall usage rate has been increasing at an average of 5 percent per year over the past 25 years. Petroleum accounted for 44 percent of the total U.S. energy budget in 1975, followed by natural gas at 28 percent, coal at 17 percent, nuclear power at 7 percent, and hydropower at 4 percent. In the same year, 31 percent of all energy produced was consumed by utilities (think of them as burning coal, oil, or gas, for example, to produce electricity), 26 percent by industry, 19 percent by residential and commercial users, and 24 percent for transportation.[2]

Two trends should be noted. First, production of electricity is claiming an ever larger percentage of energy consumption, making electric utilities more central to the economy of cities each year. Second, hidden in each of the consumption categories is a significant amount to bring food to U.S. kitchen tables. Frances Moore Lappe estimated that food production is one of the largest absorbers of fossil fuels in our economy.[3] Grown on huge corporate farms, tended by giant energy-guzzling machinery and fertilizers and pesticides made from petroleum, transported long distances, processed by high-tech methods, refrigerated all along the way, that simple pop-in-the-oven dinner represents a major energy investment. The meat-centered diet of U.S. citizens is also in itself representative of high energy imports. The lowly hamburger is actually plucked from the top of the food chain, each level of which can be visualized as concentrating more energy. Therefore, neighborhood associations seeking to deal with energy problems often address food issues in the same breath.

Energy crises are nothing new. What we call the current energy crisis is at least the *sixth* the U.S. has experienced in this century, according to Robert Sherrill.[4] In fact, Britain went through a similar economic trauma in the sixteenth century when the forests were drastically depleted and the country was forced to rely on coal for its basic fuel.[5] The essence of any energy crisis, then, is a shortage to the consumer of an essential fuel, combined with a steep hike in the price of what is actually available.

The subject of disagreement, however, is the cause or source of the shortage. One popular view of the contemporary situation is that OPEC (Organization of Petroleum Exporting Countries), a cartel of Middle Eastern, African, and South American oil-exporting countries, manipulates the supply of oil to the U.S. in order to get top dollar. The oil companies, worldwide giants that control the refining and distribution of the precious fluid, are the chief causes of the problem, according to another view. A third perspective places most of the blame on U.S. government policies that encouraged exaggerated consumption of oil and natural gas in years past and that brought about the present U.S. dependence on foreign supplies. A conservative variation on this theme places the onus on environmentalists and consumer advocates who demanded governmental price controls.[6] Still others blame the wasteful consumers themselves or the overall reliance of our industrial and agricultural systems on nonrenewable energy sources, particularly fossil fuels. (Uranium is nonrenewable, but is not a fossil fuel.)

All of these perspectives have some element of truth. They find integration, however, in the analysis of ecologist Barry Commoner.[7] The economic system of modern society, according to Commoner, has shaped our technologies. Our extreme emphasis on building and using machinery that gets ever more output for ever less labor input has led us to an almost helpless dependence on fossil fuels. Our fascination with centralized networks has tied these energy-gulping technologies into vast interdependent organizations whose failure can bring economic or physical chaos to thousands or millions of people at a time. Centralization and emphasis on the machine over human needs have led to a sort of servitude to our own technologies. Mistaken short-range government policies, corporate or national greed, and the parochialism of most of us in the industrial world have then been folded into the mix, to produce economic decline.

Commoner further hypothesizes that the capitalist emphasis on labor productivity in an era of startlingly limited energy supplies contains the seeds of its own imminent collapse. Simply put, his argument goes something like this. The emphasis on labor productivity (i.e., ever more output for the same human labor input) is a natural consequence of the desire for profit. This emphasis, however, is possible only if fossil fuel is abundant and relatively cheap. Where such fuel becomes in short supply, economic growth is hampered if not stopped altogether because dwindling profits are no longer reinvested in order to keep the industrial machine up-to-date. The result is slow or no growth and ever-increasing unemployment.

There are a number of alternative explanations for the obvious signs of economic decline in the industrialized world. They range from the *political*, usually from the conservative viewpoint (i.e., the "bankruptcy of liberalism and welfare state policies") to the *philosophical*, in which technology itself is considered to be either the culprit or the savior of humankind.[8] The advantage of a view such as Commoner's, however, is that it brings human decisions into the center of the discussion. The powerful make these decisions and implement them through organizational means: corporations and government. While government deserves criticism, it is more directly accountable to society than are large corporations. The main point is that if some people are deciding what happens to society, others—the rest of us—can make some decisions, too. The forces of change are not out of human control, although the limits of the earth's resources are being felt. People can influence their destiny.

When the neighborhood organization begins to address energy issues, it must cope with two fundamental realities. The first is that the neighborhood energy infrastructure (natural gas pipelines, electric wires, and gas stations) is just the tail end of a vast network that stretches around the globe. The other fact is that individuals—technocrats and power-brokers—control the network; it does not work by itself.

Rising energy costs drain the neighborhood of capital in ways we are only beginning to understand. A principal cause of neighborhood decline is the net loss of capital, as noted in Chapter 7. But the two facts just mentioned about energy make organizing on energy issues more difficult. The first reality implies that when the neighborhood organization wishes to attack cost escalation *directly*, it must join with other local groups to form coalitions at state, national, or even international levels. Conversely the neighborhood organization can promote efforts to decentralize energy sources by helping local residents shift to solar or wood heat, for example. The group can attack spiraling energy costs *indirectly* by promoting conservation of energy, making homes more heat efficient, or by supporting mass transit. The second fact, that people control the system, has not been lost on neighborhood organizers. The problem is *which* people? Finding the right targets for mass actions has taken diligent research. Examples of the results follow.

ORGANIZING STATEWIDE AND NATIONAL NETWORKS

Actions Against Utilities

In the Northeast and the Midwest, where home heating demands are great, grassroots organizing on energy issues has focused on utility rate reform. National community organizing newsletters, such as *The Neighborhood Works*, *Disclosure*, *Diffusion*, *NAN Bulletin*, and *The Congress Watcher*, regularly feature articles about people's coalitions' wrestling matches with their friendly local power companies over what are fair and equitable rate structures. A government survey has summarized several types of grassroots confrontations with utilities.[9]

First, grassroot organizations seek to stop automatic fuel rate adjustments. Many utility companies (75 percent of them privately owned) are allowed to automatically pass along fuel cost hikes through fuel adjustment clauses. Activists in groups such as Massachusetts Fair Share argue that this privilege removes incentives for them to shop around for the cheapest fuel available and have urged stricter audits of utilities' books. Several states now disallow this automatic passthrough.

Second, grassroots coalitions have pushed to reduce rates for small users. Energy waste is encouraged when rates are reduced for big users; small users in effect subsidize the bigger ones. A citizens' coalition in California got a state law passed in 1975 establishing *lifeline rates* for small users, whereby they have special low rates for the minimum amount of energy needed for life's essentials. Utilities are still grumbling about this one even though, or perhaps because, it has reduced residential electric bills by millions of dollars. Lifeline rates are now commonplace in many states.

Third, these coalitions want utilities to stop making customers pay for power plants that do not produce power yet. An accounting device, called Construction Work in Progress (CWIP), allows utilities to charge customers for power plants under construction. Consumers retort that CWIP makes them pay rates based on plants that are not yet providing them service. Oregonians for Utility Reform, a statewide coalition like several others in the nation, has successfully lobbied through a bill banning CWIP. Because utility companies argue that CWIP helps avoid huge financing costs and in the long run reduces consumer rates, however, several states' utility regulatory bodies have yet to act on the question. Their delay may have been the harbinger of bad news for activists. A recent federal court decision has allowed utilities to charge these costs to consumers.[10]

Fourth, activists want utilities to go slower on shutoffs. In some states, consumer groups, such as Georgia Action, have won revision of regulations that allowed utilities to shut off service in cold weather. In general, a new federal law, the Public Utility Regulatory Policies Act (PURPA), requires state regulatory commissions and large cooperative utilities to *consider* adopting cutoff procedures which specify that (1) reasonable notice must be given, as well as an opportunity to dispute the reasons for shutoff and (2) service cannot be terminated during any period when it would be especially dangerous to the consumer's health.

Fifth, grassroots groups want utilities to stop building unneeded power plants. Citizens' groups have petitioned utility commissions in some states to turn down requests for rate increases to finance construction of what they believe to be unneeded power plants. For example, in Waterloo, Iowa, Citizens for Community Improvement discovered that their electric utility, Iowa Public Service, wanted permission to build a new generating plant to be paid for by a 19.5 percent rate increase. But the Iowa Public Service Ottumwa plant was already producing 35 percent beyond peak demand.[11] The utility's existing facility was not being fully used, yet it wanted to build another one.

Two other cases of state-level tactics to make utilities more accountable to consumers deserve mention. Enterprising state organizers in Wisconsin concocted a kind of Trojan horse to get inside the utilities' own systems. The Citizens' Utility Board (CUB) won the right to enclose its own notices inside utility bills, although it pays all costs of the enclosure. These notices can even urge defeat of rate increase requests and have done so successfully. Tim Massad, who organized the Wisconsin CUB, is now coordinating a national campaign from Washington, DC, to get CUBs organized in other states.[12]

The second example occurred in Wisconsin's neighboring state, Minnesota. A grassroots farmers' rebellion against utility imposition of a high-energy powerline across their farmland gained national attention when a television docudrama based on this bitter clash aired in August 1982. Although the group that organized was rural and middle-income instead of urban and low-income, the confrontation, which continued over several years even after the governor and the media declared it dead, demonstrated two points: (1) the political clout of the utilities, which all but had the state and county regulatory agencies in their pockets and (2) the tenacity of the small farmers, whose very turf was being overrun. Even after the powerline was constructed, nonviolent protest evolved into guerilla warfare: sabotage of the line itself.

At night, towers were attacked by "bolt weevils" and fell to the ground; the land was littered with glass as an epidemic of "insulator disease" broke out; and highpowered rifle bullets (or was it "wireworms"?) splayed open the conducting wire.[13]

This last case is instructive because it highlights how a threat to one's turf can be a powerful motivator to organize resistance. It also points out how the state government used the guise of citizen participation, allowing the farmers to voice their protests at numerous hearings, to siphon off their anger while the towers were under construction.

All the protests mentioned so far have been aimed at utilities that provide electricity or natural gas. Statewide coalitions of mostly middle-income participants have been the vehicles behind the protest activity. Although these groups used the legal system as effectively as their resources allowed, few were able to rely exclusively on this tactic because of the utilities' access to expert attorneys and technicians. Strategies that allowed for much broader citizen involvement in group settings, such as hearings or picket lines, proved more effective.

Another factor influencing protest effectiveness should be mentioned. Poor planning by the utilities themselves during an era of uncertainty about energy demands created unevenness in capacity in many Midwestern and Northeastern states. Some utilities overbuilt or failed to convert to cheaper fuels; others underconstructed. This shortsightedness, connected with ever-higher prices from oil and gas producers, made utilities more sensitive to pressures for promoting conservation measures and taking steps to hold the line on rates. In several ways, many utilities found themselves in a bind, even without the burden of their white elephants, the nuclear plants.[14] Further adding to the pressure on rates for natural gas has been the conversion of large industrial users to other fuel sources (particularly petroleum during the price slump of 1982).

Utilities say they are forced to raise residential rates to cover their industrial losses.[15]

Actions Against Energy Producers

Large oil and gas suppliers, collectively though not affectionately known as Big Oil among organizers, are not nearly as desperate as the utilities. It is no accident that the wealthiest corporations in the world are likely to be oil companies (which also own and control most of the natural gas, coal, and uranium).[16] Although government policies have at times in the past kept Big Oil's profits from soaring even higher, there has been a steady cooperation between the regulated and the regulators, under the nostrum that government must support the profits of this vital industry through tax incentives, such as the oil depletion allowance. Without such help, the slogan goes, there will not be adequate reinvestment in exploration activities to find more fuel. This argument has also been recently trotted out to justify full deregulation of natural gas. While it is true that search and drilling operations have become more expensive now that the "easy" oil and gas has been found, the very unprofitability of exploration has prompted oil companies to invest in ventures wholly unrelated to energy production, such as department store chains, beef processing plants, or corporate mergers. Such diversification seeks to stabilize these huge corporations' profits in uncertain energy markets.

Whatever the disagreement over oil company profits or investments, organizers are fully aware of their impact on the price of fossil fuels. Consequently, organizing activities against these corporations and against the government regulatory agencies that have been so cozy with them have frequently occurred on the national level. For example, National People's Action (NPA), a Chicago-based coalition of grassroots groups, brought several thousand demonstrators to Chicago from around the country in October 1981, when the American Petroleum Institute held its annual conference. Although the particular focus of this protest was to counter the deregulation of natural gas, NPA's general displeasure with the arrogance and unaccountability of these corporations was evident. In a variety of dramatic gestures, including barging in on an elegant penthouse dinner for top industry executives, the demonstrators highlighted the vast gulf between themselves, as representatives of the people at large, and the powerful who concentrate ever more wealth and control as the years pass.

The NPA newsletter, *Disclosure*, regularly features this type of confrontation with multinational corporations deemed to be squeezing the average American in some way, or with federal agencies that either by commission or omission are helping them do it. The general thrust of NPA's work is to (1) educate the public about how it is being harmed, (2) enlist or bolster federal and state regulatory assistance where this has been lax, and (3) force concessions from the corporations themselves as a result of (1) and (2). NPA has been particularly successful in dealing with the housing issues of redlining. Though the oil companies have proven a much tougher nut for grassroots groups to crack, progress is being made. In a recent *Atlantic* article, for example, David Osborne, a researcher concerned with why natural gas prices have risen so sharply in recent years, lucidly discusses how the oil industry has had its way in raising those prices despite piecemeal government attempts to keep a lid on.[17] Though the issues are complex, grassroots activists from the national Citizen/Labor Energy Coalition (C/LEC), which claims to represent 300 groups, have opened new fronts in the battle against deregulation of natural gas. Osborne's description of the scope of this clash makes us realize that the energy war requires concerted action on a broad scale; and that it is happening.

During the 1982 campaigns, oil and gas political-action committees gave more than $7 million to congressional candidates, and they will no doubt be similarly openhanded this time around. On the other side, the Citizen/Labor Energy Coalition has unleashed what may be the largest genuine grassroots effort since the anti-ERA campaign; its activists claim that they knock on 50,000 doors a day. The C/LEC campaign has had such an obvious effect on congressmen from consuming states that the Natural Gas Supply Association which represents the major oil companies, has spent $3 million on its own door-to-door effort in support of decontrol.[18]

ORGANIZING AT THE NEIGHBORHOOD LEVEL

As energy prices, particularly for home heating, have leaped upward over the past decade, neighborhood residents have begun to place higher priority on energy as an issue. Local associations have developed two broad avenues for organizing. One is to promote conservation either through disseminating information to residents or, in the case of low-income homeowners, cooperating in low-cost or no-cost insulation, caulking, and weatherstripping projects. These conservation programs may or may not be in cooperation with the local utility. The second tack is to develop simpler alternative technologies to enable residents to unhook themselves (at least partially) from the end of the energy line. Though there are fewer examples of this latter strategy than of conservation programs, two are illustrative for our purposes.

The first example is the now famous "sweat equity" project in New York's Lower East Side. In rehabbing their delapidated apartment building, the tenants, in concert with technical experts and supported by a Community Services Administration grant (a program the Reagan administration torpedoed soon after it came into office), installed comprehensive insulation, along with 30 copper solar collectors for hot water heat, and a windmill atop the building. These decentralized technologies have cut the building's fuel bill by 75 percent and save the residents $1,200 annually on their electric bills. The technology itself did not generate the media interest; the low-income residents' involvement in planning and constructing it grabbed the nation's attention.[19]

The second example comes from the other side of the U.S. The San Bernardino West Side Community Development Corporation in California has effectively started its own neighborhood utility to combat high electric and gas bills. The West Side CDC had previously been in the business of rehabilitating rundown housing in the Delman Heights/ California Gardens neighborhoods, while training their residents in construction skills with on-the-job experience. In 1977, recognizing the great job potential in the new solar industry, West Side CDC decided to install a central solar heating system in a block of ten vacant houses that needed extensive repairs. Funding for this $85,000 system came from three sources, two federal (HUD and Community Services Administration (CSA)) and the State Energy Commission. Five West Side craftsmen paid by Comprehensive Employment and Training Act (CETA) funds trained 25 residents to construct and install 72 solar collectors in elevated rows along the utility right-of-way running behind the homes. A four-ton, 5,000–gallon tank with a water storage capacity to heat all ten homes for four sunless days was placed beneath an adjacent park. After the end of the first year, the homes were occupied by their new low-income owners, who now note savings of up to 70 percent on their gas heating bills. The West Side CDC is also a good example of a neighborhood group training its residents for employment. From 1973 to 1979, its staffers trained over 650 residents in carpentry, painting, and plumbing as well as solar construction. Seventy-five percent of these trainees had landed jobs with nearby California corporations by 1980.[20]

A MUNICIPAL SOLAR UTILITY

All the themes of this chapter converge in a farsighted set of programs being assembled in the city of Carbondale, Illinois, a college town (home of Southern Illinois University) of about 50,000. In 1977, the Shawnee Solar Project (SSP), a community-based nonprofit organization, began to demonstrate to Carbondale residents how to retrofit their houses with passive solar heating systems. SSP also built a community solar greenhouse. The next year SSP and the city received a grant to establish the Appropriate Technology Resource Center, which contained a modest library on community energy and whose staff gave workshops for residents on energy conservation techniques.[21]

SSP's success persuaded the city to appoint a permanent Energy Advisory Committee in October 1978, and to hire in November 1979 an Energy Coordinator, who in turn developed an Energy Division within the city's Community Development Department. Subsequently, an SIU professor conducted an Energy Impact Study to assess the effect of Carbondale's energy consumption on the town's economy. The study concluded that 85 percent of the money spent on fuel in Carbondale left the area, never to return. The result of this capital drain was the progressive decline of local business and small industry, since very few of these energy dollars were being recycled locally. It was estimated, for example, that for every one-cent increase in the price of a gallon of gasoline, four jobs were lost to Carbondale.[22]

The Energy Impact Study formed the empirical foundation for a Comprehensive Energy Plan which the city adopted in 1981.[23] This plan contains four program and two revenue measures, which other cities and their neighborhood leaders would do well to study. The program elements are as follows:

1. An Energy Audit and Quality Assurance Inspection Program. Upon request, any building in the city will be audited to determine energy needs and solar/conservation potential. If the resident wishes to have work done that the auditor recommends, he or she can get financing through either ordinary

lenders or the Conservation Loan Fund, described below. Completed work will be inspected to assure both the resident and the lender that it was done correctly. The goal is to audit every building in Carbondale. These audits will be much more thorough and reach many more buildings than those that the utilities are required to do by the federally mandated Residential Conservation Service.

2. A Community Energy Education Program. Here the goal is to provide accurate information from a credible source to as many community members as possible. The mechanism is a program of conferences, seminars, construction workshops, demonstration projects, and media programming, as well as the education that takes place during an energy audit itself.

3. Conservation Loan Fund. Under the model, the city government will become a Municipal Solar Utility (MSU). It will have the authority to manage the audit and education programs, to capitalize and manage a Conservation Loan Fund, to contract with private industry for the manufacture of solar hot water- and space-heating systems, and to levy taxes for the capitalization and operation of these programs. The Loan Fund will provide low-cost capital for energy related home improvements. It will not compete with private lenders because it will lend only to those who cannot meet the private sector's credit requirements.

4. Energy Production Systems Development. This long-range strategy will enable the city, in its capacity as the MSU, to supply residents with energy from renewable sources, such as passive and active solar hot water- and space-heating devices and production of ethanol from biomass. All such products will be scaled to community needs and will be manufactured by Carbondale residents, thus providing local employment as well as reducing dependence on large utility grids.

To insure the feasibility of this program, a startup capital fund is required. Auditors and inspectors need to be hired and trained, education programs must be undertaken; the Conservation Loan Fund must be capitalized before it can begin to revolve. The authors suggest two sources: (1) an Energy Consumption Tax, based on the *amount* of energy used, not its price, and (2) contributions from conventional utilities. The local tax is seen as a more predictable alternative than federal grants or municipal bond issues. Utilities would contribute because they would share in the detailed energy-use data generated by the MSU, thus helping them plan more efficiently. They also need the public relations in a time of soaring fuel costs, and probably their own role as central generators and distributors of energy will shift to that of brokers of energy from many decentralized sources. In any event, decentralized energy production will not eliminate the need for conventional utilities in the near future.

The MSU model makes sense for Carbondale, but there are obstacles to transporting it to other cities, as the authors themselves admit when they are contemplating the Municipal Solar Utility in Santa Clara, California. There, the climate was mild, the state had a unique 55 percent solar tax credit, and the focus of the project was to heat the city's 800 swimming pools. Carbondale's problems were far different.

The decentralization of energy production and intensified local conservation efforts do seem applicable to most Midwestern and Northeastern cities, however. With the exception of two states, Kentucky and North Dakota, the 24 states comprising this area produce much less fossil fuel than they consume.[24] The Midwest produces 39 percent of the fossil fuel it consumes; the Mid-Atlantic region, 25 percent; and New England, 0 percent. By contrast, the Sunbelt (South, Southwest, Far West) and Mountain states regions produce more than they consume. The effect of this imbalance is to drain the economies of the Frostbelt, which will pay an estimated $450 billion for imported energy between 1980 and 1985.[25]

The implications of such a massive removal of capital are devastating. Midwestern household energy expenditures (including gasoline) were 12.5 percent of disposable income in 1978 and 16.8 percent in 1980. They will certainly go to 18 percent by 1985.[26] About one million more Midwestern jobs will be lost by 1985 as well.[27] Signs of an economic depression in this area are already evident in unemployment levels 5 to 6 percent higher than the national average. Dependence on centralized fossil-fuel-based energy sources appears to be suicidal for Frostbelt residents.

Where do neighborhood organizations come in? First, the awareness that energy dependency underlies much of our economic decline must be brought home to people everywhere. Neighborhood organizations as advocates for residents can play a vital role in this educational process. Second, such organizations must advocate collectively with city governments to begin the politically thorny process of energy needs assessment and comprehensive planning. Conservation will achieve top priority for cities when they equate saving energy with keeping dollars in the local economy. Advocacy efforts at the federal level must be continued and expanded, although the present atmosphere in Washington of "let them eat cake" is not conducive to support of local initiative, rhetoric to the contrary. If a local energy consumption tax is to be employed to fund program measures, it will not come about without an intensive campaign among voters to show that it is in their own interest. Anti-tax sentiment is a major obstacle to implementing local energy initiatives and should not be taken lightly.

Another hurdle to be expected when Carbondale's model is fitted to other municipalities derives from the fact that in Carbondale activists were dealing with only one government body. In larger cities with suburban satellites, only regional or metropolitan planning makes sense. But the traditional antipathy between city and suburb will make such planning excruciatingly difficult. Grassroots groups with a common vision, however, can form a base of support for the design of a model that meets the needs of the particular area in question.

The Carbondale experiment is but one of many examples of heightened awareness in urban government, particularly in the smaller cities where changes can be expedited more rapidly. David Morris details ways that U.S. cities are coming to grips with this threat to their very existence.[28] Although he does not elaborate on the linkage between neighborhood organization and City Hall, it is clear that a climate of concern about energy issues is forming in the minds of local officials everywhere. The costs of energy, not only in terms of city budgets, but also in terms of lost employment and resulting economic damage, are grabbing their attention. Neighborhood organizations can exploit this worry by pushing for inclusion of their representatives in comprehensive energy planning and by demanding that programs developed meet residents' needs for employment and independence from Big Oil. The organizational infrastructure to achieve these advocacy goals is present and operable from local to national levels. As long as organizations can function primarily as advocates for residents and can work cooperatively with one another, energy issues, particularly in the Frostbelt, will demand more room on the agendas of neighborhood organizations. But activists must develop a common perspective on what the sources of the problem are and what solutions are feasible. That vision must combine decentralization with renewable energy sources.

Many Havenot neighborhood organizations, faced with more immediate pressures, have not yet placed energy high on their agendas. To many it still has the aura of a middle-class suburban issue. But opportunities are rapidly opening up for considerable neighborhood organization impact on city programming to promote energy self-reliance and a healthier local economy. Versions of the Carbondale plan to achieve local municipal energy independence could just as well be developed by coalitions of neighborhood groups. Cities are now in a swift transition because of the energy situation. Neighborhood organizations should move energy to the top of their activity list immediately. It is becoming a most basic bread-and-butter urban issue.

NOTES

1. David Morris, *Self-Reliant Cities: Energy and the Transformation of Urban America* (San Francisco, CA: Sierra Club Books, 1982), 106.

2. W. Jackson Davis, *The Seventh Year: Industrial Civilization in Transition* (New York: W.W. Norton, 1979), 33–35.

3. Frances Moore Lappe, *Diet for a Small Planet*, Tenth Anniversary Edition (New York: Ballantine Books, 1981), 74, 147.

4. Robert Sherrill, "The Case Against the Oil Companies," in *The Big Business Reader: Essays on Corporate America*, ed. Mark Green and Robert Massie, Jr. (New York: Pilgrim, 1980), 19–35.

5. John U. Nef, "An Early Energy Crisis and Its Consequences," *Scientific American*, 237 (November 1977), 140–51.

6. William Tucker, "The Energy Crisis Is Over!," *Harper's*, November 1981, 25–36.

7. Barry Commoner, *The Poverty of Power: Energy and the Economic Crisis* (New York: Bantam, 1977).

8. Bernard Gendron, *Technology and the Human Condition* (New York: St. Martin's, 1977).

9. *People Power: What Communities Are Doing to Counter Inflation* (Washington, DC: U.S. Office of Consumer Affairs, 1981), 259–73.

10. "Agency's Ruling to Add Billions to Utility Bills," *Grand Rapids Press*, March 11, 1983, 1A.

11. "Two Groups Challenge Iowa Utility," *Disclosure* 63 (June 1981), 3.

12. Tim Massad, "Fighting Those Unbearable Utilities," *The Congress Watcher*, May-June 1981, 10–11.

13. Barry Caspar and Paul Wellstone, *Powerline: The First Battle of America's Energy War* (Amherst, MA: University of Massachusetts Press, 1981), 5.

14. Larry Strange, former controller for the Tennessee Valley Authority, speech given at conference: "Community Energy and Economic Development," Argonne National Laboratories, Chicago, Illinois, October 3, 1981.

15. "Industry's Flight from Gas May Boost Homeowners' Bills," *Grand Rapids Press*, September 21, 1982, 3A.

16. Carl Solberg, *Oil Power: The Rise and Imminent Fall of an American Empire* (New York: New American Library, 1976); Commoner.

17. David Osborne, "America's Plentiful Energy Resource," *The Atlantic*, March 1984, 86–102.

18. Osborne, p. 100.

19. *Neighborhood Self-Help Case Studies: Abstracts of Reports on Revitalization Projects Funded by the Office of Neighborhood Self-Help Development* (Washington, DC: U.S. Department of Housing and Urban Development, October 1980), 12.

20. *People Power*, pp. 202–3.

21. Tom McMenamim, "Working Together in Carbondale, Illinois," *Sun Times*, July-August 1981.

22. Richard Archer, "National Energy Plan Testimony," Denver, CO, April 15, 1981. (Copy obtainable from Archer at Southern Illinois University, Carbondale, IL 62901).

23. Chris Robertson, Michael Besal, J. Randle Shick, and Larry Strange, *Municipal Solar Utility: A Model for Carbondale, Illinois* (Carbondale, IL: Shawnee Solar Project, 1981).

24. *Energy and the Economy*, Midwest Governors' Report, 1981, 9.

25. *Energy*, p. 10.

26. *Energy*, p. 16.

27. *Energy*, p. 17.

28. Morris, chaps. 5–9.

9

CRIME: THE BIGGEST NEIGHBORHOOD ISSUE

THE SCOPE OF NEIGHBORHOOD CRIME

As noted in the opening paragraphs of Chapter 1, U.S. cities suffer from a public image problem. At the core of that perception is that cities are dangerous places inhabited by predatory hordes that operate with impunity on darkened streets and alleys. Night in the city is no time for strolls or sightseeing; it is a time for being home and bolting the locks. Street crime is *out* there, ready to happen to you.

What is the case? One observer argues that what has increased is crime *reporting*, up 50 percent between 1970 and 1979.[1] Actual crime *rates* as measured by victimization studies and arrests for major crimes have remained about the same since 1974. Arrest rates of juveniles have actually dropped from what they were a decade ago. The rate of violent attack per 1,000 people remained at about 33 from 1973 to 1979. Robbery and aggravated assault resulting in injury saw no change between the same years, remaining at 5.5 per 1,000 people. Thus there is considerable support for the view that criminal behavior remains constant over time and that "crime waves" are a product of our imagination, perhaps enhanced by the pervasiveness of TV crime programs.

But two further points must be made. First, even if it is not really on the increase overall, there is still a lot of crime. Second, one particular type of crime *is* on the rise: murder. In California, young black males are particularly subject to this ultimate misdeed; 62 out of every 100,000 of them were murdered in 1980, four times the state average and 15 times the murder rate for young white women. In general, one is far more likely to be murdered if one is black, Hispanic, or Asian than if one is white.

Fear of crime has always been part of the urban odor.[2] But one should distinguish the fear from the fact. There is crime on the streets, but anxieties that we are experiencing a tidal wave of it are unwarranted. This distinction is essential. If a problem is to be solved, it must be defined with precision.

A recent major study of crime compared ten inner city neighborhoods in Philadelphia, Chicago, and San Francisco.[3] The study concluded that fear of crime overall in these areas was at a moderate level, although three times as many people (30%) said they were very fearful as had experienced personal contact with crime (6–10%). There were further anomalies. For example, personal crime struck young males most frequently, yet they expressed the least concern or fear. Fear of crime, to no one's surprise, turned out to be a function of feeling vulnerable. Women, the elderly, and blacks in these neighborhoods all reported stronger feelings of fear than did other groups.

Crime in neighborhoods can be split into two broad categories, those against persons and those against property. There is a third grouping of public behaviors, however, that cause concern to residents, some of which are criminal and others which somehow accompany or lead to criminal behavior. This last collection includes prostitution, pornographic pandering, gambling, and drug trafficking among the criminal activities and disorderly public behavior, such as drunkenness, loitering, panhandling, teenage rowdiness, defacing public property with graffiti, loud noises, and unrestrained parties.

James Q. Wilson and George L. Kelling advance the hypothesis that when it appears that no one cares to tend an area and the public behavior in it, this area becomes vulnerable to criminal invasion.[4] Residents witnessing these worsening conditions, they argue, modify their behavior. They walk the streets less frequently, and when they must go out, they proceed with downcast eyes and hurried steps. They do not want to get involved. The elderly fear the young. The neighborhood has gone from being a home to merely a place where one lives.

As a counterpoint, Jane Jacobs described vividly how a rich and diverse street life nurtures neighborhoods.[5] By this she meant that residential, commercial, and traffic patterns all interacted to meet a wide variety of interests. Because the neighborhood is interesting—viable— it brings people into proximity with each other, by itself eliminating the isolation that encourages crime. Jacobs' more positive thesis does not necessarily deny the more tenuous theory of Wilson and Kelling about how residents modify their behavior, but these two differing views on how neighborhoods decline are less important in their different emphases than in their common acknowledgement of the primacy of social fabric in maintaining viable neighborhoods. The social fabric has a visible counterpart. Physically well-tended neighborhoods are probably socially well tended. That is, people in such neighborhoods feel they control the neighborhood's public behavior. Abandoned buildings, on the other hand, presage abandoned social control. When 3 to 6 percent of the neighborhood's buildings are abandoned, the neighborhood is in serious trouble.

In many neighborhoods, however, even the most zealous residents are often not capable of controlling by informal means the public behaviors they encounter. It is the spreading of disorderly public behaviors together with the various criminal acts they seem to invite, that constitutes—more accurately—the crime wave engulfing cities. The fear of crime lumps these two into one, making their solution either withdrawal, what Wilson and Kelling call *atomization*, or calling the cops. Neither of these are effective strategies in themselves.

The fear of crime is thus a social problem in itself because it shapes resident behavior. The authors of the ten-neighborhood study mentioned above reasonably speculate that

the suspicion, distrust, isolation, and declining community attachment that presumably go hand in hand with high levels of fear may *retard* rather than stimulate group-based activity focused on the problem.[6]

Their study suggests that fear of crime could become a separate subject of public policy. In this regard, they echo Ahlbrandt's and Cunningham's conclusions that public policy with respect to neighborhoods should seek to reinforce social fabric and promote collective involvement, which in turn is stimulated by a vested interest in the community.[7]

This quick dissection of the crime problem avoids for the most part a discussion of what causes crime. There is no definitive answer, only evidence that bolsters one perspective over another. Liberals have long felt that unemployment led to crime or that juvenile offenses foreshadowed an adult life of lawlessness. Yet studies do not show these correlations. Belief in the moral autonomy of the individual, which places responsibility on the person for his or her acts, is woven into the substance of our culture and law. Social scientists have long known, however, that environmental pressures can affect one's decisions. One writer suggests that alienation and suppressed rage resulting from a life that sees no future can produce criminal outbursts. "Those at the bottom of society often relieve the endless tedium they face through violence, a violence which then becomes routine and banal."[8]

Those who emphasize the moral freedom of the criminal will endorse the truisms of the Right: more police, more prisons, harsher punishments. Yet the fact that there are more police and more prisons now than ever before has not deterred crime. Tougher sentences in California, including the death penalty, mandatory jailing for use of a gun during a crime, and a major program of jailing juveniles, have led to more imprisonments. But the murder rate in Los Angeles has doubled during the same time period.

One's assumptions about the causes of crime, then, lead one to embrace one set of strategies over another. The argument made here has a double emphasis. First, neighborhoods in which residents do not or cannot exert social control over public behavior by informal means are more likely to experience increased criminal activity. Second, economic deprivation partially causes crime when it increases alienation by drastically reducing the individual's options for the future. Both of these assumptions focus on the environment, but they do not deny the possibility of moral freedom, that mysterious element by which one identical twin chooses to become an outlaw and the other a saint. The principal value in concentrating on the environmental side is that it is here that something can be done, even while admitting that some people are so dangerous to society that they must be kept away from it, perhaps for the rest of their lives.

NEIGHBORHOOD-BASED CRIME CONTROL STRATEGIES

Neighborhood organizations at present may be much better able to address the need for social control of the neighborhood than they are the economic deprivation issue.[9] Crime, in fact, is often *the* motive force behind the creation of neighborhood organizations. Chapter 2 demonstrated how neighborhood organizations grow out of each community's social networks and in turn act to reinforce them. In other words, neighborhood organizations influence social fabric by their very operation.

Direct Tactics

Neighborhood organizations can deter crime in several direct ways. First, they organize residents to watch out for each other (for children, the elderly, one another's homes, and so forth) on an informal basis. A variant of this is the Whistlestop Program, in which residents buy whistles for a dollar or so at a block meeting. One blows the whistle if one is attacked; the goal is to startle and repel the offender while at the same time summoning help.

Second, some neighborhood organizations create more formal civilian patrols. These groups work closely with police, carry walkie-talkies, and do not attempt to apprehend suspects. This last point differentiates them from vigilante groups. They may walk or ride in cars; they may be tenants in a housing project or taxi drivers. They function as people taking some formal responsibility for tending to public behavior. When behavior improves, these patrols often cease.

Third, the ordinary operations of the neighborhood organization in creating block clubs, disseminating information about the neighborhood to its residents, and involving them in its neighborhood-wide activities, all help to weave the social fabric we have been discussing. The sense of neighborhood identity—that one not only resides in an area, but that one belongs to and therefore cares about it—is a less tangible but extremely important outcome of everything the neighborhood organization does.

Dealing Through Police

The fourth way that neighborhood organizations squelch crime, cooperation with police, is perhaps what residents might think of first but for a variety of reasons is the most difficult to accomplish. Police assistance is essential, of course, for those situations involving public behavior or outright criminal activity that cannot be handled by residents alone. This last strategy requires a little more elaboration because traditionally police and residents in low-income neighborhoods have had a relationship analogous to that between the white colonizers and black African natives: police have been seen as "motorized bwanas cruising, hunting, and foraging among the natives in the urban jungle.''[10] In short, tension existed between the two sides, and it still does to a great degree in many cities.

Police-initiated programs in response to neighborhood crime have been of two kinds: (1) beefed up but conventional mobile patrols in high crime areas, and (2) Neighborhood Watch programs in which an officer meets residents in a block club setting, advises them about reporting suspicious activity and improving their home security, and leaves.[11] Neither of these tactics by itself has had much impact on urban crime rates, although reporting of crime often increases.

Citizen groups on the other hand have regularly sought foot patrols and citizen boards that review police activity and that offer advice from the neighborhood perspective. While initially neighborhood groups might have welcomed increased police patrols or special strike forces in high crime areas, these operations have often worked to increase community stress rather than relieve it because more innocent people fell victim to police tactics than before.

A citizen review board that exerts formal control over police policy is an unlikely creature. Most local governments are loathe to share or delegate their power in this most sensitive area. But *advisory* boards have come into being and gained credibility in a number of cities. Their effectiveness is entirely dependent upon the receptivity of top police administrators, however. Wise police officials and community leaders know that setting up such a board is only a small part of the overall effort needed to improve the communality of the neighborhood by tending to its public behaviors. The advisory board concept has its particular usefulness in providing a citywide forum and promoting citywide citizen concern with police operations.

The other demand of neighborhood groups for police patrols has been the subject of isolated experiments. For instance, the state of New Jersey funded police forces in 28 cities to put officers on walking beats in the mid–1970s. Five years later the Police Foundation evaluated the project.[12] Although crime rates were not reduced, citizens felt safer, and officers on foot had higher morale and a more favorable attitude toward the citizens in the neighborhoods than did those police assigned to patrol cars. The officer on the beat, it was found, was able to elevate the level of public order in these neighborhoods by keeping an eye on the strangers (people passing through) and enforcing a set of informal but widely understood rules for the *regulars*, who included both ''decent folk'' and drunks and derelicts usually in the area. Although the police were white and the neighborhoods predominantly black, both parties seemed satisfied with the way things worked out.

Foot patrols do increase positive contact between police and citizens, though many city governments feel that this benefit does not outweigh their expense or their reduction in officer mobility. Other cities have experimented successfully by having patrol officers walk part time and drive part time. Whenever police activity increases markedly to restore and maintain order in a neighborhood, however, it runs a great risk, even in the best of situations, of becoming a harassment of innocent citizens. In the worst cases it becomes a legitimization of police brutality and other victimizations of residents, such as police burglaries, which have not been uncommon in some cities.

Nonetheless, more comprehensive cooperation between police and citizens seems necessary. Detroit's successful drastic reduction of its horrendous murder rate and other major crimes is due to several factors. Movement of blacks into key government positions and many police openings under Mayor Coleman Young was a first step. The decentralization of police operations to 50 ministations in storefronts and church basements was a second. The third was the creation with the help of the police of some 4,000 Neighborhood Watch block clubs. In the final analysis, we return to the social fabric issue: "All that has changed in Detroit and elsewhere is that people who once believed they had no control over their lives or their community seem now to believe that real change is possible."[13]

An even closer type of cooperation between neighborhood associations and police can be found in Grand Rapids' Safeguard Program. Since 1980, the city signed contracts with several inner city neighborhood associations to hire community organizers. These staff people organize at the block and the neighborhood level around crime issues. They function as liaisons with police and occasionally as ombudsmen. They write articles for the neighborhood newsletters, publish crime statistics for their target areas, give psychological support to victims and witnesses, and do the legwork necessary to raise citizens' awareness of their collective ability to reduce crime by actively watching out for each other. The source of the funds is the CDBG (Community Development Block Grant) Program. Although the program's effectiveness in reducing crime has not been formally assessed, citizen reporting of crime has increased, and police, the associations involved, and city officials all expressed general satisfaction at the increased levels of citizen involvement and activism in deterring crime after two years of program operation. A later informal assessment of the six organizers' effectiveness, however, indicated that there should be a more structured orientation, supervision, and evaluation plan—assisted by the police department—than had previously been in place. The neighborhood associations would continue as the principal employers, however, under contract with the city.

Neighborhood organizations reduce or prevent crime in two general ways: through independent action and in concert with police. Their organizing activities increase the cohesiveness and identity of the community. At the same time, these activities dampen the climate for crime and increase residents' sense of security. Organizing also ameliorates the conditions that breed crime, by improving housing and commercial districts, demanding jobs, and creating alternative economic institutions. Just cleaning up the physical appearance of the neighborhood can have positive effects. Neighborhood groups can also organize block clubs specifically on crime issues and keep the neighborhood informed on the incidence of crime. Working with police can mean involving them in block organizing, demanding foot patrols and advisory status, and hiring organizers in the neighborhoods to concentrate on crime concerns. These and other strategies should work together, not separately.

THE EFFECTIVENESS OF NEIGHBORHOOD-BASED CRIME CONTROL STRATEGIES

Studies of the effectiveness of neighborhood-based organizations in lowering crime rates in their areas are relatively rare. A main reason for this scarcity is that it is difficult to show a direct connection between the main activities of an organization and criminal behavior in the neighborhood. In some instances, of course, patrols organized by a neighborhood group have helped apprehend lawbreakers, but generally the work of a neighborhood organization is supplemental to that of the police in controlling public behavior. A 1979 national survey of 45 community organizations showed that although the concern they had about the crime issue was paramount, they were not well organized programmatically to address it.[14] Of five major issues categories, crime had the greatest differential between advocacy and programmatic approaches. An organization was three times more likely to advocate citizen voice in making plans to deter crime than it was to create its own program, probably because of a shortage of funds. Neighborhood organizations had taken some action, however, to deal with what they considered major crimes, such as breaking and entering, juvenile crime, burglary, drug abuse, vandalism, and assaults. These actions emphasized residents' activity, rather than reliance on social services and the criminal justice system. Such direct action included mounting political pressure on City Hall and the police department, as well as organizing patrols and crime watches.

In the national survey just mentioned, success in fighting crime was judged by the organizations themselves. A key finding, though, was that success depended upon the application of methods that fit the particular neighborhood's problem. For example, COACT, a coalition of seven neighborhoods in Philadelphia, acknowledged that each neighborhood's crime problem was unique. In one, juvenile crimes against the elderly were the most urgent. In another, burglaries by drug addicts were most serious. In a third, police-community relations took top priority. Contextual variables also included the attitudes of the police and local government officials, the character of the area, and the kind of crime most plaguing the residents. This idea, that the local context ought to be the principal determinant of neighborhood revitalization strategies, is a theme heard often in scholarly works about the care and feeding of neighborhoods.

A study in St. Louis by C.W. Kohfield, Barbara Salert, and Sandra Schoenberg explored whether there was a correlation between neighborhood association organizing and reduced crime rates in sections of that city.[15] Having overcome the difficulty of matching crime statistics, demographic data, and neighborhood organizational information, the authors acknowledged that a simple relationship between presence or absence of a neighborhood organization and crime rates says little about the *effect* of that neighborhood organization on the rates. The community conditions that spawn the organization could also produce lower crime rates apart from the organization's actions. Kohfield, Salert, and Schoenberg concluded that if they could statistically control for these differences in neighborhood conditions, they could isolate the impact of the organization. The conditions to be considered included the percentage of nonwhite population, percentage of heads of household who were unemployed or retired, percent net change in occupied housing units, and percentage of commercial addresses. Three other independent variables were neighborhood organization, umbrella organization, and community corporation. The crime data was an average of 1976 and 1977 figures "to ensure stability in low crime categories."[16]

The initial data analysis concluded that where neighborhood associations operate, violent crime is reduced 55 percent and property crime 25 percent when other condition variables are controlled for. A second, more conservative, analysis that allowed for the fact that conditions do affect crime rates still showed an overall reduction of 16 percent in those neighborhoods with organizations: 30 percent reduction in violent crime, 15 percent in property crime. So there appeared to be a relation between the presence of a neighborhood organization and a lower incidence of criminal activity, particularly of an assaultive nature.

The authors then investigated the effect of an active crime watch program on crime statistics. Surprisingly, they found no significant difference between *organized* areas with and without crime watch activities. On the basis of this finding, they could not conclude that such programs are effective in reducing crime. Their data sources included neighborhood group self-reports and outside expert reports. A more sophisticated analysis of this data revealed that although the differences between neighborhoods with crime watch and those without were not large, they did favor areas with crime watch programs. That is, when neighborhood conditions were controlled for, those areas in which a neighborhood association ran an active crime watch program experienced lower numbers of crimes.

The authors hypothesized that neighborhood organizations can influence both the instrumental and social sources of crime. Instrumental sources refer to (1) perceived opportunities for crime and (2) criminals' perceived chances of getting caught. Social sources of crime refer to (3) community cohesiveness and (4) environmental conditions that breed crime. Their study suggests that, on the one hand, a neighborhood organization can minimize the environmental conditions and opportunities for crime perceived by criminals. On the other hand, it can enhance community cohesiveness and the criminal's perception that he or she might be caught. The St. Louis study suggests that when neighborhood organizations direct their attention programmatically to these factors, they can reduce crime inside their borders by 10 to 25 percent.

Studies of neighborhood organization effectiveness in reducing crime, though few, suggest that when such groups address the issue by establishing a program to deal with it, they can have some impact. These programs, however, should be tailored to the context in which they operate, implying that the neighborhood groups themselves ought to be the principal consultants on program goals and strategies.

NOTES

1. Frank Browning, "Nobody's Soft on Crime Anymore," *Mother Jones*, August 1982, 25.

2. Alfred Kazin, "Fear of the City: 1783 to 1983," *American Heritage*, February-March 1983, 14–23.

3. Wesley Skogan and Michael Maxfield, *Coping with Crime: Individual and Neighborhood Reactions* (Beverly Hills, CA: Sage, 1981), chap 4.

4. James Q. Wilson and George L. Kelling, "Broken Windows: The Police and Neighborhood Safety," *The Atlantic*, March 1982, 29–38.

5. Jane Jacobs, *The Death and Life of Great American Cities* (New York: Random House, 1961), 68.

6. Skogan and Maxfield, p. 240.

7. Roger S. Ahlbrandt and James V. Cunningham, *A New Public Policy for Neighborhood Preservation* (New York: Praeger, 1979), chap. 12.

8. Browning, p. 29.

9. James V. Cunningham, "Assessing the Urban Partnership: Do Community Forces Fit?," *National Civic Review*, November 1981, 521–26.

10. Melvin Levin, *The Urban Prospect: Planning, Policy, and Strategies for Change* (North Scituate, MA: Duxbury Press, 1977), 240.

11. A recent study by the National Institute of Justice suggests police cannot keep citizens safe without their cooperation. Besides reporting on police-initiated participation efforts in Detroit and Chicago, the manual includes information on neighborhood police beats, police ministations, street observation programs, crime hotlines, citizen crime patrols, escort services, witness assistance programs, and others. "Report Suggests Police Rely on Citizens' Aid," *Grand Rapids Press*, January 20, 1983, 2A.

12. Wilson and Kelling, p. 29.

13. Browning, p. 40.

14. Gerson Green, *Who's Organizing the Neighborhood? Community Organizations: A Report on Their Structure, Accountability, Finance, Personnel, Issues, and Strategies* (Washington, DC: U.S. Department of Justice, 1979).

15. C.W. Kohfield, Barbara Salert, and Sandra Schoenberg, "Neighborhood Associations and Urban Crime," *Journal of Community Action*, November-December 1981, 37–44.

16. Kohfield et al., p. 38.

10

NEIGHBORHOOD SCHOOLS

The U.S. . . . has never, on any large scale, known vital urban schools.
—Charles Silberman[1]

Neighborhood organizations in low-income urban areas have ordinarily been less concerned with school issues than with those discussed in the previous three chapters. The nature of the school process, the complex organization of public education, and the press of other needs are all reasons why advocacy activity with regard to schools is not widespread in the neighborhood movement. Nonetheless, there have been enough studies of interaction between community organizations and public schools in low-income and minority neighborhoods that we can begin to flesh out the potential of the neighborhood organization to promote effective school change.

Why should the neighborhood organization be concerned about the local schools? Three related reasons come to mind. First, the section on crime discussed the ability of the neighborhood organization to repair the social fabric of a residential area as one of its strongest attributes. Therefore, the neighborhood organization is a medium of localized social control. The school, since it convenes large numbers of youth over the years of their maturation, is another key agent of social control in a community. Although their methodologies and structures are radically different, both types of organizations have a lot to do with whether the people in the community feel that they still control it. When school is viewed as a *source* of drug trafficking, vandalism, purse-snatching, and rowdyism, when it is *not* in control of the neighborhood children from the residents' perspective, then the neighborhood organization will be interested in working to restore order.

Second, the school is one of the major institutions influencing the neighborhood. Since it lies within the neighborhood boundaries and directly provides services to local residents, it is more visible and vulnerable to protest than are other institutions that mold the contours of the neighborhood but are beyond its pale, such as lending institutions, large corporations, or government. In larger cities, however, this immediacy is deceiving because of centralized control of budget, personnel, and curriculum matters.

Third, and perhaps most important, the parents of children in a poor district are just as interested in their sons' and daughters' success in school as are those in a wealthier area. Although the debilitating effects of their poverty may hamper their participation in school matters, they still care about their children and what is happening to them inside the school building. There are many reasons why parents would not see education as an issue, including the fact that they themselves do not directly experience the boredom or violence that may be the lot of their offspring during the school day. But there has been enough upset over the poor quality of urban education to have provoked many organized protests over the past 20 years. The neighborhood organization, then, is not only concerned about neighborhood social order and control of institutions affecting the community, its members want the same quality public service afforded the more affluent.

This chapter explores the control relationships influencing the urban school, with a primary focus on the relation between it and the neighborhood organization. The first question addressed is whether schools can be effective in teaching the children of the poor. We then examine links between school effectiveness and how the school is controlled; a case is made that power imbalances, whereby educators exclude parents from shared influence in schools, promote school failure. The chapter then reviews studies of neighborhood groups' attempts to influence local school policy, and closes with an analysis of a case study that suggests dos and don'ts for other groups.

CAN SCHOOLS MAKE A DIFFERENCE IN POOR CHILDREN'S ACHIEVEMENT?

One would not be concerned about making a service better if one thought it to be a useless service in the first place. Before attempting to unravel the control controversy surrounding urban education, we should resolve the matter, to the extent it can be resolved, of the influence of schooling on children. The past two decades have witnessed a hot debate, at least in academic circles, over whether schools make any difference in the lives of their students. Do they function as elevators of upward mobility for those in the lower social strata, or do they act to preserve the inequitable status quo? Those who hold that schools reinforce present economic and social disparities cite the analyses of James Coleman and Christopher Jencks, based on enormous data pools.[2] These widely quoted studies purport to demonstrate that equalizing quality in elementary and secondary schools has little effect on children's later economic and social status.[3] Bring a child of low socioeconomic status (SES) to any school, they said in essence, and at the end of it all, the child will most likely stay low SES. Conversely, the children who go to college come from parents who went to college. The exceptions were put down to chance, heredity, or unique environmental factors.

This liberal view of the failure of public schools to promote low-income student achievement reinforced federal initiatives to expand schools' activities to alleviate family malfunctioning among the poor, through such programs as school breakfasts and lunches, Head Start, and other compensatory education projects. A quieter neoconservative trend was building as well, beginning in 1970 with research into the differences between inner city schools where students achieved and those where they did not. In the early 1980s, the public outcry against poor schooling reached a crescendo. In 1983, *A Nation at Risk*, a report of President Ronald Reagan's National Commission on Excellence in Education, headed a list of dozens of reports and studies, most of which had a traditionalist emphasis, chronicling the sorry state of American education in the U.S. What was in the 1960s a mainly liberal concern with inner city school failures has broadened in the 1980s to a national upset with virtually all schools.

This new national consciousness of school problems, coupled with the research in the past decade on what factors make a school effective, provides new opportunities for parents and other community members to improve their local schools. The currently predominant view is that schools can make a difference and that certain organizational factors, lumped under the heading of *ethos*, are pivotal in the effective school. These factors include strong leadership by the principal, high expectations for student achievement by everyone (including students and parents), schoolwide emphasis on cognitive learning, and frequent monitoring and evaluation of student progress.[4] These elements can all coalesce only when the school is a controlled environment. Two recent studies on school effectiveness describe how this concept might work, for it does not necessarily imply a return to the birch rod and hard bench of yesteryear.

SCHOOL EFFECTIVENESS: THE SCHOOL UNDER CONTROL

Michael Rutter and his associates conducted a three-year study in a dozen secondary schools in inner London.[5] Although these schools varied considerably among themselves in the average behavioral patterns and academic achievements of their pupils, the authors concluded that the *process* of each school affected student outcomes. That is, the way the school was organized did seem to be a causal influence on the children. Such factors as the degree of academic emphasis, instructional methods, availability of incentives and rewards, and the opportunity for students to take responsibility were all significantly related to outcome differences between the schools. School organization shaped student attitude and learning to an appreciable extent. These social factors were far more important than the size of the building, its age, or the space available in it.

Another finding of the Rutter study is of particular importance to parents' groups. Although schools that had large proportions of less able students did have higher average rates of delinquency and lower achievement scores, the ''process of school functioning'' was not affected. This meant that, in the authors' words,

Schools have a considerable degree of choice in how they are organized, and that teachers have a similar choice in their decisions on how to respond to the children they teach. Our results suggest that these decisions on how to respond are likely to affect the chances of the children improving in their behavior and attainments.[6]

Rutter and his associates do not argue that schools are the most important influence on children's development or that education can compensate for the inequities of society. They do suggest that schools constitute a major area of influence, one which is susceptible to change.

The Rutter study identified several factors in the social organization of school that appeared to be important in promoting student progress.

The first factor was the group management technique of the teacher. The better teachers employed positive reinforcement and avoided punishment. The second factor identified was the normative atmosphere (*ethos*) of the school. In the more successful inner city schools, teachers communicated clear expectations to the students, gave them accurate feedback, and consciously acted as role models for them. In addition, these norms showed consistency from class to class. Third, the students who made progress had opportunities for positions of responsibility within the school. Finally, peer group influence that would subvert school success was countered by deliberately manipulating the pupil mix.

A larger study closer to home supported the London findings. Extensive investigation of 91 Michigan elementary schools concluded that *cultural normative climate* and *student status-role definition* explained most of the variance in academic achievement and other behavioral outcomes.[7]

Cultural normative climate refers to teacher expectations and student norms for achievement. In a supportive climate, teachers believe students are able to learn, and they expect them to learn. In such an atmosphere, teachers are more likely to commit themselves to instructional tasks and provide appropriate reinforcement for learning behavior. Students also support one another in achieving academic mastery, whereas in all too many city schools students ridicule their academically achieving peers because of their own alienation from teachers and school.

Student status-role definition refers to the student's feeling of control over mastery of academic work. This feeling is not the same as self-concept. One can have confidence in one's own ability, but still feel a lack of control over one's academic life. I recall a bright ninth-grader in my math class in an inner city school several years ago who complained bitterly that the constant chaos in the class was keeping her from learning. Although she undoubtedly (in my estimation) had a good self-concept, she was developing a sense of futility about her school experience. Other students in the class had developed this feeling much earlier and had come to expect little of themselves within the school setting. It is this futility which is at the core of much alienation in the schools. I *alone*—and I felt very much alone—could do little to deal with the alienation I sensed around me. In turn I felt frustrated, and many other teachers at our school indicated to me that they felt as I did.

The effective school, then, embodies an achievement ethic within a social framework that is simultaneously tight and loose. On the one hand, the principal provides strong, supportive leadership, there is communication and consensus among staff about the mission of the school, the curriculum, and discipline codes, and all its students are expected to achieve and behave well. These central shared values, on the other hand, provide teachers a secure domain within which to go about their learning/teaching tasks with some degree of professional autonomy: enriching the curriculum with their unique insights and experimenting with different methods of instruction. Achievement can be pursued down many avenues precisely because things are under control in the school environment. The school under control is now seen as the effective school. But how can Havenots get the school under control?

POWER IMBALANCES AND SCHOOL INEFFECTIVENESS

Historically, urban education has been a battleground on which many groups have fought for dominance, or at least a share of influence, in school policy. Elected boards of education and their top executives, traditionally the school power elite, have been challenged from new directions in recent decades. The federal government, the courts, teachers, and parents have each mounted campaigns to share control of education. What follow are brief comments designed to analyze how the contemporary urban school is out of control, how present power positions among the various actors in urban schools are out of balance. A critical assumption here is that while much of the political struggle over policy-setting has not directly affected student achievement, current power imbalances that deprive parents and students of a sense of shared control work against establishing the achievement consensus essential to the effective school.[8]

Teacher Unions

Mario Fantini, a recognized author on issues that result from the bureaucratization of education, analyzed the rise to power of teacher unions, particularly during the 1960s.[9] School boards and administrators held sway prior to this period, but with the rise in expectations for schools, what Fantini called the rise of the *educational consumer*, teachers found themselves squeezed. Their reaction was to give more allegiance to their unions and to escalate collective demands for control over their working conditions. The effect was to give teachers, through their union leaders, approximate parity with board members and top administrators in the setting of school policy. That they also lost some autonomy to innovate in their own classroom procedure was a regrettable but necessary consequence of collectivization.

The militancy of teacher unions is slackening in a national climate of economic recession and growing taxpayer reluctance to put more dollars into government services. But this small diminution in teachers' collective power should not hide the reality of their considerable leverage in school policy. As union negotiators gained parity with education officials in deciding school policy, the gap in communications between teachers and parents widened, and parents often have come to feel as thwarted as teachers did before they unionized. Still largely unorganized with regard to local school issues, parents and other community members have experienced little involvement in decisions that matter in their local schools. Groups that have organized in low-income areas have tended to define their issues progressively; they maintained that the schools oppress them and their children in various ways and that solutions should stress liberation through community involvement. This view parallels the teachers', but it has not resulted in stronger parents' organizations on a widespread basis.

The case that best highlights this collision between Haves and Havenots in education is the community control experiment in the predominantly black Ocean Hill–Brownsville district of New York City in the late 1960s. Parents and community members were given power over local school budget, personnel, and curriculum matters under a plan funded by the Ford Foundation. When they summarily transferred several white teachers from the district, the the United Federation of Teachers (UFT), which had been watching the process nervously, was outraged. Led by their audacious president, Albert Shanker, the UFT struck the entire New York City system. This muscle-flexing by the teachers' union proved the ultimate undoing of the community control concept in urban education.[10] Although less potent experiments in decentralization continued through the 1970s, especially in Detroit, a demonstrated model for empowering parent/citizen organizations *vis-a-vis* schools has yet to be developed.[11] Whatever local arrangements do evolve, however, they must acknowledge the right of *all* the actors to a share in influencing the outcome.

Parent Involvement

Public schools represent a paradox. They are distant yet immediate, impenetrable yet vulnerable, bureaucratic yet extremely sensitive to public opinion. This irony exists because public education is a political institution; it needs the support of the very people it serves.[12] The resolution of conflict lies in this organizational symbiosis.

A conservative viewing the mess in urban schools is likely to feel that low-income parents already have too much power, not because they are organized, but because the school itself is so vulnerable.[13] From this perspective, schools have had to develop their rhino-hides of bureaucracy to insure impartial decision making and to avoid knuckling under to the pressure tactics of a few strident parents. Yet this argument, played against a background of scenes of angry parents yelling at administrators, ignores a basic human reality. If a person, a Havenot, sees that this opportunity is the only one he or she may get to voice a sense of frustration built over a lifetime, it is unlikely that he or she will speak in modulated tones. On the other hand, the U.S. Constitution is founded on the belief that when citizens are afforded long-term structural avenues to voice their opinions and to exert control in their own spheres, they will act responsibly and with concern for the rights and needs of others. Furthermore, to hold that low-income parents are incapable of wise counsel to the professional educators of their children is not only to deny the fact that the parents themselves are the primary educators, it is also blatantly elitist, a vestige of aristocracy.

Curriculum and Student Sense of Control

Students also need to sense that they control their own achievement in the school. Though they should not gain the upper hand in setting policy for their classroom or school, the curriculum method should be consonant with the positive school atmosphere factors mentioned earlier, and it should increase the students' self-reliance and eradicate feelings of futility. Much current discussion assumes the traditional stance that the teacher should direct and the students follow. Many low-income parents take this position as well. Where all the other effectiveness factors are present, such as a school climate that fosters achievement, security, and strong linkages with the community, teacher-directive methods can promote academic mastery. But what has been learned from progressivism, even from its mistakes, since the early part of the century should not be precipitously thrown out. The open or informal classroom structure *can* be a potent instrument for avoiding the sense of futility so prevalent among urban students and teachers. Under such a method, each student develops his or her own learning objectives, with the teacher's guidance. In the Montessori form of open structure, attractive materials fill the classroom, inviting curious children to explore them, the teacher's role is to allow each child to become her or his own teacher. There is not mere permissiveness; structure and purpose underlie every activity. This method boldly addresses the inconsistency plaguing most schools: how can one teach democracy and self-discipline by using an authoritarian technique?

As the founder and first administrator of an independent, community-controlled, early elementary Montessori school in Milwaukee's inner city, I am a firm believer in the power of open education. But too much of what has been called open education practice in many schools is ineffective because it fails to match the needs of many urban children as they develop. That is, one cannot suddenly open one's classroom without any result but chaos.[14] Moving to positive strategies with students who are accustomed to restrictions, threats, and punishments as the principal means of keeping order will cause them to react negatively if such means are replaced too quickly.[15] In addition, the development of self-reliance and self-direction is a complex set of learned behaviors that takes into account not only the individual student's needs but also the class's evolution as a group.[16] Classmates have to *learn* to support one another and to work on their own, and teachers must spend considerable time at the beginning establishing appropriate norms and leadership patterns in the group, as the transition is made from teacher-centered to teacher-and-student-centered curriculum approaches.

Open classroom structure, practiced within a milieu of high expectations and an ethos of achievement, can be a solution to the problem of boredom plaguing urban students. To paraphrase G. K. Chesterton, it is not that open education is a failure, it just has not been tried yet.

Appropriate method, however, whether it be traditional or progressive, is a necessary but not sufficient condition for a successful school

program. Increasing student academic self-reliance, which in turn reduces parent frustration, is the result of more than merely changing
teaching method. If school practice changes under demands for excellence, it must forge new links with the neighborhood community. We
now turn to studies of past attempts by neighborhood groups to influence
change in their schools.

STUDIES OF NEIGHBORHOOD ORGANIZATION
INFLUENCE IN SCHOOL ISSUES

Published research on the effectiveness of neighborhood groups organized to cope with school issues is quite limited. Perhaps one of the
reasons is that such associations are a relatively recent phenomenon and
usually address a wide variety of other issues as well, making experimental design more difficult.[17] Another reason might be that the nature
of neighborhood organizations is not widely or uniformly understood.
Finally, the view that parents are or should be partners with educators
in the socialization process has surprisingly only recently begun to
capture attention in professional writing.[18]

A major study in the field was done under the guidance of Marilyn
Gittell in Atlanta, Boston, and Los Angeles during 1977 and 1978.[19]
The majority of the 16 local grassroots organizations selected in these
three cities were low-income and principally interested in school issues.
But other groups that addressed several issues, went beyond neighborhood boundaries for membership, were middle-income, or had been
established by government mandate were included for comparative purposes. Several findings are significant.

First, most of the low-income groups had moved from advocacy or
protest modes to providing services for residents, a shift described in
other studies of low-income organizations.[20] The middle-income associations, on the other hand, retained their militancy. Gittell and her
associates assumed that this shift from protest to program is a necessary
one in the life cycle of every neighborhood organization of the lower
working class, a theme that is reminiscent of the Frances Fox Piven
and Richard A. Cloward thesis.[21] Their hypothesis that the form any
citizen organization takes is determined by the social class of its members appeared to be confirmed.

Second, organizations that retained their protest orientation not only
were middle-class in makeup but had no paid staff. The authors therefore

distinguished between successful advocacy groups and those that had begun to provide direct services to their members on the basis of the type of leadership in each kind of organization. Paid staff, charismatic figures, or leaders imposed on an organization by an outside funding agency were all less effective than rotating leadership in maintaining a militant cast to the organization. To Gittell and her associates, empowerment of the poor required militancy, which in turn demanded continuous development of new leaders. Paying staff or relying on the original leadership for too long seemed to be the kiss of death. The organization's leaders in these latter cases came to view members as clients rather than compatriots in a common task. Internal democracy suffered as a result, and the power in organized numbers weakened because fewer members mobilized.

Third, the influence on school policy of all the organizations studied depended to a great degree upon their access to the public school system; access required that the system display bureaucratic openness. Since none of the three systems revealed this trait, the effectiveness of even the middle-class advocacy groups was severely limited. The fact that each of the three cities was considerably different in economic and political atmosphere did not appear to affect the outcomes of neighborhood group action.

The Gittell study pessimistically concluded with a paradox. Community organizations of the poor had to be militant to achieve institutional changes that would benefit their members. But since they were underfinanced, of necessity they diverted their attention to getting funding from institutions that wished to blunt their political thrust and coopt them into providing services for their members. This dilemma seemed always to doom the work of low-income organizations to effect social change. Yet even those higher-income groups that maintained their confrontational stance were still relatively ineffective in producing school system changes.

The Gittell pessimism seems too complete. While many of the study's conclusions appear sound, its dichotomizing leadership (volunteer vs. paid staff) and organizational typology (advocacy vs. service) is simplistic. It contains little or no analysis of organizational changes within the school systems themselves and no acknowledgement of social and economic pressures impinging on these megastructures. It is entirely possible that, at the time they acted, these neighborhood organizations were not structured in ways designed to take advantage of fissures and niches appearing as the public school systems adapted to demands on them from their social and political environment. The Ocean Hill–Brownsville case is an example of community people organizing to take advantage of an opening in the largest school bureaucracy in the country, a slot created by social upheaval, civil rights consciousness, and liberal sentiment in high places. Unfortunately, the community group discounted the firepower of the young teacher union as they moved too rapidly to secure their beachhead.

Another case of neighborhood organization impact on local public schools was contained in John Fish's study of The Woodlawn Organization (TWO) in Chicago.[22] TWO had gained the respect of both the University of Chicago and City Hall through its confrontations with both powers. But before the university sought to establish a $10–million education research center, TWO had no leverage with the public school system. The interests of the university created an opening in the school system's defenses that TWO was quick to exploit.

TWO eyed increased control by the community over the schools in Woodlawn, institutions widely perceived as not only ineffectual but harmful to their students. In spite of an ambiguity in its goals (overhaul or merely upgrade programs), TWO was able to insert itself as an equal representative on the board of control for the new Woodlawn Experimental Schools Project (WESP). Seven representatives each from TWO, the public school system, and the University of Chicago comprised the 21–member Woodlawn Community Board. Thus constituted, WESP received a $1.35–million grant to upgrade two Woodlawn schools. Much of the money was to be used to organize Woodlawn parents and other residents to become more involved in the schools in various ways, including acting as teacher aides.

Fish reported that impressive achievements were made in the classroom (in the form of improved reading scores) and in the community (in the form of greatly increased parent participation). But because TWO had never gained clear authority over the project, recalcitrant teachers remained to subvert gains, and the public school administration dragged their feet at every opportunity. Fish summed up the mixed results:

In spite of these accomplishments WESP was severely limited by a variety of constraints imposed by the prevailing authority structure of the school system. ... That is, the intent to demonstrate possibilities of community control was subverted.[23]

Parents and other community residents interested in having a positive impact on their neighborhood school should take these findings into consideration. Changing a school is not a matter of simply demanding change, although the process must begin there.

That schools can make an important difference in the lives of low-income children seems beyond doubt. Yet most school personnel still suffer from a kind of schizophrenia: they invest themselves in this belief but act to deny it when confronted with their failures. Ideas for linking schools more completely with their communities are not in short supply, and many have been around since the community school movement of the early decades of this century.[24] What has been lacking is the will on the part of the system's professionals to make these connections. This short-sightedness is a product of both a defensive posture and an inability to see the community as a resource pool.

Even where local educators are receptive to making connections, however, the neighborhood organization must be sophisticated in forming partnerships. The following case represents an attempt by a neighborhood organization to create a working relationship in which parents and other community members might have more significant influence in the local school than the existing parent advisory committee afforded. Though the attempt failed, it provided insight into what should have been done.

A CASE STUDY OF LINKAGE BETWEEN COMMUNITY AND SCHOOL

The case involved the Eastown Community Association (ECA) of Grand Rapids, Michigan, and Sigsbee Park Elementary School, a nearly all-black school within ECA's boundaries.[25] ECA was a long-established neighborhood organization; Sigsbee was a stereotypical inner city school in that it was predominantly low-income and low-achieving, with a white-majority staff living outside the area. As the President of ECA, I approached the Sigsbee principal with a proposal to form a committee of representatives from the Sigsbee parents, educators, and ECA members. The purpose of the group, broadly put, was to bring neighborhood resources together in solving perceived problems centered on Sigsbee. Three meetings of the group led to sharing perceptions of problems, but blaming was the chief way it was done: parents blamed prejudiced teachers, teachers blamed disorderly students (and by implication the parents), and both sides viewed ECA's interest with suspicion, unsure why ECA had initiated this group in the first place.

The first activity the group planned was a presentation to parents at the upcoming open house of the upper elementary teachers' new discipline code. The teachers seemed to want the parents' views on their proposed code. Another activity suggested was that the ECA organizer, who was black and had some experience in such training, might organize several sessions for Sigsbee teachers on cross-cultural perceptions. This idea was left for further discussion and never materialized. More than 70 parents attended the open house, a much larger number than usual, due to the contact work of the ECA organizer. Discussion in small groups (four parents and one Sigsbee staff person each) had been carefully prepared for. A short survey instrument to gauge parent concerns prompted animated conversation about several issues. But any real differences over what went on in the school never surfaced. The meeting ended with a resolution to ask the school board for a new playground fence. Throughout the remaining months of the school year, a few parents would come to the weekly faculty meetings but maintained a shy silence for the most part. The committee never met again.

The presence of an established independent neighborhood organization was not enough to overcome some basic communication gaps within the neighborhood. Although ECA had organized in the area for several years, its organizers and leaders had never been settled residents with children in the Sigsbee school. ECA was a predominantly white, mostly middle-class organization (although some of its leaders had from time to time been black or white working class). ECA leaders had no direct investment in a better Sigsbee. Attempts to draw Sigsbee parent leaders into the ECA structure were fruitless, for the most part, because ECA was not their primary reference group in the neighborhood; the Sigsbee Parent Advisory committee and their own block clubs and churches were. One or two of the Sigsbee teachers were willing to continue meeting, but they could not carry the burden of the organizing. Individual interest, present in all concerned, never overlapped enough to form a common interest. Clearly, if the neighborhood organization is going to be effective in bridging the moat between school and community, its leaders ought to be parents with children in the school.

Many of the failed attempts by neighborhood organizations to breach the walls of the local public school establishment were due to a lack of what Gittell called bureaucratic openness, a cultural receptivity to new structures allowing for parent and citizen empowerment. The new chorus of calls for school improvement, coming from every sector of society concerned with schools, is creating the openings community groups have long sought. Local boards of education everywhere are appointing citizen study committees to examine how schools could be improved. And they are listening to what these groups have to say. Academics, excellence, mastery, and achievement are the catchwords of the mid 1980s. Thoughtful conservatives and liberals alike, though they still differ philosophically, are both supporting many of the new initiatives to reform schools. It appears that there has been no time like the present for neighborhood/parent groups to make their voices heard. If they do not do so, the school as a mediating institution is a bankrupt concept, and the potential partners in the socialization of the young cannot cooperate to build the viable neighborhood.

NOTES

1. Charles Silberman, *Crisis in the Classroom: The Remaking of American Education* (New York: Random House, 1970), 59.

2. J.S. Coleman, E. Campbell, C. Hobson, J. McPartland, A. Mood, F. Weinfeld, and R. York, *Equality of Educational Opportunity* (Washington, DC: Government Printing Office, 1966); C.S. Jencks, M. Smith, H. Ackland, M.J. Bane, D. Cohen, H. Gintis, B. Heyns, and S. Michelson, *Inequality: A Reassessment of the Effect of Family and Schooling in America* (New York: Basic Books, 1972).

3. "Equalizing quality" referred to achieving consistency in teacher credentials and pay, facilities, curriculum materials, and other measurable aspects of school operation.

4. Gilbert Sewall, *Necessary Lessons: Decline and Renewal in American Schools* (New York: Free Press, 1983), 139–40.

5. Michael Rutter, Barbara Maughan, Peter Mortimer, Janet Ouston, with Alan Smith, *Fifteen Thousand Hours: Secondary Schools and Their Effects on Children* (Cambridge, MA: Harvard University Press, 1979). In an extensive review of the school effectiveness literature, Stewart Purkey and Marshall Smith, "Effective Schools: A Review," *The Elementary School Journal*, March 1983: 427–53, culled essentially the same conclusions as did the Rutter study.

6. Rutter, pp. 181–82.

7. Wilbur Brookover, C. Beady, P. Flood, J. Schweitzer, and J. Wisenbaker, *Schools Can Make a Difference: A Study of Elementary School Social Systems and School Outcomes* (East Lansing, MI: College of Urban Development, Michigan State University, 1977).

8. See Randall Eberts and Joe A. Stone, *Unions and Public Schools: The Effect of Collective Bargaining on American Education* (Lexington, MA: Lexington Books, 1984) for an assessment of the negligible effect of teacher unions on student achievement.

9. Mario Fantini, *What's Best for the Children? Resolving the Power Struggle Between Parents and Teachers* (Garden City, NJ: Anchor Press/Doubleday, 1975).

10. Mario Fantini, Marilyn Gittell, and Richard Magat, *Community Control and the Urban School* (New York: Praeger, 1970); David Bresnick, Seymour Lachman, and Larry Polner, *Black, White, Green, Red: The Politics of Education in Ethnic America* (New York: Longman, 1978).

11. Thomas Glass and William Sanders, *Community Control in Education: A Study in Power Transition* (Midland, MI: Pendell Press, 1978).

12. Donald Tobias and Donna Hager, "Community Education: A Means for Developing Micro-Political Processses for School Governance," in *Community Participation in Education*, ed. Carl Grant (Boston: Allyn and Bacon, 1979), 224–39.

13. Hadley Arkes, *The Philosopher in the City* (Princeton, NJ: Princeton University Press, 1981).

14. James Comer and Alvin Poussaint, *Black Child Care* (New York: Pocket Books, 1976).

15. Edward Ladd, "Moving to Positive Strategies for Order-Keeping with Kids Accustomed to Restrictions, Threats, and Punishments," *Urban Education* 6 (January 1972), 331–47.

16. Richard Schmuck and Patricia Schmuck, *Group Processes in the Classroom*, 3rd ed. (Dubuque, IA: William C. Brown, 1979).

17. Gerson Green, *Who's Organizing the Neighborhood?* (Washington, DC: Department of Justice, 1977).

18. Mario Fantini and Rene Cardenas, *Parenting in a Multicultural Society* (New York: Longman, 1980).

19. Marilyn Gittell, Bruce Hoffacker, Eleanor Collins, Samuel Foster, and Mark Hoffacker, *Limits to Citizen Participation: The Decline of Community Organizations* (Beverly Hills, CA: Sage, 1980).

20. Joan Lancourt, *Confront or Concede: The Alinsky Citizen-Action Organizations* (Lexington, MA: D.C. Heath, 1979), 159; Paul David Wellstone, *How the Rural Poor Got Power: Narrative of a Grassroots Organizer* (Amherst, MA: University of Massachusetts Press, 1978), 179.

21. Frances Fox Piven and Richard A. Cloward, *Poor People's Movements: Why They Succeed, How They Fail* (New York: Pantheon, 1977).

22. John Fish, *Black Power/White Control: The Struggle of The Woodlawn Organization* (Princeton, NJ: Princeton University Press, 1973), chap. 4.

23. Fish, p. 234.

24. Jacqueline Scherer, "School-Community Linkages: Avenues of Alienation or Socialization," in *School Crime and Disruption*, ed. Ernest Wenk and Nora Harlow (Davis, CA: Responsible Action, 1978); Tobias and Hager.

25. Michael Williams, "The Urban School and the Neighborhood Association: Toward Building a Working Relationship," paper presented at Western Michigan University, AERA Regional Conference on the Social Context of Education, September 13, 1980. (Copies available from author at Aquinas College, Grand Rapids, MI 49506). For a detailed description of the development of the Eastown Community Association, see Linda Easley, Thomas Edison, and Michael Williams, *Eastown!* (Battle Creek, MI: Kellogg Foundation, 1978), chap. 2.

PART IV

The Promise of Neighborhood Organizations

11

THE ORGANIZATION AS CONFLICT MANAGER

Neighborhood organizations in depressed areas of the city must engage in conflict or suffer the fate of the irrelevant. The view that poverty is the result of personal inadequacy is still alive and well in middle America, and many of the poor themselves hold this opinion. But the slogans of self-help and antipathy toward the excesses of big government have taken on cultural momentum. Neighborhood organizations, only one result of this rolling tide, may be inward in their world view, but as they swing into action to defend or revitalize their communities, they confront the inevitable barriers of unequal economic distribution and class discrimination. Despite the enormous internal pressures to provide services for their constituents and the presence of many in their membership who would make them totally service-oriented, the organization's leaders intuitively understand that they are locked in a struggle with the Haves. If they do not understand this from the beginning, they come to know it sooner or later, as we see in the following instance.

Florence Scala was a grassroots leader in Chicago in the 1960s who came of age when City Hall decided her neighborhood, one of the oldest in the city, was dispensable. Much of it was to be razed to make way for a Chicago branch of the University of Illinois. She learned in a bitter way the difference between Haves and Havenots. Hull House, a famous settlement house established in 1906 by Jane Addams, had "saved the neighborhood," in her words, in its earlier days. Now its board of trustees threw in their lot with the city. Florence Scala, suddenly aware of her Havenot status, describes these Haves to Studs Terkel:

I'm talking about the Board of Trustees, the people who control the money. Downtown bankers, factory owners, architects, people in the stock market. The jet set, too. The young people, grandchildren of old-timers on the Board, who were not really like their elders, if you know what I mean. *They were not with us.* There were also some very good people, but they didn't count so much any more. This new crowd, this new tough kind of board members, who didn't mind being on such a board for the prestige it gave them, dominated. These were the people closely aligned to the city government, in real estate and planning. And some very fine families, old Chicago families. (Laughs.) The nicest people in Chicago. [Italics mine.][1]

This working class woman was no 1960s radical. She continues:

When the announcement came in 1961, it was a bombshell. What shocked us was the amount of land they decided to take. They were out to demolish the entire community.

I didn't react in any belligerent way until little kids came knocking at the door, asking me to attend a meeting. That's where the thing got off the ground. . . . Though we called the Mayor our enemy, we didn't know he was serving others. It was a faceless thing.[2]

Scala's awaking to this fundamental struggle between Haves and Havenots was particularly poignant because the Haves she portrays controlled the very agency, the settlement house, that had provided social services to her neighborhood for so many years. They had appeared to be sympathetic to the neighborhood Havenots, yet ultimately their allegiance was elsewhere. When new opportunities came to exploit neighborhood land by building a university, the basic conflict between these Haves on the Hull House board and the resident Havenots surfaced.

This chapter therefore explores, first, a theoretical view of interorganizational conflict. It then examines whether conflict can be institutionalized in the neighborhood organization, given its considerable lack of resources in comparison to its Have counterparts. This institutionalization of protest refers to *managing* conflict. The final portion of the chapter is a case study of successful conflict conducted on a win-win basis, whereby the neighborhood organization and its original antagonist, the city government, each achieved victory as a result of their confrontation.

A THEORETICAL VIEW OF INTERORGANIZATIONAL CONFLICT

The Maximization Principle

One respected textbook on organizational theory points out that a basic property of bureaucratic systems is that they move toward growth and expansion.[3] This virtually universal phenomenon is called the maximization principle. An organization seeks not only to maintain itself, but to grow, expand, and thus change itself. There are several reasons for such a system dynamic. First, the organization's tendency to get the job done leads to an increase in its capacities to do so. Second, expansion is often the simplest way of dealing with problems of internal stress. Third, expansion is also a direct method of handling problems of a changing social environment. Fourth, the rules and roles in a bureaucracy are quite susceptible to ever more elaboration. And fifth, the very ideology of organization encourages growth. This discussion adds to what was said in Chapter 1 about urban bureaucracies *vis-a-vis* the neighborhood. On the one hand, the maximization principle has supported an increasingly affluent lifestyle in the U.S. Most people take for granted adequate housing and diet, autos, even TV and telephones. On the other hand, this principle of organizational growth has led to awesome concentration of power and resources in all phases of politics and the urban economy. These giant systems are not committed to the general welfare, even though they affect it considerably.

Another trend in organizational evolution is the explosion of formal systems to deal with problems traditionally handled by individuals, families, friendship and neighborhood groupings, and other less formal structures. One has only to glance back at the sections on crime and schools to recognize the implied dependence we have developed on large bureaucratic systems to educate our children, police our neighborhoods, and by extension, tend to our health, take care of our poor, find employment for our jobless, and so on. One could almost say the contemporary urban dweller is a mere point at the juncture of overlapping systems: political, economic, *and* social.

Ironically, the neighborhood organization may be the urbanite's reaction to overorganization. One of the principal tasks of this book has been to investigate how a neighborhood organization functions precisely as an organization—beginning, growing, maturing, or declining—in an organizational environment, an environment dominated by complex and often hostile bureaucracies. But there is usually more to the reality of neighborhood organizations than reaction to bureaucracy. Our main focus has been with the organizing of inner city Havenots. If the city is an arena of competing interests, then Havenots have heretofore been unable to compete successfully. Whether the development of this new kind of organization enables them to compete for resources is the question at issue.

Competition implies a struggle among powers. When the struggle involves a great discrepancy between these forces, we say the competition is unfair. The interaction may or may not lead to open conflict when the competition is fair. But it most certainly will when it is patently unfair. As frustration due to continual failure deepens, a community becomes riper for organizing. Once organized, it is more likely to publicize its grievances. Under the maximization principle, the Have organizations have grown at the expense of the Havenots.[4] The goals of the large systems have not been compatible with those of neighborhood residents. Conflict was inevitable.

The Havenot neighborhood organization seeks therefore to *destroy* the institutional emphasis in society on the maximization principle. This orientation is not the same as seeking to destroy the institutions themselves. Nor is it necessarily a naive adherence to the "small is beautiful" ideology. The neighborhood organization, whether it lives or dies, is the embodiment of political resistance appropriate to our time and culture. Its insistence on new forms of citizen participation in political and economic decision making is an alternative to current authority structures. Commentators such as Joan Lancourt and David J. O'Brien have faulted Alinsky for being merely reformist.[5] But they have not acknowledged that when one proposes and pushes for significant alterations in the ways that decisions about resources are made, one is a *revolutionary* in terms of institutional change. Andre Gorz calls this transition "revolutionary reform" because there is a transfer of power as well as resources.[6] Those in power understand this threat, where it actually is a threat, and they know why conflict attends the very operation of an effective neighborhood organization.

The basic purpose of a neighborhood organization is to affect power relations: to protect the turf against governmental or corporate invasion, to make service systems serve, to get an equitable share of sustenance from the organizational lions of society. The control of power relations extends by corollary to the social conditions of the neighborhood itself. The organization simultaneously seeks to enhance resident control over public behavior in the neighborhood, a requisite for the building of community. This social fabric cannot be built without resident involvement, however, so a subpurpose of the organization is to overcome the temptations of privatism, withdrawal, or noninvolvement. These internal and external purposes are but two views of the same phenomenon: the increase in neighborhood self-control is inherently political. At our present state of human development, it appears that internal community may be strengthened by external conflict. When Edward Schwartz made his distinction between neighborhood groups that seek primarily to enhance community and those whose purpose is doing battle with great institutions, he simply pointed out a confusion in the minds of some leaders and organizers.[7] There should be no confusion. Neighborhood organizing is a political act, inevitably fraught with the potential of conflict and necessary for the rebuilding of neighborhood community.

The Elements of Intergroup Conflict

Let us return to a more general model of interorganizational conflict. Katz and Kahn specify six main variables that comprise the process of conflict between the groups.[8]

1. *Organizational properties.* Organizations differ in their tendencies to engage in conflict. Some organizations have special substructures to conduct conflict (e.g., nation-states have military forces); these groups are more likely to engage in conflict than organizations that do not have such units or specialized personnel. In addition, one organization might have an ideology of conflict while another might be more arbitration-oriented.

2. *Conflict of interest.* When the good of one organization precludes that of another in a substantive area, they have a conflict of interest. Conflict often involves more than two groups. The conflict may be objective (independently assessed) or only subjectively perceived by the parties. Conflict behavior can proceed from both conditions. Stuart Klein and Richard Ritti add that not only must the incompatibility of goals be felt, but also each side must have the ability to interfere with the goal achievement of the other group, which implies in turn some degree of interdependence.[9]

3. *Role expectations.* Organizations in conflict are represented by relatively small numbers of people in certain boundary positions. The behavior of those people is determined to a large extent by the expectations of the

members of the organizations whom they represent. Boundary roles are particularly stressful and may require a special personality disposition for their effective performance.

4. *Personality and predisposition.* Aggressive traits and hostile behavior in the conflict interaction both affect and are affected by the boundary role expectations of the membership. Constituencies tolerate such behavior in that role performance, although they depend on such people to manage these aggressive tendencies appropriately.

5. *Norms, rules, and procedures.* There are constraints outside the organizations themselves that influence their conflict behavior. These limits may be legal or cultural, more or less formal.

6. *Interaction.* This term refers to the behavior of the people actually conducting the conflict. Initially, it is predicted by the preceding five sets of variables, according to Katz and Kahn. However, the very process itself has its own dynamic, so that action and reaction also become a function of this sixth variable.

The conflict dynamic itself is perhaps the most important variable of the six. Escalation until one side or the other either backs down or is overcome is a universally understood and typical conflict interaction. Escalation increases the tendencies of the hostile parties to (1) make sure the other does not win, as opposed to emphasizing one's own gain; (2) close off communication; (3) spread the conflict to other issues; and (4) end the relationship. Simple escalation, in the case of a neighborhood organization confronting a large institution, is likely to work to the local group's disadvantage. Keeping the pressure on does not mean constantly building it to the point of explosion or rupture. Having put the squeeze on, the organization must be aware of what further behaviors will be most likely to achieve its goals. A switch to unconditional conciliatory behaviors, for instance, may lead to exploitation by the other party. Katz and Kahn suggest three other conflict-controlling initiatives, which have varying degrees of effectiveness. Least effective, according to experimental research, is making *threats. Promise*, in which the future behavior is positive, is more likely to reduce conflict than threat would. *Conditional cooperation*, in which a cooperative move is made and at the same time a reciprocal act of cooperation is requested, has proven the most effective way of these three to alleviate the conflict to the benefit of both parties.

The stage is now set for understanding how a neighborhood organization can manage conflict. Chapter 3 discussed such conflict in ideological terms, to explore where it was and was not compatible with the leftist tradition. Good organizers know that the tidal waves of disruption documented by Piven and Cloward are not what neighborhood organizations promote. Escalation of conflict, as the theory implies, is risky business, although at times it may be the only recourse. But it can be poison to the Havenots' cause and is a cure for the disease of poverty only when used in infinitesimal quantity, a swift and painful death in amounts much larger. Low-income residents are instinctively wary of any organizer with a martyr complex who insists on leading them to the barricades unless they are sure all else has failed. Appropriate confrontation strategies should flow from the application of the six general elements of interorganizational conflict to neighborhood group confrontations with the establishment.

APPLYING THE THEORY TO NEIGHBORHOOD ORGANIZATIONS

Organizational properties refers to an organization's tendency to engage in conflict. That neighborhood organizations in low-income urban areas exist as a citizen response to oppression is an assumption not always warranted. Many leaders of the poor find the pressure to provide services for their fellow residents impossible to withstand. The desperate need of their neighbors pulls them, while proffered funds from powerbrokers may push them. Nonetheless, the short-term track record of most of these organizations indicates that if they were born out of protest, they will retain that characteristic even if they begin to provide some degree of service. As Paul David Wellstone and others point out, the provision of service, especially advocacy for the individual, need not reduce the organizational ethos of militancy, although it could severely diminish organized thrusts toward institutional change by eating into the time and energy of the leaders.[10]

Another point concerns the tendency of most people to be nice and to work within the system. However, as Lamb showed, the poor have fewer options to redress their grievances, which accounts for the political cast of most organizations in poor areas. Authentic Havenot leaders are more likely, therefore, to organize in opposition to oppressive institutions than to act to dampen the fires of insurrection, as Piven and Cloward claim. Neighborhood organizations are like unions in their consistent suspicion of those whose hands control the economic and political levers. The psychological properties of the two types of organizations are the same, even if their structural properties are very different.

Conflict of interest, the second variable, must be sharply defined by the neighborhood organization. Sometimes the residents of the area do not see exactly how their interests are at odds with the oppressive institution until it is too late to do anything. Or they may not perceive *how* several institutions (government, lenders, realtors, developers) interact to devastate their neighborhood. In other words, they may have *subjectively* perceived that their interests *are* compromised by institutions, but they may not have a way to *objectively* assess *how* they are compromised. It is the work of the neighborhood organization's leaders to gather the facts and to illustrate to the members the exact process by which they are oppressed. Only on the basis of this careful research can effective action be planned.

Role expectations and personality characteristics of people conducting the conflict may become confused in the neighborhood organization only in the case of the organizer. This person usually has the degree of institutional alienation necessary to plan and coordinate confrontation, but the organizational ideology of citizen participation demands that others enact it. It is not unusual, however, for the confronted institution to perceive the organizer as the true "point man" and bring their forces to bear on him or her as the principal boundary role person. If this occurs and the organizer is an effective leader, other neighborhood leaders and members will come forward to present a united front.

External norms, rules, and procedures governing civil conflict in U.S. society usually have to do with the legal limits that neighborhood organizations may encounter. I know of no case in which the neighborhood organization has incorporated civil disobedience, vandalism, or more injurious activities into its regular operations. Alinsky made a point of always staying within legal limits when he planned strategy. Individuals may have stepped over those bounds occasionally, but it was not the intent of the organization that they do so.

On the other hand, attention-getting devices often deliberately flout social mores. Alinsky recounted a situation in which his organization was attempting to impress on the power elite that the city's minority poor needed employment. To make his people more visible and to score the point that business (in this case, pleasure) as usual could not continue, his group planned to obtain a hundred symphony tickets, eat great quantities of beans before the performance, and give their own unique performance after filing into the hall in their grubbiest clothes. The degree of outrageousness of such tactics probably correlates with the disrupters' level of alienation from the institution(s) being confronted.

The sixth variable, the conflict dynamic itself between neighborhood organization and institution, contains the potential for much more flexibility than that between labor and management. This wider range for action follows from the multi-issue nature of neighborhood groups and their members' varied access to these institutions. If it is government, for example, that they challenge, they are voters or taxpayers. If it is a commercial establishment in the neighborhood, they are consumers. If it is a nonprofit institution such as a hospital or a college, they are neighbors sharing the adjoining space and affected by land-use decisions these nonprofit organizations make. To escalate and then control the conflict implies that there is a relationship between the neighborhood group and the institution in question. This relationship is often buttressed by third parties such as government institutions, foundations, churches, or other interest groups, even unions. Successful conflict management often includes third-party support.

Now that the neighborhood group is into the fray, organizational theory suggests how to increase their chances for success. The neighborhood people should constantly keep their eyes on their own gain and the particular goal they have set for themselves, not letting their anger draw them into trying to count coup by embarrassing the institution in some way or letting the conflict spread to other issues. This stance lessens the tendency to shut off communication and end the relationship. Lapsing into guerilla warfare is a symptom of lost hope.

It is not enough to be pesky or vexatious, one must be intelligent about it, always asking, "What's in it for them as well as for us?" The self-interest of neighborhood residents is served when they achieve victories in matters they are interested in, such as obtaining capital improvement loans, better security on the street, or improved public services. But the institutions' interests can also be served in a variety of ways, such as lowered costs, increased efficiency, good public image, opportunities to expand, improved security, a skilled workforce, or the ability to deal effectively with citizen concerns through its authentic representatives in the neighborhood organization.

The effective neighborhood leader manages conflict by thinking in terms of tradeoffs with the institutions being confronted. The neighborhood organization is simply not in a position to demand changes without understanding that the challenged institution seeks to gain something as well. Since the neighborhood organization has come into existence as a reaction to the maximization principle of bureaucratic development, it must stand against this blind tendency by deliberately offering itself as an alternative form of organization, a largely decentralized or less coordinated institution.[11] Acknowledgement of one's organizational limits does not mean abandonment of the struggle and ultimate cooptation. To provide further understanding of how a neighborhood organization institutionalizes protest and manages conflict, the following section compares it with a labor union.

CONTRASTING UNION AND NEIGHBORHOOD GROUP APPROACHES TO CONFLICT

One observer of neighborhood groups employed the union model as a contrast to the Alinsky-style neighborhood organization.[12] He did so in order to analyze why, from their perspective, these latter groups had failed to institutionalize protest. Institutionalizing protest means managing perpetual conflict. If the interests of two categories of people are fundamentally at odds, as they are in the case of Haves and Havenots, there will always be a tension in relations between two groups representing them.

The union acts as an organizational instrument, to preserve the ongoing conflict between labor and management in some sort of balance. The union can coerce its members to pay the costs of this conflict, and by doing so it has considerable clout in dealing with management. It can thwart management goals by withholding its input into the production or service process. Union members have access to the production system. The two organizations are interdependent, and a type of cooperation underlies the conflict of interests. Members are willing to underwrite the costs of participation, by paying dues, going to meetings, going without pay or with less pay for a period of time, picketing, or enduring harassment, because they can envision a personal benefit that will result from their sacrifice.

The Wagner Act of 1935 shored up the strength of unions immeasurably by legitimizing bargaining and establishing a body of law to protect their members against unfair labor practices. Whatever the current deficiencies of unions, the role of the federal government in nurturing the movement should not be underestimated. Although federal initiatives in the past 20 years have had quite a bit to do with heightening the national awareness of citizen participation, there is no Wagner Act counterpart for neighborhood associations.[13]

Neighborhood organizations are not able to coerce residents to pay the costs of organizing, a fact that discourages some. These costs are not only financial, they are, like unions', the costs of conflict: time, energy, harassment, and perhaps demonstrations. Active members are constantly tempted to look about themselves and see others reaping benefits they have not paid for. Poor people especially may find it hard to pay these costs. To institutionalize conflict, neighborhood organizations must therefore devise ways to get more and more residents to pay for the effort. Crassly, this is what organizers really mean by "involving more people."

In general, one must ask about neighborhood organization access to target organizations or systems and about the benefits accruing to participants as well as internal structural variables. The analysis becomes more complex than the union structure because the target systems are many, and differ from one locale to another. In addition, the part played by the altruistic motivations of participants and outside institutions alike seems to confound the simple cost-benefit perspective of economic analysis. Evidence indicates that altruism is a principal motive of effective neighborhood leaders. This evidence does not deny the pressure of other motives, since people rarely operate from pure motivation of any kind; it is stated to avoid the trap that economically-oriented skeptics may have inadvertently set. While some political behavior can be explained by self-interest, much cannot. Credible leaders of the poor appear to project a concern for others, despite their alienation from institutions and their somewhat higher income and educational background.[14] A study of 11 neighborhood organizations in Indianapolis found that activists are *not* motivated primarily by a desire for their share of collective goods.[15] Rather, ethical commitment to their work is their principal source of satisfaction.

If the most involved neighborhood organization members are altruistically motivated, perhaps this attitude can be aroused in a significant number of residents along with self-interest, even though such a pool of people will always be small in proportion to the total population of the neighborhood. The hypothesis about the motivation of organization members is open to dispute, then, if it focuses solely on self-interest.

This brief discussion of some similarities and contrasts between the union and the neighborhood organization approaches to institutionalizing conflict is summarized in Table 11.1. The following section provides an actual case of effective conflict management by a neighborhood organization.

A CASE STUDY OF SUCCESSFUL CONFLICT MANAGEMENT BY A NEIGHBORHOOD ORGANIZATION

The city is Grand Rapids, Michigan, whose conservative Dutch heritage is tempered by a social mobility that has raised its minority—mostly black—population to about 22 percent of the 185,000 residents. Its moderate size and cultural background support taxpayer expectations that public systems will work; minor corruption in public office is still cause for scandal.

The neighborhood organization is the Eastown Community Association (ECA), which has been the accepted voice of the Eastown area since 1972.[16] Its boundaries encompass about a square mile of single-family and duplex houses built 50 to 85 years ago, with a commercial focal point in the Wealthy–Lake Drive business district. Owner-occupancy rates average 75 percent. Most of the black residents live in the area of Eastown bounded by Wealthy, Ethel, Franklin, and Fuller streets (WEFF), its southwest quadrant. Since WEFF has been a special target area for CDBG funds during the past several years, many of its homeowners have qualified for loans and grants for housing rehabilitation. In 1980, Jane Rice was hired to coordinate this Target Area program under ECA's auspices. She quickly became aware of a large number of houses that certain landlords refused to maintain. She also learned how difficult it was to get corrective action taken by the city in any of these cases. Although a coalition of city neighborhood groups had successfully lobbied in the recent past for passage of a strict housing code, it was only selectively enforced. Uniform housing code enforcement became her central issue.

Harassing the City Housing Inspection Department, organizing tenants to protest to landlords, and demanding punishment when the worst

Table 11.1
Two Models of Institutionalizing Protest

	Union	Neighborhood Organization
SIMILARITIES		
Access to Institution(s) (Interdependence)	Provides necessary element in production/service process: labor	Pays taxes, votes, consumes goods and services, "shares neighborhood space"
Typical Power Tactics	Can disrupt production/ service by withholding labor	Can legally disrupt, "business as usual," boycott, vote
Ideology	Sees constant conflict of interest between management and labor goals	Sees continuous conflict of interest centered on neighborhood land use or economic or exploitation
Organizational Goal	"Manage" conflict through bargaining threat, cooperation, and negotiation	Control conflict thru combination of implied
Self-Interest of Members	Higher pay, better working conditions (some unions do look beyond immediate bargaining and self-interest goals to "social conscience" issues, however.)	Improved service, economic gain, improved social fabric
DIFFERENCES		
"Involving" members	Often can coerce to join union--at least to pay dues	Cannot coerce involvement; must rely on self-interest, altruism, or social needs motivation
Range of Issues	Single-issue: employment conditions	Multi-issue by necessity

violators finally did chance to fall into the machinery only served to bring home to her that the enforcement system itself was a bureaucratic mess. No one seemed to understand it entirely or know how to make it work consistently. Patiently, diligently, she and another woman from the neighborhood began to build a model of the enforcement process. They sat in courtrooms, interviewed prosecutors, inspectors, and administrators, and plowed through files. They formed a small group of Eastown residents to meet regularly with key administrators in the Housing and Community Development Department. At these gatherings, the administrator whose job it was to coordinate enforcement would present updated flowcharts on the process, and all would comment on problem areas that had been uncovered.

As the months rolled by, several flaws in the enforcement process became apparent. First, the "paper trail" on any given case was woefully inadequate. Bench warrants for the arrest of housing code violators who did not appear for trial simply disappeared into police files. Housing inspection officials did not know the disposition of cases, or even whether the city attorney had decided to prosecute. Second, citizens interested in a particular case did not have ready access to records or trial or sentencing dates. If the bureaucracy itself suffered from faulty communication, the problems were compounded for an irate resident attempting to get a notorious landlord to clean up his or her act. Third, the five district judges themselves differed considerably in their attitude toward disposition of housing code violations cases. Two felt they should be fully prosecuted, one opposed prosecution, and the other two would levy only fines, not jail sentences. The court's autonomy meant it could probably ignore the stiff minimum penalties in the housing code.

Coordination among the departments involved in the code enforcement process became the first priority. The ECA requested a meeting on its premises between city officials and the several residents who had pushed the study. The meeting was extraordinary in its dynamics, a study in successfully blending confrontation and cooperation by the neighborhood organization.

The following people were present: from the 61st District Court: the chief judge, the court administrator, and the chief probation officer; from the Housing and Community Development Department: the director, the neighborhood improvement administrator, and the housing inspection supervisor; from the City Attorney's Office: the city attorney and his assistant attorney in charge of prosecuting housing cases; from the ECA: Jane Rice and Margaret Carlson, who had done most of the study, the ECA executive director, the current WEFF organizer, and two other residents, one a landlord in WEFF who was upset with absentee landlords who were hurting his neighborhood.

Jane Rice chaired. On the wall behind her was a six-foot high flowchart of the code enforcement process; those present had smaller copies in front of them. This chart was the agenda for the meeting. ECA had pinpointed 11 places on the flowchart where there were either questions or requested changes. Throughout the meeting, the city officials talked more to each other than to the ECA members, asking information and showing surprise at the occasional ignorance of procedures in another's department. The residents themselves felt free to share their frustration in a nonthreatening way. As each successive point was brought up, appropriate background information was offered by those whose area was under discussion.

ECA had originally sought the establishment of a housing court as its main objective in this issue. Under this plan, a permanent room and judge would be assigned housing cases. The chief judge opposed this idea, stating that random assignments of judges to cases and courtrooms was necessary for impartiality and could not be done away with. The neighborhood improvement administrator had hoped that such a room and a specific weekday would be set aside for hearing housing cases. Nonetheless, the judge was in favor of publishing regular notice of housing cases so that citizens could provide their input. Several other agreements were also struck having to do with improving communication, especially the collection of all pertinent case information in the housing inspection office.

The meeting ended amicably, and the director of Housing and Community Development made an astonishing remark. Praising the ECA's work on this project, he acknowledged that "this problem had to be solved by a group that had its goal that the entire system worked." Apparently no department at City Hall had such a goal.

The meeting was instructive in several ways. First, the domain of concern for both sides overlapped; there was consensus on where authority lay. Stephen Weissman used the domain concept to analyze power relations between an Alinskyite organization in San Francisco and other agencies it dealt with.[17] City government and neighborhood organization were both interested in bringing houses up to code. One way to effect this had been to punish code violators. When an ECA resident at the meeting offered that "the people who frustrate us are the chronic ones," the housing director and the city attorney shot back in unison, "Us, too!" The problem was to devise a flexible system of enforcement that meted out justice as deserved. The city's authority underlay the enforcement process; the interest of the neighborhood group was that it actually work. There was no competition between city and neighborhood to offer this service to citizens. Grand Rapids city officials had come to expect informed citizen input on improvement of city services. In other words, all agreed that while the city government had the legal authority to prosecute and punish housing code violators, the residents had the authority to demand that it be done effectively.

Second, this meeting cannot be understood except as the culmination of numerous smaller consultations and hours of tedious research by both residents and city officials. Throughout all of this, however, it should not be forgotten that ECA was indeed applying direct pressure, but the pressure was more in the form of a businesslike project than a quick punch in the stomach. ECA was confronting remiss city officials, but was saying, "Let's do this together," rather than "You do it for us."

Third, the demands of the neighborhood organization dovetailed with the needs of certain of the city departments, so that when they were put on the table, one or two city officials were already in favor of them and prepared to argue for them with their fellow bureaucrats. Housing inspection also saw the neighborhood association as an ally, for example, in lobbying with the city commission to retain departmental funding levels. Thus the two sides were interdependent to some degree, although not in the same sense as the city departments themselves were interdependent. As corollary to this point, one cautions grassroots change-agents against thinking of the large institutions they are confronting as monolithic. Such megastructures are in all likelihood an amalgam of subgroups integrated by task but struggling among themselves for scarce resources in order to perform their part of the task. Chief among those resources is information. This internecine strife can be exploited by canny research, as the previous example illustrates. The very interdependence of subgroups or departments within a large organization is a source of internal conflict. The neighborhood organization may have the advantage, then, by virtue of its very smallness.[18]

Fourth, the boundary role persons in this conflict, Rice and Carlson from ECA and the supervisors from housing, were uniquely qualified to succeed. Their adroit social skills augmented their sense of purpose, and the interaction dynamic afforded each side the opportunity to gain something. In addition, the neighborhood organization provided a support mechanism for Rice and Carlson, with its legacy of citywide leadership in housing matters, its staff on call to provide technical help, and its capacity for quick communication with large numbers of residents.

Successful prosecution of the confrontation depended on transforming the original conflict of interest into common concern. The ECA first accused housing inspection of dragging its feet. Housing inspection cried foul, claiming ECA did not know what it was talking about, so ECA people found out more than any single city department knew and helped educate the bureaucrats themselves. One should not conclude that this is a model for all neighborhood-institution conflicts, however. It merely demonstrates that such a conflict does not always have to follow a stereotypical path toward a win or lose conclusion. It is possible for both parties to win sometimes, hard as that idea may be to accept at the outset.

NOTES

1. Studs Terkel, *Division Street: America* (New York: Pantheon, 1967), 4–5.

2. Terkel, pp. 5–6.

3. Daniel Katz and Robert L. Kahn, *The Social Psychology of Organizations*, 2nd ed. (New York: Wiley, 1978).

4. Occasionally the Havenot neighborhood organization has encountered indirect opposition from the Have *neighborhood* organization as well as from large corporations. The neighborhood groups of the middle and upper-middle class will fight fiercely and effectively to keep their turf intact, often at the expense of low-income areas. For example, proposals to put subsidized housing or halfway institutions in higher-income areas have historically met with widespread resident anger, which says in effect, "Not in *my* neighborhood, you don't!" Attempts to seek cooperation between low-income and high-income neighborhood groups have rarely succeeded.

5. Joan Lancourt, *Confront or Concede: The Alinsky Citizen-Action Organizations* (Lexington, MA: D.C. Heath, 1979), 34; David J. O'Brien, *Neighborhood Organization and Interest-Group Processes* (Princeton, NJ: Princeton University Press, 1975), chap. 7.

6. Andre Gorz, *Strategy for Labor: A Radical Proposal* (Boston: Beacon Press, 1967), 6.

7. Edward Schwartz, "Neighborhoodism: A Conflict in Values," *Social Policy* 9 (March-April 1979), 8–14.

8. Katz and Kahn, pp. 618–20.

9. Stuart Klein and Richard Ritti, *Understanding Organizational Behavior* (Boston: Kent Publishing Company, 1980), 274.

10. Paul David Wellstone, *How the Rural Poor Got Power: Narrative of a Grassroots Organizer* (Amherst, MA: University of Massachusetts Press, 1978), 192.

11. Katz and Kahn, p. 682.

12. O'Brien, chap 7. Similarities between an Alinsky People's Organization and a union are probably no accident, since Alinsky was formerly a labor union organizer.

13. See Robert A. Rosenbloom, "The Politics of the Neighborhood Movement," *South Atlantic Urban Studies*, September 1979, 118, for the place of the National Neighborhood Policy Act and the Community Reinvestment Act, both of 1977, in the history of the national neighborhood movement.

14. Roger S. Ahlbrandt and James V. Cunningham, *A New Public Policy for Neighborhood Preservation* (New York: Praeger, 1979), 43; William Ellis, *White Ethnics and Black Power: The Emergence of the West Side Organization* (Chicago: Aldine, 1969), chap. 2; Curt Lamb, *Political Power in Poor Neighborhoods* (New York: Schenkman, 1975), 86.

15. Richard C. Rich, "The Dynamics of Leadership in Neighborhood Organizations," *Social Science Quarterly* 60, No. 4 (March 1980), 570–87.

16. For a full description of the development of the Eastown Community Association, see Linda Easley, Thomas Edison, and Michael Williams, *Eastown!* (Battle Creek, MI: Kellogg Foundation, 1978).

17. Stephen R. Weissman, "Environmental Constraints on Neighborhood Mobilization for Institutional Change: San Francisco's Mission Coalition Organization, 1970–74," ed. Robert Fisher and Peter Romanofsky, *Community Organization for Urban Social Change* (Westport, CT: Greenwood Press, 1981), 187–216.

18. Katz and Kahn, p. 762.

12

THE ORGANIZATION AS MEDIATING INSTITUTION

If residents of the community want information about how to deal with the outside world, they are likely to come to WSO [The West Side Organization]—their buffer against the world.

—William Ellis[1]

For decades if not centuries, reversing urban social disorganization has been a goal common to mayors and slum dwellers, radicals and do-gooders, academics and streetworkers. But though the goal be common, its achievement has been splintered among a potpourri of viewpoints that give rise to nearly contradictory strategies. Recently a major attempt has been made to unify the social work and political activist traditions under the concept of *mediating institution*.[2] This phrase refers to a group structure that *stands between* the private life of the individual and the giant megastructures of modern society, such as large corporations, governments, and other bureaucracies. Generic examples of mediating institutions are family, church, school, neighborhood, and voluntary association. One author suggests that all such institutions are mere extensions of the family; in fact, the characteristics of some are different enough to warrant separate analysis.[3] This chapter applies the idea of the mediating institution to the neighborhood organization, holding that the organization serves a dual function: looking inward toward the residents and looking outward toward the megastructures. Internally, the organization enhances community through education; externally, it advocates neighborhood needs through confrontation with oppressive or at best indifferent institutions. Since Chapter 11 analyzed interorganizational conflict and the institutionalization of protest, public policy requires that we now emphasize ways to connect local government with the neighborhood organization, in order to establish and maintain mutually beneficial relations.

THE TWO FUNCTIONS OF MEDIATION

How does the neighborhood organization stand between the individual and the public sphere? Chapter 1 states that the megastructures of society are a source of alienation to urban dwellers, especially Havenots. As these complex agencies of the public sphere either remotely oppress or directly obstruct citizens in their attempts to fulfill their needs, they often respond by withdrawing into their private worlds. They stop trying to influence the social sphere, primarily on their own behalf and secondarily for others, and turn to escapism, fantasy, crime, or other activities in the underlife of the community. This privatism can stunt the growth of community-minded leadership, much as grass shaded from the sun shrivels up. At best, justice and public order are left to the care of others; at worst they are directly attacked.

The mediating structure, a manageable group within which people can form close relationships, enables individuals to express their personal values and needs, while at the same time it provides them with a framework in which they can experience the realities of community life. Standing between means both standing *with* the individual *vis-a-vis* the outside world as a shelter, an advocate, and an immediate community, and standing *before* the individual as a teacher of social responsibilities. Through the mediating structure a person both acts and learns: the structure itself is both instrument and instructor.

Each of these two functions, educator and advocate, involves a fundamental tension. Education implies the unification of widely diverse individuals. It requires attraction of at least superficial opposites across racial, class, and ideological boundaries. Since the seeds of internal dissension are ever present, the neighborhood organization must use all the means of communication at its disposal to bring residents together, psychologically as well as physically. The second tension results from the organization's competing with other interest groups in the urban arena. Its resistance to encroachment by destructive megastructures, not to mention its launching assaults to recapture lost capital and services, create strained relations with outside agencies. The neighborhood organization must employ finesse in these encounters.

The successful neighborhood organization continually adapts to stress and tension.[4] It mediates among its members and between them and institutions external to the neighborhood. We first examine ways that the organization acts as internal mediator and ultimately as educator in social responsibility.

THE FIRST MEDIATING FUNCTION: INTERNAL COMMUNICATION AND EDUCATION

We have already discussed Saul Alinsky's concept of "education through activism," whereby citizen participants grow in understanding of the political process and their own inherent power by working on the resolution of neighborhood issues. This form of education affects a relatively small percentage of the residents of any neighborhood, simply because only those few will become so involved. And leadership studies indicate that these individuals probably have some background of activism already, or are at least active in other civic organizations.

The neighborhood organization also instructs or teaches the neighborhood residents in other ways. The most pervasive mode is through the dissemination of the neighborhood *newsletter*. Whether it is crude or slick, brief or lengthy, its very choice and treatment of subject matter speak to the residents in didactic ways. If the subject is local crime and efforts of neighbors to combat it, the message is that public safety should be an important value for the area and that people can do and are doing something about it. The house organ defines the issues, gives them an order in priority, and continuously injects the theme of self-reliance or self-dependence for the neighborhood. If it is regularly distributed, the newsletter also informs the public on the progress of issue resolution. Because it has the potential to reach every neighborhood household, some activists consider it a basic function of any neighborhood organization, a partner in the very process of organizing itself.

A few authors have written some how-to-do-it precepts about putting out an effective newsletter, but it goes without saying that it is easier said than done.[5] The logistics of production (from writing and getting advertising to layout, printing, assembly, and distribution) vie with hard policy questions for precious volunteer energy. Who should edit? What length should it be? How much should it emphasize neighborhood social news vs. political and economic news? What should be the balance between local items and citywide or national developments? Should it merely supplement city newspaper coverage or reinterpret what those papers report? How much editorializing should it do? In general, how open should the newsletter be to diversity of input and opinion?

Just as the neighborhood organization itself must develop direction and structure if it is to be effective, so must its newsletter. Editorship should be in competent hands, probably not a volunteer or a committee, although such an arrangement may have to be endured in its infancy. Since the editor is in all probability also the publisher and factotum, volunteer or committee editorship can rapidly dissipate energy under the stringent demands of monthly or bimonthly production. But the drudgery is well worth it. The newsletter is the principal means whereby the organization communicates with everyone in its geographic area and is the foundation upon which future local fundraising and issue-involvement will be based.

Another way in which the neighborhood organization acts as educator or instructor is through the *block meeting* and social networks that result. While it is true that the very localized concerns discussed at the meeting, such as barking dogs and speeding cars, hardly lend themselves to lofty discussion of ideology, these problems provide entry into broader social issues. If the people on the block, already acquainted with each other, can experience a higher level of interactive problem solving, they become open to new views and one another's concerns. On my block years ago, for example, a black welfare recipient who lived at the corner with her five children had been the target of criticism by several of the elderly whites who had lived on the street for up to 20 years. When the local organizer called a meeting in our home, everyone attended, black and white. During the course of the evening, the welfare recipient took on a personality and made us aware of her troubles with the landlord, a man who had let his house deteriorate and had allowed large piles of dead tree limbs to clutter up the side yard. Trivial concerns, one might say, but they upset the nearby residents enough to be a barrier to further communication with the woman. After she had told her story, three of the former complainers volunteered to phone and write the landlord about his negligence. The mess got cleaned up, and more significantly these neighbors had learned a valuable social lesson.

The neighborhood organization, therefore, can function as an *adju-*

dicator of disputes and petty grievances neighbors have with each other. Such an approach has received formal foundation support in six San Francisco neighborhoods.[6] In this case, a paid staff of 14, together with 300 volunteers, make contact with neighborhood antagonists, conduct visitations and hearings when necessary, and do followups. Police support the idea.

Neighborhood disputes may require other solutions besides sitting down and reasoning through to a mutually satisfactory compromise. Sometimes neighbors just get out of line. Activist leaders can then function as *disciplinarians*, given the proper set of circumstances. Recently, an angry neighbor confronted a group of young people living nearby who began their weekend parties at 3:00 AM. Calling the police had achieved little, since soon after the patrol car passed the shouting, loud music, littering, and revving of motorcycles and mufflerless junkers began again. This woman went to their house with a coat over her nightclothes and announced to the tenants that unless they quieted down, she was prepared to do battle to get them evicted. Citing violations of exterior and interior housing codes and noise, litter, parking, and public indecency ordinances, she vowed to summon the police and press charges against the tenants, as well as to harass their landlord every time they made such a disturbance. The parties ended soon afterward. Whether such tactics will always work is questionable, but they represent an improvement on the standard reliance on telephoning the police. The woman, by the way, was a former executive director of her neighborhood association, a person who had refined techniques for handling people in her role as an activist leader. She had become a teacher of social responsibility partially as a result of her participation in the neighborhood organization.

The process of education of the residents by the neighborhood organization has therefore several facets: from active learning through participation in actions, to more passive learning from newsletters and contact with leaders. The very stands taken by the organization's leadership or governing body are educative. As Fish has pointed out, they represent the considered opinion of leaders about not only what can or cannot be done but more important, about what *ought* to be done. The neighborhood organization is more than an information processor and disseminator and certainly more than a disciplinarian of rowdy residents. It is, or should become, a *moral educator*, a corporate body that seeks to elevate the judgments and reasoning of its constituents. For this reason, it must reflect diverse opinion, while always engaging in dialogue with its members about the best course of action.

The disputes within a neighborhood are not always petty or trivial. Cases abound in which residents have reacted only on the basis of their prejudice, harassing racially different newcomers, setting old people against young, blocking small-scale progressive efforts to deinstitutionalize the mentally ill, ex-offenders, addicts, or foster children.[7] In these cases, the neighborhood organization has a particularly powerful role as the arbiter between threatened residents and otherwise oppressed individuals who heretofore may not have even had a chance to reside in the area. Organizers who pander to the prejudices of the established residents in order to get them involved in directing the affairs of their neighborhood give up a great deal to achieve this end. They may develop an organization, but it will have no soul, no vision of the better, more socially harmonious future. Saul Alinsky is often wrongly accused of seeking sheer power for the powerless, no matter what the means. But in the preface to his first book, reissued after two decades, he reflects moodily on how the Back of the Yards "progressed" to the point where it embraced the oppressive values of the larger society. It had turned its back on the needy and the poor and had embraced the upwardly mobile materialism of U.S. culture. He would do it all over again, he writes, but though the outcome be undeniable, he would not ever set Havenot against Havenot for the sake of an organization.[8]

When the neighborhood organization is effectively acting as moral educator, it has reached the zenith of its maturity as a mediating institution with respect to the neighborhood residents. It probably will also have achieved success in reversing neighborhood decline. Perhaps at this point in its development the two functions of socializer and advocate blend into each other. We have seen how the neighborhood organization can morally educate in its role of information provider, interpreter, and adjudicator. Conversely, when one is an advocate, one has the opportunity to present the moral alternatives to the broader public. Is this not moral education also?

Let us return from these lofty ideals to the pragmatic questions about how neighborhood organizations can mediate in the second sense, as *advocate*. Specifically, how can these localized sources of confrontation be accommodated by public policy in a way that does not dilute their autonomy, credibility, and effectiveness in revitalization efforts? We

have investigated from the neighborhood perspective how to institutionalize protest. What remains is a discussion of how society, through
its representative government, can help institutionalize advocacy, the
second mediating function of the neighborhood organization.

THE SECOND MEDIATING FUNCTION: ADVOCACY

Recent Federal Initiatives Affecting Citizen Participation

A spate of writings in recent years has been concerned with creative
public policy that will nurture the young neighborhood movement.[9]
Suppose for the sake of discussion that we were sincere public officials,
elected or appointed, who wish to support the efforts of neighborhood
activists to improve the seedier areas of the city. What could we do to
enhance the mediating activities of their neighborhood organizations?
Why would we want to? How have bureaucracies dealt with these
questions in the past? What are the obstacles, dangers, and constraints
within the governmental bureaucracy itself and outside of it on giving
such support? A recent history of the idea of neighborhood participation
and control at the federal level begins to answer these questions.

The Economic Opportunity Act of 1964, with its call for "the maximum feasible participation of residents of the areas and members of
the groups to be served," was the first formal recognition of the need
to include the voices of the poor in planning their "reclamation."[10] It
was the inevitable result of previous decades' worker and civil rights
movements. But from the beginning Office of Economic Opportunity
(OEO) Director Sargent Shriver's demands that local poor be represented on policy-making boards drew bitter opposition from the League
of Cities and the Conference of Mayors, both of which enlisted the
support of Hubert Humphrey, then Vice President. The net result was
that the idea of control over poverty programs at the neighborhood level
never became a reality on a widespread basis. The Green Amendment,
passed by the House in 1967, provided local governments with the
option of running the Community Action Programs (CAPs), established
by Congress in 1964.

The Model Cities legislation of 1966 demonstrated that Congress was
more aware of the political implications of citizen participation than it
had been just two years before. Hence it was more cautious, although

urban renewal had envisioned some influence in an advisory role for citizens planning their services. The Congress now vested community responsibility in the "principal local executive officer and elected governing body." In other words, City Hall would now control the poverty programs.

Roy Innis of Congress of Racial Equality (CORE) pushed the introduction of a more radical proposal to give ghetto residents more control over their neighborhood destiny in the late 1960s, the Community Self-Determination Act. This legislation sought to establish locally-owned community corporations, community development banks, staff funding for these corporations, use of profits from subsidiary businesses for community services, and use of tax credits to induce established corporations to contract with these fledgling local companies. The established private sector and labor unions saw unfair competition in this proposal, local governments feared the independent power base of such corporations, and civil rights groups resented its overtones of separation. The Community Self-Determination Act emerged stillborn.

In 1974, however, a block grant program, the Community Development Act, replaced Model Cities. It brought new potential for citizen involvement in planning distribution of funds for community redevelopment. Although in some cities local government and corporations kept their stranglehold over use of such federal funds, in other cities there emerged citizen advisory bodies with some clout to direct money to needy areas and away from downtown or affluent neighborhoods.

One forecast of the impact of President Reagan's New Federalism reviewed several studies of the Community Development experience from 1975 to 1979.[11] Although there were problems with civil rights compliance in some cities and inevitable administrative inefficiency, most surveys found that the percentage of funds going to low- and moderate-income census tracts had increased on the average from about 60 percent in 1975 to 70 percent in 1979. The Reagan approach, which sought to reduce the number of block grant categories from 60 to six and to let the state governments dole out funds to municipalities, will probably make the CDBG program less effective. There will be a greater tendency to scatter the funds rather than target them, which in turn will lead to greater waste and abuse. The reduction of funds by 25 percent overall will hamper already inadequate city administrative staffs. Finally, because the 3,000 local governments have poorly evaluated what they have already done, it is probable that the evaluation process will only get worse.

Three other programs have had an impact on citizen participation in the neighborhood movement. Volunteers In Service To America (VISTA) in the late 1960s and the decade of the 1970s acted as organizers (among other types of work) in numerous inner city neighborhoods, and some CETA workers have done the same. In addition, neighborhood organizations sometimes hired young people to supplement their organizing activities under the Neighborhood Youth Corps program. All these programs have come under severe attack and have been reined in.

The Equal Credit Opportunity Act of 1976, the Community Reinvestment Act of 1977 that rested on it, and the Home Mortgage Disclosure Acts of 1975 and 1980 required lending institutions to be more equitable in granting credit and included provisions for citizens to monitor lending practices. Although this thrust did not grant funds to citizen groups, it did provide an instrument to reinforce the citizen involvement movement.[12]

The past two decades have seen a number of major urban initiatives from Washington. For the most part, involvement of citizens was limited to advice. Despite the legions of critics of these programs, however, Howard Hallman's review of studies of their effects on citizen participation indicated that, overall, the level and breadth of resident input increased as a result of their existence.[13] It is tempting to hypothesize that a major effect of these federal programs has been to whet citizen appetite for deeper participation, a growing expectation that underlies the neighborhood organization movement of today.

Forms of Local Government Affecting Citizen Participation

Two general forms of local government structure have evolved in urban areas since World War II to address the teeter-totter movement of city decline and suburban growth. The first has emphasized amalgamation of government functions, the second their decentralization.

Metropolitanism

Calls for centralization rest on a view of the suburbs as parasites on the central city. Suburbanites often work in central cities, enjoy their amenities, avoid their problems, and do not contribute their taxes to the cities' support. Three proposals to reverse this imbalance have been (1) *consolidation* of several local governments into one supergovernment, (2) two-tier *federation* in which one umbrella level dealt with certain technical systems, such as water, transportation, or waste disposal, while local units retained their autonomy on other matters, and (3) *regional planning* for land use and development, which was to be advisory only.

Consolidation does not appear to be an idea whose time has come. Several areas where it has been tried, such as Miami–Dade County in Florida, Nashville–Davidson County in Tennessee; Lexington, Kentucky; Anchorage, Alaska; Jacksonville, Florida; and Indianapolis, Indiana, give evidence that consolidation has not made much impact on urban blight in those areas.[14]

Federation seems to be a more workable concept. A unique multi-county federation has emerged in the Twin Cities area of Minnesota. The Metropolitan Council there is autonomous of other units of local government, but it levies a small property tax (less than .07 cent per dollar of assessed value) on all its seven member counties to finance its basic operations. Since 1974, its 16 members are appointed by the governor, one each from the districts created by the state legislature. Its principal responsibility is the preparation of a guide for orderly development of the entire area. It has review and approval power over development plans of the 245 local governments in its jurisdiction. Although to date the effectiveness of this body has not been clear-cut, it has gained a measure of legitimacy and respect. In addition its metropolitan policies, especially in waste management and mass transit, have had noticeable impact; and there has begun a regional political process, a political interaction that transcends the narrower interests of local units.[15]

Regional planning may be the least potent of the three forms of local government centralization. Since it has been only advisory in nature and was largely a creature of federal legislation, regional planning has been unable to readjust gross imbalances in local land use and economic distribution.[16]

Decentralization

A centralized form of government offers drawbacks to the operation of effective neighborhood organizations, not the least of which is the increased difficulty of citizen participation. Even Minnesota's innovative Metro Council idea does not allow for election by district. Retention or creation of smaller governing units, a move collectively known as decentralization, has seen more experimentation than centralization. In most cases, this change has occurred at the neighborhood level, where neighborhoods and small municipalities are similar in size (5,000 to 25,000).

Administrative decentralization occurs where the local district manager of a branch office has discretionary authority without citizen involvement. Varieties of these little city halls have popped up in several cities in the past two decades, among them Los Angeles, San Antonio, Kansas City (Missouri), Chicago, Norfolk, New York, Atlanta, and Boston.[17] In 1970, 72 cities in the U.S. had some form of little city halls.[18] One commentator admits that decentralization in some form in large cities is a structural imperative, but such decentralization is likely to be of the administrative type which does not enlarge citizen participation.[19]

Delegation of some decision-making power by local governments to neighborhood groups has seen a number of diverse experiments, two of which are instructive here. The following examples lie at opposite ends of a continuum of government-initiated citizen participation mechanisms: At the one end is *complete decentralization* and autonomy, and at the other end is a body limited to *advice-giving* but with legislative stability and consultative legitimacy.

The most publicized instance of community control was the creation in 1968 and subsequent dissolution of New York City's Ocean Hill-Brownsville school board. The board of education, as an experiment, had delegated to the neighborhood group power over school budget, personnel, and curriculum matters. When the newly elected citizen school board members in this black community fired thirteen district faculty, the teachers' union struck the entire New York Public School System until the experiment was terminated. Since then, much of the written criticism of community control has zeroed in on this particular failure as evidence of the folly of giving power to the people.

The second case was the 1975 establishment in Washington, DC, of advisory neighborhood councils (ANCs). Delegation of power was limited to consulting on neighborhood planning. The 333 unpaid, locally elected commissioners who sat on the 36 ANCs were recruited heavily from citywide political organizations, principally the Democratic party, rather than from neighborhood organizations.[20] When these activist volunteers began their ANC involvement, they believed in the responsiveness of city government and felt confident in its ability to solve problems. However, considerable conflicts developed within the ANCs over the nature of their mediating position between City Hall and the neighborhoods. After two years, they had begun emphasizing physical and economic development concerns over service issues and as a result tended toward a more technical planning approach to decision making by relying on experts and research. Little effort had gone into building constituencies for their plans, promoting citizen participation, and developing issues.

The ANC leaders' perceptions, two years later, were that these organizations were only moderately effective; only one third thought they made a substantial difference. To those polled, success was most obvious in the areas of information dissemination, outreach, and advisory roles. ANCs were seen to be less effective in community mobilization, development of specific projects, and representing the neighborhood to local administration. Bette Woody, who studied these ANCs, made three concluding recommendations for improvement in the operation of the advisory neighborhood councils. There should be (1) improved communication with city government, (2) clearer definition of the formal role and authority of the ANC, and (3) stronger efforts to develop neighborhood constituencies.

We have sketched three types of political decentralization: (1) administrative, which as mere dispersion of bureaucratic authority has little to do with citizen participation; (2) community control, which approaches Milton Kotler's idea of autonomous neighborhood government; and (3) advisory neighborhood councils, a vehicle whereby City Hall can hear the people more efficiently. What was said earlier about the two functions of mediation is applicable to these types of decentralization, especially the latter two. The advocacy aspect of mediation was strong in Ocean Hill-Brownsville, but the internal educative one was weak. On the other hand, the ANCs overemphasized the educative aspect (information dissemination, outreach) and neglected the advocacy aspect (community mobilization, representation). Only when both of these are in balance can the local citizens' group—what we have called the neighborhood organization—be effective.

Any local government contemplating its relationship with neighborhood groups can learn from these two cases. The New York example involved neighborhood control of a neighborhood service, schooling. The new local school board had not made the transition from being a confrontational advocate for the residents to being a service provider. If the municipal government and the grassroots group are agreed on the objective of neighborhood control of some services, it is incumbent upon the government body to prepare the neighborhood organization for assumption of such authority, including providing the means to help the organization educate its community about the transition. Both the New York City school administration and the teachers' union failed to understand the oppression they themselves represented. An enlightened city administration will bring along the neighborhood association step by step to a mature control of development and services that these organizations can monitor in their unique settings.

Local control does not have to refer only to services. Many neighborhood groups do not want such control. Generally, control will indicate effective advocacy power. This power was missing in the case of the ANCs because the organizations did not see as a main task their building of a grassroots constituency. They informed the residents, but did not try to mobilize them to action on their own behalf.

The Tense Partnership

The nub of the issue now becomes apparent. How can City Hall nurture grassroots organizations that, as they exert their autonomy, often conflict with it? One city planner put the dilemma in stark terms:[21] if citizens do not participate, planners risk large mistakes in meeting neighborhood needs; if they *are* organized to participate, there may be conflict. Yet his solution is clear.

Planners . . . have more to gain than to lose in embracing the sharp horn of the citizen participation dilemma. Like all sharp objects, it needs to be treated with respect. But it need not gore. And there may not be any choice.[22]

Consistent with the new thinking about mediating institutions is the idea of partnership. Books and articles have begun to appear detailing innovative proposals for cooperation in various combinations of city, state, and federal governments, grassroots groups, and third parties in the private sector. Few of these proposals, however, address tension as a fundamental consideration. One model, federated partnership between neighborhood and City Hall, does institutionalize their adversary relationship.[23] It allows for the local group to mount pressure on central administration to change and adapt social programs and public services as that local community defines its specific needs. This ability to clash with downtown implies that the neighborhoods have jurisdiction or para-jurisdiction over these services, a control not to be confused with full autonomy.

If the practical configurations of this *para-control* are confusing, it is because working models have yet to be developed. An analogous relation exists between the federal government and the individual states. Disputes historically have been adjudicated by the court system. Even now courts are dealing with balancing the powers of majority rule with the rights of the minority and the equitable distribution of tax revenues across large regions. With the courts as umpires and neighborhood associations able to press their demands legitimately (i.e., from a jurisdictional geographic base) on central government, the potential for citizen participation in government increases markedly.

There are instances, of course, where city governments have tried to reinforce the notion of neighborhood self-development. New York City created 62 local planning councils to screen proposals for development in their respective neighborhoods or districts. Cincinnati formally recognized its self-generated neighborhood organizations by drawing up official boundaries for its 44 neighborhoods after consulting with them. Washington's ANCs have already been mentioned. Baltimore and other cities provide money and technical assistance to neighborhood organizations.

Therefore, a first step that city governments could make is to officially designate the areas that neighborhood organizations represent. This has already been done in some cities, while in many others the process has begun through creation of special target areas for CDBG funds in consultation with existing neighborhood organizations. The 1980 census allowed cities to indicate that information should be collected by neighborhood where those boundaries were different from previously established census tracts. The formal geographic designation of neighborhoods seems to be an idea whose time has already arrived. Appointing neighborhood organizations as official representatives of these areas cannot be far behind. What follows from this appointment has to be vastly different from city to city, however.

Theoretically, neighborhood associations might become legal and formal partners in the building and passage of the city budget and the creation or adaptation of ordinances affecting their areas. In practice, some neighborhood organizations already do these things through pressure tactics and negotiations, but no city government has granted them veto power in such matters.

Neighborhood groups might also tax their own areas both for commercial or residential development purposes as well as for maintaining their own staffs and paying their own bills. State enabling legislation to allow these new governmental partnerships would probably be required, but the real fights would occur within the cities themselves, where city finances are already hard pressed.

Partnerships in Service Delivery

Much has been written about the decentralization of city services, some of which might be performed by neighborhood associations themselves or else contracted for with private firms. Such services could include some forms of health care, garbage collection, day care, building inspection, housing rehabilitation, property management, crime surveillance, recreation, and employment counseling.[24] Complete decentralization of police, housing development, and schools is problematic, however. That many neighborhoods would not wish to take over these services is not at issue. The creation of such options might make delivery of these services more effective than they currently are, especially in declining neighborhoods. Not only could they increase local employment, they would improve the neighborhood's desirability in the eyes of its residents, a major factor in neighborhood stability and revitalization.

Although some neighborhood organizations perform these services and others as well, there is a fundamental difference between the city's initiation of a contract and the neighborhood organization's initiating it. City Hall might want to fob off services they find onerous and expensive onto residents before the latter are either willing or able to perform them.

If the neighborhood organization is to share in service delivery, administrators have an obligation to see to it that the organization is strong and sophisticated enough to handle the job. There are several further considerations, however, in shifting services toward neighborhood jurisdiction.[25] First, different social services require different combinations of centralization and decentralization. Therefore, the city should evaluate each service separately and spell out regulations clearly. Second, inequities in levels of service may demand changes in state law. Third, it should be convenient for citizens to appeal actions of the new local service purveyors. Fourth, there should be neighborhood service areas but citywide taxation to balance differences between need and ability to pay. Fifth, residents could be given vouchers to purchase services directly. Neighborhood corporations, formed by the neighborhood organizations, might compete for these vouchers with private suppliers.

Variations on these themes are beginning to surface around the country.[26] City Hall in Kansas City, Missouri, has contracts with three neighborhood organizations to perform all inspections for health and safety code violations in their respective areas. Portland, Oregon neighborhood groups are repairing streets; such groups in Louisville, Kentucky are constructing sidewalks. In Jacksonville, Florida, some of them manage social service centers; in Boulder, Colorado, they operate shelters for the poor. In Baltimore and Grand Rapids, Michigan, they maintain parks. In Woodbury, New Jersey, a group has contracted to rehabilitate housing; and in Canton, New York, other groups from the neighborhood help children and the disabled. It is becoming apparent to some city administrators and elected officials that it is efficient in the short run to involve neighborhood organizations in the work of managing the city. In the long run, the increased citizen involvement and subsequent commitment of residents to their neighborhoods cannot but help to stave off area decline or move it toward rejuvenation.

Complications in the Federated Partnership Model

The feasibility of sharing governmental authority with self-generated local organizations has drawn many skeptics. They cite differences between charismatic yet idiosyncratic grassroots leaders and the city bureaucracy's need for uniformity. There is the natural parochialism or localism in the viewpoint of residents when it comes to allocating scarce resources. This narrowmindedness can be the source of even greater inequities than now exist, critics say. Service delivery cannot simply be shifted to neighborhood organizations that are not capable of taking over these functions. Even if these criticisms were met, there remain the political problems of actually devolving the power. The entrenched interests in municipal government would resist fiercely. And since not all neighborhoods would profit by such changes, especially more affluent ones, they themselves might join the resistance movement against creating what they perceive to be another layer of government.

These are all valid objections. Some insight into resolving them might be gained by investigating the relation between the public interest movement (consumer and environmental advocacy groups) and government. There are important differences between public interest groups and neighborhood organizations, however. The issues that bind the neighborhood organization are multiple and specific to the local community, whereas the public interest group focuses on one issue and boasts a regional or national constituency. Furthermore, activists in public interest issues of a technical nature, such as nuclear arms or environmental preservation, are likely to be middle-class, middle-aged or older, well-educated, active in other civic affairs, and knowledgeable about the technology in question.[27] This profile does not fit that of grassroots leaders in declining neighborhoods, except insofar as they are broadly active and knowledgeable about the issues.

Despite the differences, there are similarities between the two citizen movements in their organizational techniques and the way they push their causes. One study of public interest groups in 12 states showed that their effectiveness in influencing administrative and legislative decisions correlated positively with their budget and staff size and their technical expertise. The reputation that preceded them was important, but was secondary to the persistence of their organization over time, their preparation of a sound case, and pressure from a large constituency.[28] Another study of a more localized *hunger lobby* suggested that the successful public interest group convinces bureaucrats of its value to them and gets itself institutionalized into the decision-making process.[29] A third commentator on public interest group effectiveness emphasizes that the higher the perceived citizen expertise, the greater the bureaucratic tolerance for citizen participation.[30] It helps, apparently, if you have eight lawyers in your group. If the public interest comparison is valid, therefore, incorporation of the neighborhood group into municipal jurisdiction will require of this group that it have existed for some time, that it actually represent a large portion of its constituency, and that it manifest a degree of expertise, making it appear valuable to the bureaucracy.

One criticism of the public interest movement, however, is that these groups want influence in public affairs, including federal support for their activities, but avoid control by governmental agencies.[31] They say, in other words, "we want to control, but we don't want to be controlled." Alinsky and other militants traditionally resolved the dilemma by pointing out that those seeking power through community organization were merely trying to achieve a balance, to get their fair share. But our earlier discussion of interorganizational conflict made clear that a long-term adversarial relationship is based on a wary cooperation. The instability of confrontation coexists with the stability of partnership. Although vestiges of militancy and skepticism may remain between the two partners, the maturing relationship will contain mutual contracts and entanglements. The very process of exerting control on City Hall will impose self-constraints on the neighborhood organization. The local group will have to develop sophistication, technical expertise, and the ability to cooperate. Sharing control implies mutuality of control.

Its connections to municipal government need not make the mature neighborhood organization merely a little city hall, as long as its staff is of the neighborhood. This is not to say staff must reside or have grown up there, although that may be desirable. It means that neighborhood organization leaders have as their first allegiance the people of the neighborhood, not their own self-aggrandizement. It is to be expected that some of the best neighborhood organization staff will move into the larger bureaucracy. This is normal attrition from the neighborhood's point of view and may in fact be a healthy phenomenon for both neighborhood and central government.

The meaning of mediation when speaking of the neighborhood organization is clearer now with respect to "standing with" the people of the neighborhood as an advocate. The us-them mentality of the urban guerilla or the insurgent militant organization must change to a more formal jurisdictional relationship with local government, somewhere between mere administrative decentralization and full neighborhood autonomy. There will always be vestiges of the us-them antagonism, but if city governments can find ways to shore up neighborhood organizations with funds and technical assistance without coopting them, the potential exists for a lasting partnership that will benefit both sides.

Underlying this whole conceptual scheme of federated partnership is the assumption that the local bureaucracy and the populace itself support the idea. As neighborhood organizations become more truly representative of urban residents, and pressure mounts for federation, government cannot resist for long. The avenue to success lies in grassroots organizing, not in cozy deals with urban politicians and bureaucrats. Let it be clear that the partnership will always be a tense one, even though it is cooperative at the same time. Trust and mistrust must coexist.

ADVOCACY WITH LOCAL NONGOVERNMENTAL INSTITUTIONS

Advocacy questions so far have focused on the relationship between local government and neighborhood groups because this connection is fundamental. Citizens use the immediacy of this level of government to meet many of their neighborhood's needs; City Hall can also be a lever against private sector incursions into the neighborhood and a stepping stone to broader units of government. When coalitions form to press issues at state and federal levels, even when they are composed largely of neighborhood activists, these groups take on the characteristics of public interest groups. They become single-issue by necessity. Their internal communication network has to expand to encompass the geographic jurisdiction of the governmental body they are confronting or pressuring. Their expertise and logistical requirements increase in similar proportion. To speak of citizen groups operating on these broader scales, then, is to cease talking about neighborhood organizations. The same holds true for discussion of organizing against large corporations. Such semantic qualifications are not meant to deny the necessity of such wider organizing, merely to encourage realism about the effectiveness of neighborhood organizations as such.

Many nongovernmental institutions that influence change in neighborhoods are accessible to neighborhood organization advocacy, however. Hospitals, schools, colleges, churches, small and medium-sized businesses, light industry, and social service agencies shape the neighborhoods they share with residents. The chapters of Part III posed some examples in which neighborhood organizations mediated with local institutions to revitalize aspects of the neighborhood. Current jargon glibly employs the word *partnership* to designate many of these relationships, but the reality may not be so easily labeled. Assuming that fundamental tensions between Havenot and Have groups will characterize all their relationships, not every case of mediation will be successful, even where the institution's leaders are well-intentioned and savvy. Most institutions, of course, will be either indifferent neighbors or big bullies, in which cases the neighborhood organization will engage in overt confrontation, much the same as it does with City Hall. But let us approach the issue of mediation from the viewpoint of an institution seeking to help a neighborhood group revitalize the neighborhood they both share. Shifting to this perspective may add further nuances to the meaning of partnership.

Basic to every institution-neighborhood community relationship is the fact that each affects the other. Institutional impact ranges from benign to malicious. Church bells awaken; auto traffic pollutes, congests, and makes a din; concentrations of employees or students distort housing patterns and influence commercial development; expansion of institutional building razes older structures and shoves residents aside. The neighborhood influences an institution as well, especially if it is in decline. Crime may beset employees and besmirch the institution's public image, losing it business. Inner city churches have seen their white congregations flee as blacks move into the neighborhood. City plans to reroute traffic and raze old buildings to create new land uses have spelled doom for small businesses or nonprofit organizations.

If there is to be a cooperative interaction between an institution and the community organization, this mutual impact must be understood, especially by key individuals in the institution. These sensitive institutional leaders are the door of access for the neighborhood group.[32] To make the potential partnership effective, institutional leaders must not only comprehend the systemic sources of the neighborhood's people problems or physical deterioration, they must also be committed to a philosophy of neighborhood self-determination.

Putting sympathy into action, however, will require even more of these individuals.[33] First, their professional self-image must be consistent with a cooperative effort. Too many professionals (managers, administrators, faculty) view their work as separate from community involvement. They might be more disposed to cross this psychological bridge if they resided in the area and if they saw their involvement as an intrinsic element of their job, for example, if revitalizing the community meant to them enhancing business opportunities or public image. The altruism attributed to the leaders of the poor in Chapter 5 is also likely to find a parallel in these people. If they can be motivated only by some direct benefit, such as a consultant fee, a research project, or publicity, they will not remain long at the arduous task.

Second, even the most well-intentioned official must avoid the *agency mindset*. This phrase refers to the tendency of people in large organizations to impose a premature structure and set of expectations on the neighborhood people. Professional people are sophisticated in the intricacies of organizational bureaucracy; they value efficiency highly and want to get on with business. This experience tends toward manipulation of the community organization and obstructs the necessary role-reversal all institutional leaders must undergo before achieving effectiveness in the interaction. Officials must become more listeners, and less problem solvers. Their confidence in their knowledge and ability must be restrained before the sometimes halting and unsophisticated comments of residents. The temptation of officials to decide *for* the residents is almost irresistible. But if it is not resisted, the residents do not become more self-determining, and the organization is not truly theirs.

This point about resisting the desire to impose order on the community cannot be overemphasized. Writers on the education of the poor continually stress the need to bolster their confidence by refraining from giving answers or making decisions without them.[34] It follows that the institution should strive to be a supportive partner, rather than dominate the planning as it so easily can do, even where the neighborhood organization is relatively mature. The main function of the institutional leader is to educate the neighborhood people on how best to utilize the institution's resources. For example, could the institution provide a day care center and if so, how should residents devise a proposal and approach the institution's board of directors with it? What are the *real* limits of the institution's resources? Could its leaders and other professionals act as brokers to involve other leaders in the proposal program? The lending of direct aid by an individual professional, such as an accountant setting up a food cooperative's books, is relatively easy to understand and execute. But where the institution must reorganize itself to some degree, considerable difficulties can arise.

Who in the partnership controls the changes in the neighborhood is of ultimate importance. The greatest danger inherent in the relationship is contained in the *culture of professionalism*. The professional is a candidate for paternalism. Another danger is the pressure on the resident leaders themselves to become professional. Douglas Biklen, a veteran organizer on social service issues, counsels grassroots groups against wholeheartedly embracing the tenets of professionalism.[35] Just as the concept of charity—doing good for the poor—has shown no signs of eradicating poverty despite the giving by Americans of over $80 million a *day* to charitable organizations (including religion), professionalism harbors the risk of perpetuating, rather than solving, social problems.

Champions of the professional approach have stressed the need for theory as a ground for problem solving, for autonomy connected to responsibility, for continuous updating in one's field. Though at first glance these appear praiseworthy, their effect has been to create experts and specialists who operate within institutions closed to those outside the profession. These professions institutionalize problems, rendering the public dependent upon them for solutions. They are, in essence, conservative, antidemocratic bureaucracies. Biklen is not speaking only about bankers, attorneys, engineers, or doctors; he means also teachers, social workers, and police officers.

The siren of professionalism lures neighborhood leaders and organizers who know they must become expert enough in a field so that they can translate its esoteric ideas and language into lay terms.[36] Their sole purpose must be the demystification of the field for the residents—to enable them to penetrate the profession's decision-making monopoly. Organizations that achieve success in improving the housing of their residents, revitalizing commercial districts, promoting energy conservation, and influencing local education or social service agencies, including police, have done so by avoiding the isolationism of professionalism even while gaining its expertise. Yet just as the modern city has come to be governed in large part by professional managers, so the pressure will grow on the maturing neighborhood organization to be governed by the professional organizer. In both cases, the structure officially gives power to the elected representatives. Yet such representatives are often at the mercy of the full-time technocrats who see themselves as really in the know. Only organizers committed to empowerment of their constituents can sidestep these temptations. Many have done so quite successfully.

This chapter has explored a number of ways that the concept of the mediating institution can be applied to the neighborhood organization. In standing between the individual and the giant systems of society, the neighborhood organization performs an educational, socializing function for its constituents and an advocacy function for them *vis-a-vis* these outside agencies. It is these elemental functions that enlightened city governments will seek to bolster by incorporating neighborhood organizations into a jurisdictional relationship with the central municipal authority that is somewhere between complete autonomy and mere advice giving. This relationship, if properly balanced, holds the promise of revitalizing urban neighborhoods and the cities they comprise.

NOTES

1. William Ellis, *White Ethnics and Black Power: The Emergence of the West Side Organization* (Chicago: Aldine, 1969), 114.

2. Peter L. Berger and Richard J. Neuhaus, *To Empower People: The Role of Mediating Structures in Public Policy* (Washington, DC: American Enterprise Institute, 1977).

3. Virginia Satir, *Peoplemaking* (Palo Alto, CA: Science and Behavior Books, 1972).

4. This notion of the group dynamic as a continuous adaptation to stress and tension is elaborated in Rodney Napier and Matti Gershenfeld, *Groups: Theory and Experience* (Boston: Houghton Mifflin, 1973), 255.

5. For example, Robert Cassidy, *Livable Cities: A Grassroots Guide to Rebuilding Urban America* (New York: Holt, Rinehart, and Winston, 1980), 111–21; Si Kahn, *Organizing: A Guide for Grassroots Leaders* (New York: McGraw-Hill, 1982), 230–31; Greg Speeter, *Power: A Repossession Manual* (Amherst, MA: Citizen Involvement Training Project, 1978), 94.

6. Shirley Fogarino, "The Community Board Program: Neighbors Helping Neighbors," *Community Jobs* 4 December 1981–January 1982, 3–5.

7. See, for example, Ed Marciniak, *Reversing Urban Decline: The Winthrop-Kenmore Corridor in the Edgewater and Uptown Communities of Chicago* (Washington, DC: National Center for Urban Ethnic Affairs, 1981), chap. 2. Marciniak points out that the release into this area of 7,000 mental patients from state institutions within a period of one year contributed significantly to the decline of the Uptown neighborhood. There were far too many of them to be accommodated. On the other hand, Cassidy recounts the successful integration experience in Chicago's Beverly Hills-Morgan Park area. The Beverly Area Neighborhood Planning Association (BANPA) actively promoted and sought control of racial integration in the housing of a previously all-white neighborhood.

8. Saul D. Alinsky, *Reveille for Radicals* (New York: Vintage, 1965), xi-xii.

9. For example, Anthony Downs, *Neighborhoods and Urban Development* (Washington, DC: The Brookings Institution, 1981); Sandra Schoenberg and Patricia Rosenbaum, *Neighborhoods That Work: Sources for Viability in the Inner City* (New Brunswick, NJ: Rutgers University Press, 1980); Roger S. Ahlbrandt and James V. Cunningham, *A New Public Policy for Neighborhood Preservation* (New York: Praeger, 1979); Cassidy.

10. Roland James, "National Strategies for Neighborhood Control and Citizen Participation," in *Neighborhood Control in the 1970s: Politics, Administration, and Citizen Participation*, ed. George Frederickson (New York: Chandler, 1973), 183.

11. Donald Kettl, "Blocked Out? The Plight of the Poor in Grant Reform," *Journal of Community Action* 1 (1981), 13–18.

12. David Bartelt, "Neighborhood Reinvestment Strategies: The CRA Experience," *Journal of Community Action*, November-December 1981, 5–12.

13. Howard W. Hallman, *Small and Large Together: Governing the Metropolis* (Beverly Hills, CA: Sage, 1977).

14. Hallman, p. 182.

15. John Harrigan and William Johnson, *Governing the Twin Cities Region: The Metropolitan Council in Comparative Perspective* (Minneapolis, MN: University of Minnesota Press, 1978).

16. David Morris, *Self-Reliant Cities: Energy and the Transformation of Urban America* (San Francisco, CA: Sierra Club Books, 1982), 79.

17. Joseph Zimmerman, *The Federated City: Community Control in Large Cities* (New York: St. Martin's, 1972).

18. Hallman, p. 165.

19. Henry Schmandt, "Decentralization: A Structural Imperative," in *Neighborhood Control in the 1970s: Politics, Administration, and Citizen Participation*, ed. George Frederickson (New York: Chandler, 1973), 17.

20. Bette Woody, Ronald Walters, and Diane Brown, "Neighborhoods as a Power Factor," *Society*, May-June 1980, 49–55.

21. Robert Seaver, "The Dilemma of Citizen Participation," in *Leadership and Social Change*, ed. William Lassey and Richard Fernandez (La Jolla, CA: University Associates, 1976), 336–44.

22. Seaver, p. 344.

23. George Frederickson, "Epilogue," in *Neighborhood Control in the 1970s: Politics, Administration, and Citizen Participation*, ed. George Frederickson (New York: Chandler, 1973), 263–82.

24. Downs, p. 179; Milton Kotler, "Partnerships in Community Service," *Journal of Community Action* 1 (1982), 45–50.

25. Downs, pp. 180–81.

26. Vanessa Waters, "Increasingly, 'City Workers' Not Listed on City Payrolls," *Grand Rapids Press*, July 3, 1983, 1E.

27. Allan Mazur, *The Dynamics of Technical Controversy* (Washington, DC: Communications Press, 1981), chaps. 4–5.

28. William Gormley, "Public Advocacy in Public Utility Commission Proceedings," *Journal of Applied Behavioral Science* 17 (1981), 446–62.

29. Jeffrey Berry, "Beyond Citizen Participation: Effective Advocacy Before Administrative Agencies," *Journal of Applied Behavioral Science* 17 (1981), 463–77.

30. Susan Hadden, "Technical Information for Citizen Participation," *Journal of Applied Behavioral Science* 17 (1981), 537–49.

31. David Vogel, "The Public-Interest Movement and the American Reform Tradition," *Political Science Quarterly*, Winter 1980–81, 607–27.

32. Recall Marilyn Gittell's requirement for "access" to the bureaucracy by neighborhood groups in Chapter 10.

33. Most of the generalizations in the following four paragraphs are drawn from Michael Williams, "The Institution in the Aquinas-Eastown Relationship," in *Eastown! A Report on How Aquinas College Helped Its Local Community Reverse Neighborhood Transition and Deterioration*, ed. Sr. James Rau (Battle Creek, MI: Kellogg Foundation, 1978), 41–54.

34. John Egerton, "The Highland Center: A People's Mosaic," *Community Jobs*, February 1983, 3–6.

35. Douglas Biklen, *Community Organizing: Theory and Practice* (Englewood Cliffs, NJ: Prentice-Hall, 1983), 68.

36. Biklen, p. 87.

13

THE PROMISE OF NEIGHBORHOOD ORGANIZATIONS FOR URBAN VITALITY

It is becoming apparent that vital cities depend on vital neighborhoods and that vital neighborhoods depend on vital neighborhood organizations.
—Janice Perlman[1]

URBAN VITALITY AND QUESTIONS OF AUTONOMY

The United States has always been ambiguous about her cities. The Founding Fathers, especially Thomas Jefferson, feared cities as threats to political stability.[2] Today, as Chapter 9 illustrates, fear of urban crime far outstrips its actual incidence. The city is still perceived as a holding pen for the propertyless, an arena for mob action, a powderkeg. On the other hand, as technologies such as sewers and water lines, steam engines, autos, mass production techniques, and the steel frame building developed to suit its needs, the city beckoned industrialist and worker alike to partake of the benefits it could offer. Yet rarely have these benefits and drawbacks achieved a balance. The liberty to pursue one's economic dream has not resulted in equality for all. The quality of life in U.S. cities suffers to the extent that some groups have exploited or oppressed others. The outcome is a patchwork of urban places, some poor, others rich, stitched together only by the common need to get and spend.

The vital city is not necessarily the stereotypical sprawling megalopolis of rapid movement, hustle and bustle, smart boutiques and tall buildings. The largest cities are losing population to the suburbs, the suburbs to areas outside the SMSAs. Small cities are growing larger; the number of U.S. cities with populations between 25,000 and 100,000 increased by 50 percent in the past two decades.[3] Urbanization has become synonymous with mobility and the separation of work, play, commerce, and residence. Such geographical dispersion aggravates social disharmony and promotes the loss of a feeling of community that cannot be replaced by mere allegiance to professional sports teams.

The neighborhood movement, however one describes it, is at bottom a reaffirmation of the human need for social contact, consistency among the sectors of one's life, and some degree of autonomy in one's personal sphere. It is a challenge to the atomization of modern culture that makes us all middle class in outlook and uninvolved with each other in our daily lives. A truly vital city is therefore one that not only sees growth (or at least stability) in population and employment but also roots its quality of life in social connectedness: the concern of the group for the individual's welfare and of groups for each other's welfare. It is a city, Janice Perlman suggests, in which *fraternity* has subsumed both equality and liberty.[4] Admittedly, such a city is an ideal.

The achievement of fraternity, ironically, is the result not only of cooperation but also of competitive struggle, although the precise meaning of the latter term varies infinitely with the context. The neighborhood organization is vital when it both advocates the needs of the residents and educates them in the art of building community, when it functions as mediator. Yet the neighborhood is not a place unto itself. Just as the walled city is no longer possible, neither is the walled neighborhood. What happens in each neighborhood affects the whole city. Impoverished communities, however, have to be selfish in their goals, competing with the Haves for resources. Only when all have reached some reasonable level of economic functioning can each neighborhood be said to be vital. There is no inconsistency betweeen this competition for equity and the demand for cooperation among all urban groupings. They are but two sides of the same coin of fraternity.

Vital neighborhood organizations are identified by their drive for influence in the neighborhood's life. They represent an emerging form of organization seeking jurisdiction in those affairs of the city that most closely concern them. Recall Figure 1.1 in Chapter 1 that traced over time the relative amounts of influence of federal, state, and local government in municipal decision making, on which was superimposed a projection of the influence of neighborhood organizations on cities' policy decisions. The influence of these organizations in municipal affairs appears to parallel the influence of the city government itself. This hypothesis is somewhat speculative because of the difficulty in linking levels of neighborhood group activity to their influence on municipal decisions. Neighborhood organizations are not legal jurisdictional bodies. It is reasonable to assume, however, that when the locus of decision making is more readily visible, as in city government itself, the activity of organizing to influence that decision process is more likely to affect it than if it were less accessible. In other words, as cities become more self-reliant, neighborhood organizations should gain in authority over the affairs of their neighborhoods. It is intriguing to hypothesize whether the reverse may be true: that as neighborhood organizations gain leverage, cities will become more self-reliant. Matthew Crenson, in his recent study of 21 Baltimore neighborhood *polities* makes the point that where this informal political activity operates vigorously—taking care of grassroots business—it gives municipal officials breathing space to attend to the longer-term needs of the city.[5] This increase in governance at the neighborhood level actually helps municipal executives consolidate their authority. Crenson, however, distinguishes between *polity*, or informal governance, and formal neighborhood organization, holding that these latter organizations have little to do with building community. This book argues that neighborhood organizations do build community when they are effective, though they do so by often indirect means, by managing conflict, advocacy, and education.

Interactive effects between neighborhood organizations and city governments are being played against the swiftly changing backdrop of the national and world scene. For instance, a main cutting edge of technology is being applied to decentralized renewable energy sources, such as photovoltaic, low-head hydroelectric, and biomass applications. Computers are intimately involved in a commmunications revolution that could minimize urban transportation requirements. The shift of wealth from one region to another creates stresses that demand change. Yet there is no guarantee that change will mean progress. The promise of the neighborhood organization for revitalizing neighborhoods and cities is tied to the vision of its leaders and to the receptivity of urban systems and institutions to its input.

Just as expectations of city governments have grown in recent decades, so expectations of neighborhood organizations have risen and will continue to rise as they themselves mature. City officials may come to see them as partners in the governance of the city, a result which is both blessing and curse. But an effective partnership cannot occur if both sides do not see that they are engaged in a parallel struggle for independence and autonomy. Almost every chapter so far has mentioned that neighborhood organization structure and operation are sensitive to context. Context has included the geographic, demographic, and cultural characteristics of the neighborhood and, by extension, of the city itself. The new element of the context is the authority of city government. If it is true that when city government is more self-reliant, neighborhood organizations stand to gain more influence in local decision making, speculating about the future of municipal authority may prove useful.

Diminishing the federal support of city budgets would seem likely to push local governments to think more in terms of self-sufficiency, although the current status of urban dependency on the federal dole is a complicated one and not easily dissipated. U.S. cities' even more dangerous tether to energy companies and foreign suppliers of fossil fuels—especially those cities of the Frostbelt—has begun to heighten official awareness of the need for energy self-reliance through conservation and localized production of energy. The traditional antipathy of state governments toward their larger urban centers still remains, but the metropolises have gained clout in state politics as their populations grew. On the other hand, dominance by multinationals of the U.S. economy, the long-lived national disdain for the poor (who increasingly are found in cities), and the political lagtime to introduce the technologies necessary for self-sufficiency, all oppose the expansion of municipal autonomy. The future direction of that autonomy is uncertain, therefore, but one can hope that insurgent organizing at the neighborhood level will bolster it.[6]

FUNDING AND NEIGHBORHOOD JURISDICTION

Havenot neighborhood organizations must have paid organizers if they are to function properly. The degree of citizen participation is directly correlated with the presence of organizers; the more organizers there are (within limits) to hold things together, the more people will be involved. Spontaneous outbursts of citizen energy do happen, of course, especially among the middle class. But there will not be self-sustaining organizations among the poor unless there are paid staff to continually breathe life into them. How then should Havenot neighborhood organizations be funded?

Let us assume for the sake of discussion that neighborhood groups in a given city have been organized for several years and that in the Havenot districts, paid organizers have staffed these associations during most of that period. The expenses of the organizations, principally to pay the organizers' salaries, have been met by funds coming from outside the neighborhoods, since poor areas are by definition characterized by a dearth of financial resources. Foundations and church groups provided some of the funds, but the bulk has come from Community Development Block Grant program funds for citizen participation. Before CDBG money, CETA and VISTA money supported organizing. Some neighborhoods, though low- to moderate-income, possessed an extensive internal network, usually through churches, that enabled them to conduct effective intramural fundraising campaigns. But the proceeds from these voluntary efforts supported only a fraction of any neighborhood group's budget. Therefore most of the organizers and leaders in these areas have had to concern themselves to some degree with fundraising.

The chief difficulty with receiving money from outside sources is that they have had a claim to shape the neighborhood organization's goals. Organizers have long had to match wits, especially with federal bureaucrats, to keep from being fatally compromised, a normal outcome of well-intentioned federal legislation originating at great distance and insensitive to local differences in need. A second problem is always the instability of such funding, particularly foundation grants. Neighborhood leaders are now asking themselves a basic question: what would be the ideal source of financial support for neighborhood organizations? The answer to this question will determine the future direction of neighborhood organization.

Advocates of voluntary action will minimize the need for money. In most cases, this response will insure that the most militant organizations will be those of the middle classes who will band together only when their turf is threatened by some local government actions. These citizens can afford to drop ten or 20 dollars in the hat at mass meetings. They number among them lawyers to file briefs, people with the leisure time to collect petition signatures, individuals who know the people in power. Their personal bank accounts would support large mailings or the printing of flyers, brochures, and newsletters. Sometimes their actions are praiseworthy; sometimes they are divisive, racist, or preservative of the status quo. The point to be made, however, is that neighborhood organization without paid organizers is unlikely to *re*vitalize urban areas. Activity will be restricted to those neighborhoods that already possess the resources for spontaneous and sustained organization, those neighborhoods that in many ways are already vital.

A second answer to the question about the ideal financial support is that it should be diversified; the organization should not be dependent on any one source, whether it be government, private sector, or resident contribution. Successful organizations advocating among Havenots hew to this line of thought. Their assumption is that such a method will maximize their autonomy, enabling them to speak out against injustice, no matter who the antagonist might be. They are not necessarily wrong in their thinking. But if they are seeking to share jurisdiction over their turf with local government in some sort of federated partnership, as Chapter 12 outlined, that authority to govern their internal affairs would parallel that of the city itself. The city legislates and taxes. Could the neighborhood organization participate in that process? Should it?

A third answer to the funding question, then, implies that if the residents want significant influence over the conditions of their neighborhood, they must be willing to tax themselves to gain it. Neighborhood participation may mean taxation in the future. Much of the recent literature about neighborhood autonomy as a necessary condition for neighborhood revitalization speaks of the need to retain the precious dollars of its residents, to keep this capital working in the community. Many neighborhood groups now approach this problem by voluntary means: pledge drives, paid membership campaigns, fundraising events. Other means of recapturing local capital include newsletter advertising for neighborhood retailers and the kinds of programs for rehabilitation and conservation mentioned in Chapters 7 and 8.

Neighborhood self-taxation would parallel in some respects current city government practices. City Hall collects property and, in some cases, income taxes to support its own organization. It also uses a variety of borrowing schemes to raise funds for public capital projects. The neighborhood organization could receive a small percentage of the property taxes raised from the neighborhood to pay for its own operation. In cities where a local income tax exists, contributors to neighborhood associations could get a tax credit up to a specific ceiling. City income taxpayers could also check off on their form a box specifying that five dollars, for example, would go to their neighborhood organization, similar to the campaign contribution boxes now on federal tax forms. Other variations are limited only by the imagination. A technique to generate capital for neighborhood rehabilitation projects might be to designate the neighborhood as a development district. As the property value of the area increases due to development (this method does not address the matter of startup funds), the taxes that would be paid the city on that increased value are instead plowed back into the district for further development. This method, called tax increment financing, has to date been applied only to commercial areas, usually downtowns.

The exact technique of taxation is really not the point, however. Whether it should be done at all is the real issue. State legislation to enable it would have to be lobbied through. Once that was passed, each municipality would have to consider the sharing of its already eroding tax pool with these localized jurisdictions. Opposition would be fierce. After all, does not local government already function to redistribute wealth from affluent to poor areas by providing uniform public services? Would not this process of sharing tax revenues further balkanize the city, exacerbating its divisions? Would not the resulting neighborhood organizations become little bureaucracies in the (negative) image and likeness of City Hall? Will the citizens stand for another layer of government? If the concept were to apply to poor neighborhoods only, why should the affluent areas, those containing the highest percentages of voters, support what smacks of socialism? On the other hand, if every neighborhood could participate in recapturing some more of its tax dollars, what is to stop the building of more public swimming pools and other amenities in the Have areas?

How the Havenot neighborhood organization responds to these objections is critical. There can be no guarantee that divisions among Havenot communities would not be heightened with the creation of little fiefdoms by unscrupulous neighborhood leaders. Under other systems, the political patronage machine, for example, or Model Cities agencies, this abuse has happened. Clearly, the city government, in order to make the move politically acceptable, must retain the right to terminate any contract with a neighborhood group that abuses it. City Hall, in other words, would act as supervisor of neighborhood jurisdiction under the federated partnership model.

Limiting the planned recapture of taxes to Havenot neighborhoods requires that the idea be sold on the basis that the entire city will gain by it. The present financial straits of cities are a result of eroding local tax bases and increasing dependence on outside sources of capital (state and federal government and private corporations). Revitalization of Havenot areas includes making public services and rehabilitation efforts more efficient. This efficiency can best be acomplished by resident involvement in neighborhood revitalization, which will in turn evoke feelings of community ownership and pride. But Havenot residents need *their own* localized organizations through which to make these decisions informed and competent, as the failure of government-initiated citizen advisory groups has regularly demonstrated in the past. Citizens who are patronized and oppressed will either function as hostile social outcasts, as public dependents, or both. These Havenots must have a stake in rebuilding their city, or they can only be anchors to drag it down. The maintenance of a large, disenfranchised underclass in a city is too expensive. Cities cannot achieve self-sufficiency when many of their citizens are not self-sufficient. A simple cost-benefit analysis demonstrates that radical change must occur if the urban place is to be resuscitated and breathe freely. The roots of this radical change are stirring in the neighborhood movement, but whether the movement will burst into the bloom of a new partnership in governing the city is uncertain. The risks are high in sharing urban authority; but the costs are higher still if the risks are not taken.

THE FUTURE OF NEIGHBORHOOD ORGANIZATIONS: A REVIEW OF WHAT WE KNOW

Havenot neighborhood organizatons to date have concentrated on their *domestic policy:* the bettering of conditions on their home turf. Things are so bad there that they have had little choice. This book argues that neighborhood organizations need to develop a *foreign policy* as well, especially toward local government, if they are to survive in the future. They must revitalize the city if they are to revitalize their neighborhood, in other words. It is a paradox that they must strengthen municipal autonomy if they are to enhance their own independence and control of their own community.

The concentration of poverty in central cities is the result of complex forces, embodied in public and private institutions of capitalism, which both shape and are shaped by the values of racial and class separatism. The residents of Havenot areas have always been aware of their disadvantaged position and that the system operates constantly to drain capital resources from their community. Recent decades have seen increasingly sophisticated organizational attempts to redress these grievances by militant advocacy. Saul Alinsky, in particular, created a legacy upon which later organizers have built.

Neighborhoods most likely to see formally active neighborhood organizations are of moderate size with distinguishable boundaries or an identifiable center. Their inhabitants are somewhat homogeneous in background, lifestyle, and income. They perceive their territory as more desirable to live in than bordering areas, even though it may be quite deteriorated. They feel threats to the neighborhood's stability, yet they are optimistic about its future, based on their sense of control of the community's social order. Organizational networks already exist in the community. These preconditions support the development of a *critical consciousness*, a psychological staging area upon which committed citizens form the neighborhood organization. Although a clear dominance of what cultural values would shore up neighborhood organizing cannot be demonstrated, the very presence of these groups within the volunteerist-citizen action tradition of our country indicates that collective resident militancy on their own behalf is a widely acceptable activity. Leftist ideologues must come to terms with the inherently conservative localism of much of the movement, however.

Most of the literature about neighborhood organizing is set in the large cities of the Frostbelt. There the problems have been most severe, and the social scientists of the local universities have been on the scene to record and analyze events, especially during the riot-torn years of the 1960s. Despite this bias, urban neighborhood organizations share certain universal characteristics. Each is geographically localized and takes its strength from residents' identification with the area. It is a democratically oriented, citizen-initiated action group that seeks greater voice in decisions that affect the neighborhood. It maintains its broad base by addressing several issues simultaneously and uses three general strategies, sometimes in combination, to achieve its goals: (1) making demands on public and private institutions, (2) using electoral politics, and (3) developing alternative institutions. Successful Havenot groups employ paid organizers, are well funded, operate with sophistication in communications and research matters, and work well with other similar groups.

Authentic leaders of Havenot organizations are products of their environment to a marked degree. Their neighborhoods are experiencing serious economic and social problems that are not being addressed by politicians. The residents are alienated from government and feel powerless to change their community conditions. Resident leaders share this alienation, but their orientation toward social participation, their personal resources (education, interpersonal skills, stamina), and their history of grassroots activity are greater than their neighbors'. They are more likely, then, to analyze what ought to be done and to initiate action. They become the organizers of the neighborhoods. Members join such groups for a variety of motives, ranging from altruism to simple social belonging needs. The most effective members will make the necessary sacrifices out of commitment to the neighborhood, a form of public responsibility. They seek to make the organization accountable to all the residents and to gain tangible neighborhood improvements. Organizational norms that support advocacy must mesh with ways to reduce or control internal stress, yet the organization must maintain a militant cast. As the organization matures, it must remain flexible when new members' objectives and needs clamor for attention. On the other hand, as senior leadership pragmatically makes room for new people and ideas, it must continue to give preeminence to advocacy for the community's needs.

Neighborhood organizations have shown they can be effective in addressing major issues of importance to their local community. Some tasks have been more amenable to grassroots action than others, however. The traditional sources of funding (the federal government and foundations) have tended to support project activities, such as housing programs, food stores, day care centers, energy conservation programs, and other service operations under the control of the neighborhood group. While much of this capital infusion has been immediately beneficial to the community, it has not increased the neighborhood's ability to control its internal affairs. Much of the energy of the organization's leaders has gone into the technical administration of these alternative institutions, while breadth of participation has narrowed. Some groups have solved this difficulty by retaining their original participative structure and "spinning off" the project or program as a separate entity.

Other groups, especially those in large cities, have been able to focus on just one issue, such as housing, and build participation through programs addressing it. Such a group, however, is but one neighborhood group among others, and is not a true candidate for the jurisdictional authority spoken of earlier until it branches out to include the full range of problems facing the neighborhood.

Energy issues offer the opportunity for neighborhood groups to coalesce in moving the city toward policies favoring energy—and thus economic—independence. Local crime and school issues require the neighborhood organization to focus on internal social fabric building perhaps even more than on their external advocacy with police and school systems. Crime, especially against people, seems able to be decreased by citizens organized to watch out for each other's behalf, but solid school-community organizations, in which Havenot parents and students have a programmatic stake in making schools work, are rare occurrences, due largely to the bureaucratic inaccessibility of the school system. As the value of neighborhood autonomy sinks into the cultural core, however, school personnel should come to see that they can be more effective by working *with* parents and students rather than against them, which is now all too often the case. Current nationwide criticism of schools is an unsettling force that may hasten this perception.

The essential feature of neighborhood organization is that it represents a new form of organization through which the disenfranchised of the city can gain access to the megastructures. The Havenot organization not only confronts government and corporations in their local manifestations, it manages the conflict in ways advantageous to the neighborhood. Its mediating characteristics include both the formation of neighborhood networks and advocacy with these megastructures. If it remains true to these purposes and is not distracted by petty parochialism or management of institutions it cannot adequately handle alone, it holds great potential to revive neighborhood and city.

NOTES

1. Janice Perlman, "Grassroots Empowerment and Government Response," *Social Policy*, September-October 1979, 19.

2. Jefferson is often quoted on this point. See, for example, David Morris, *Self-Reliant Cities: Energy and the Transformation of Urban America* (San

Francisco: Sierra Club Books, 1982), 57; Alfred Kazin, "Fear of the City: 1783 to 1983," *American Heritage*, February-March 1983, 16.

3. Morris, p. 26.

4. Perlman, p. 21.

5. Matthew Crenson, *Neighborhood Politics* (Cambridge, MA: Harvard University Press, 1983), 297.

6. It may be of interest to note that the National Municipal League now makes its "All American City" awards on the basis of citizen participation criteria.

BIBLIOGRAPHIC ESSAY

The literature dealing with neighborhood organizations and of interest to them is multidisciplinary; categorizing it is a task in itself. This essay therefore organizes the more important readings by chapter as a way to maintain consistency and coherence in handling the wide variety of pertinent topics. A few readings are mentioned more than once since they are central to more than one chapter.

REDEFINING URBAN DECLINE AND REVITALIZATION

Urban Decline and the Future of American Cities (Washington, DC: Brookings Institution, 1982), by Katherine L. Bradbury, Anthony Downs, and Kenneth A. Small, is a broadscale attempt to bring objectivity to analysis of urban decline. Its academic tone, however, contrasts sharply with that of many Havenot leaders, for example, Saul D. Alinsky in his two books, *Reveille for Radicals* (New York: Vintage, 1965) and *Rules for Radicals* (New York: Vintage, 1972). Both groups agree, however, that social and political systems embody the cultural value contradictions of society.

I have chosen the following books as sympathetic to Havenot progressive critiques of urban decline in their focus on systematic evils: Barry Commoner, *The Poverty of Power: Energy and the Economic Crisis* (New York: Bantam, 1977), points the finger at corporate capitalism. Richard Morris, *Bum Rap on America's Cities: The Real Causes of Urban Decay* (Englewood Cliffs, NJ: Prentice-Hall, 1980), blames federal policies for urban decay. Langdon Winner, *Autonomous Technology: Technics-out-of-control as a Theme in Political Thought* (Cambridge, MA: MIT Press, 1977), explores the contradictions of bureaucracy itself as a source of social decline. Joseph P. Viteritti's analysis of the New York Public School bureaucracy, *Across the River: Politics and Education in the City* (New York: Holmes and Meier, 1983), disagrees somewhat with Winner, however, in focusing on the external (political) environment of an urban system rather than on its internal characteristics as its chief determinants.

Not all Havenot critiques of urban decline are progressive, as Harry C. Boyte cautions in his book, *The Backyard Revolution: Understanding the New Citizen Movement* (Philadelphia: Temple University Press, 1980). Nonetheless the political cast of many Havenot leaders, documented by Curt Lamb, *Political Power in Poor Neighborhoods* (Cambridge, MA: Schenkman, 1975), indicates that conservative analyses of urban decline, such as those offered by Edward C. Banfield, *The Unheavenly City Revisited* (New York: Little, Brown, 1974) and Hadley Arkes, *The Philospher in the City* (Princeton, NJ: Princeton University Press, 1981), are not widespread viewpoints in Havenot communities.

THE MEANINGS OF *NEIGHBORHOOD*

A historical overview of how *neighborhood* has changed in meaning over the past century can be found in Zane Miller, "The Role and Concept of Neighborhood in American Cities," in *Community Organization for Urban Social Change: A Historical Perspective*, ed. Robert Fisher and Peter Romanofsky (Westport, CT: Greenwood Press, 1981), 3–32. Although Milton Kotler, *Neighborhood Government: The Local Foundations of Political Life* (Indianapolis: Bobbs Merrill, 1969), provides the classic polemic on the neighborhood as a political entity, Matthew Crenson, *Neighborhood Politics* (Cambridge, MA: Harvard University Press, 1983), argues that certain social structures must be present for a neighborhood to be a polity or "political society." Social functions and types of neighborhoods are categorized in Rachelle Warren and Donald Warren, *The Neighborhood Organizer's Handbook* (Notre Dame, IN: University of Notre Dame Press, 1977). The marks of neighborhood viability are outlined by Sandra Schoenberg and Patricia Rosenbaum, *Neighborhoods That Work: Sources of Viability in the Inner City* (New Brunswick, NJ: Rutgers University Press, 1980). Levels of resident identification with the neighborhood are highlighted by William P. Hojnacki, "What Is a Neighborhood?," *Social Policy*, September-October 1979, 47–52. Howard Hallman, *Neighborhoods: Their Place in Urban Life* (Beverly Hills, CA: Sage, 1984), devotes nearly half of his book to a review of the literature on neighborhoods as personal arenas, social and political communities, physical places, and minieconomies. Roger S. Ahlbrandt and James V. Cunningham, *A New Public Policy for Neighborhood Preservation* (New York: Praeger, 1979), contributed to a better understanding of the complexity of resident feelings and attitudes in their study of six Pittsburgh neighborhoods.

DEMOCRATIC CULTURE AND LEFTIST IDEOLOGICAL REMNANTS

The concepts of core culture, cultural innovation, and privatism are ably presented and documented by sociologist Rodman Webb, *School and Society* (New York: Houghton Mifflin, 1981). Harry C. Boyte, *The Backyard Revolution: Understanding the New Citizen Movement* (Philadelphia: Temple University Press, 1980), provides extensive documentation and analysis of ideological shifts in mainstream U.S. culture that both support and obstruct neighborhood organizing. The simultaneous presence within a single culture of antithetical trends is explored by Stuart Langdon, "Citizen Participation in America: Reflections on the State of the Art," in *Citizen Participation in America: Essays on the State of the Art*, ed. Stuart Langdon (Lexington, MA: D.C. Heath, 1979), 1–12. Bruce Stokes, *Helping Ourselves: Local Solutions to Global Problems* (New York: Norton, 1981), gives extensive evidence of the diversity of local organizing activity throughout this country as well as in many other parts of the world.

In this chapter, I have included only leftist critics of the ethic of protest, since right-wing critics are unlikely to be sympathetic to Havenot militancy. Frances Fox Piven and Richard Cloward, *Poor People's Movements: Why They Succeed, How They Fail* (New York: Pantheon, 1977), provide the sternest criticism of community organizing efforts by contending that they blunt the effectiveness of protest. Martin Carnoy and Derek Shearer, *Economic Democracy: The Challenge of the 1980s* (New York: M.E. Sharpe, 1980), argue that Piven and Cloward's conclusions do not follow from their historical data. Carnoy and Shearer themselves document a multitude of cases wherein "little people" have taken control of their own workplace or service institutions against great odds through carefully organized efforts. Joan Lancourt's study of eight Alinsky organizations, *Confront or Concede: The Alinsky Citizen-Action Organizations* (Lexington, MA: D.C. Heath, 1979) discusses Alinsky's ideology at length and finds it wanting because none of the organizations moved beyond protest and program to politics. But Robert Dahl's concept of "political slack" provides the missing connection between revolutionary fervor and organized reform in "The Analysis of Influence in Local Communities," in *Social Sciences and Community Action*, ed. Charles R. Adams (East Lansing, MI: Michigan State University Press, 1960), 25–42.

HISTORICAL ANTECEDENTS AND PRESENT CHARACTERISTICS

Community Organizing for Urban Social Change: A Historical Perspective, ed. Robert Fisher and Peter Romanofsky (Westport, CT: Greenwood Press,

1981), offers an excellent introduction to the history and varieties of community organizing during the past century. Saul Alinsky's two books, *Reveille for Radicals* (New York: Vintage, 1965) and *Rules for Radicals* (New York: Vintage, 1972) are not history but give the flavor of his work over a three-decade span. Two articles by Janice Perlman, based on her studies of 60 grassroots community organizations in the mid–1970s, lend some precision to the definition of neighborhood organizations; the articles are "Grassrooting the System," *Social Policy* 7 (September-October 1976), 4–20, and "Grassroots Empowerment and Government Response," *Social Policy* 9 (September-October 1979), 16–21.

LEADERSHIP: THE DRIVING GEAR IN THE NEIGHBORHOOD ORGANIZATION

Several classic studies and reviews of research on leadership in general can be found in *Group Dynamics: Research and Theory*, 3rd ed., ed. Dorwin Cartwright and Alvin Zander (New York: Harper and Row, 1968). Three other general reference works employed in this and the following chapter were Rodney Napier and Matti K. Gershenfeld, *Groups: Theory and Experience* (Boston: Houghton Mifflin, 1973), *Leadership and Social Change*, ed. William Lassey and Richard Fernandez (La Jolla, CA: University Associates, 1976), and Seymour B. Sarason, *The Creation of Settings and the Future Societies* (San Francisco, Jossey-Bass, 1972). Neighborhood leadership studies include Curt Lamb, *Political Power in Poor Neighborhoods* (Cambridge, MA: Schenkman, 1975), a study of 100 cities; Robert Bailey's Chicago study, *Radicals in Urban Politics: The Alinsky Approach* (Chicago: University of Chicago Press, 1972); and Richard Rich's study of eleven Indianapolis neighborhood groups, "The Dynamics of Leadership in Neighborhood Organizations," *Social Science Quarterly* 60 (March 1980), 570–87. An organizer whose experience concurs with leadership research is Si Kahn, *Organizing: A Guide for Grassroots Leaders* (New York: McGraw-Hill, 1982). An organizer who is contemptuous of much leadership research, yet is uniquely insightful, is Steve Burghardt, *The Other Side of Organizing: Resolving the Personal Dilemmas and Political Demands of Daily Practice* (Cambridge, MA: Schenkman, 1981).

OTHER GROUP PROCESS VARIABLES IN THE NEIGHBORHOOD ORGANIZATION

Bruce Ballenger examines motives why people join neighborhood organizations in "Why People Join," *Community Jobs*, April 1981. Joan Lancourt teases out levels of their organizational goals in *Confront or Concede: The Alinsky Citizen-Action Organizations* (Lexington, MA: D.C. Heath, 1979). Saul

Alinsky himself best analyzes what is involved in defining issues in *Rules for Radicals* (New York: Vintage, 1972). Norms specifically applicable to neighborhood organizations can be culled from William Bryan, "Preventing Burnout in the Public Interest Community," *The Grantsmanship Center News*, March-April 1981, 15–77. A comprehensive recent discussion of norms, goals, and tactics is to be found in Douglas Biklen, *Community Organizing: Theory and Practice* (Englewood Cliffs, NJ: Prentice-Hall, 1983). The neighborhood organization's change over time has been inadequately studied, primarily because both the concept itself and the organizations are new. A good general book on organizational evolution is John R. Kimberly and Robert H. Miles, *The Organizational Life-Cycle* (San Francisco: Jossey-Bass, 1980). Specific studies include Linda Easley, "The Development of a Neighborhood Organization," (Unpublished Ph.D. dissertation, Michigan State University, Department of Anthropology, East Lansing, 1983), and Jeffrey R. Henig, "Community Organizations in Gentrifying Neighborhoods," *Journal of Community Action* 1 (November-December 1981): 45–55.

NEIGHBORHOOD REINVESTMENT STRATEGIES

A readable, up-to-date textbook on the many aspects of housing, including historical perspectives, federal programs, and housing law is Mildred Deyo Roske, *Housing in Transition* (New York: Holt, Rinehart, and Winston, 1983). This chapter, however, focuses on the conflicts that swirl around the matter of urban housing. Rolf Goetze, *Understanding Neighborhood Change: The Role of Expectations in Urban Revitalization* (Cambridge, MA: Ballinger, 1979), has clarified through his studies how certain types of landowners exploit perceptions of neighborhood change to their own advantage and to the disadvantage of neighborhood dwellers, especially low-income people. Information about neighborhood direct action tactics is usually found in local and national newsletters. See, for example, "High Interest Rates—Organizing to Win!," *Disclosure* 63 (June 1981). More cooperative and sophisticated ventures, such as "greenlining," housing cooperatives, and Neighborhood Housing Services, are discussed lucidly in Robert Cassidy, *Livable Cities: A Grass-Roots Guide to Rebuilding Urban America* (New York: Holt, Rinehart, and Winston, 1980). Displacement has received considerable attention recently. Sandra Solomon, *Neighborhood Transition Without Displacement: A Citizens' Handbook* (Washington, DC: National Urban Coalition, 1979), offers a comprehensive view of the issue. Shirley Bradway Laska and Daphne Spain edited a collection of research essays on the matter, *Back to the City: Issues in Neighborhood Renovation* (New York: Pergamon, 1980) that demonstrate the "gentrifiers" come from other sections of the city. Several dozen partnerships in commercial revitalization are reported in *Neighborhood Self-Help Case Studies* (Washington,

DC: U.S. Department of Housing and Urban Development, 1980). Analysis of the essential factors in such partnerships can be found in Hans Spiegel, "The Neighborhood Partnership: Who's In It? Why?," *National Civic Review*, November 1981, 513–20, and in James V. Cunningham, "Assessing the Urban Partnership: Do Community Forces Fit?," *National Civic Review*, November 1981, 521–26. A comprehensive article on the Enterprise Zone plan is George Humberger, "The Enterprise Zone Fallacy," *Journal of Community Action*, September-October 1981, 20–28.

THE ENERGY CRISIS

The position that oil companies are primarily responsible for huge price increases over the past decade and a half is argued by Barry Commoner, *The Poverty of Power: Energy and the Economic Crisis* (New York: Bantam, 1977). The counterargument, that government controls, which were the result of consumer advocate pressure, are chiefly responsible for exorbitant price hikes, can be found in William Tucker, "The Energy Crisis Is Over!," *Harper's*, November 1981, 25–36. Grassroots activists, however, have correctly understood how the energy producers control the supply and price of fossil fuel, and have targeted them as the principal cause of the problem. David Osborne, "America's Plentiful Energy Resource," *The Atlantic*, March 1984, 86–102, reveals the web of control that the Citizen/Labor Energy Coalition, an alliance of 300 grassroots groups, seeks to counter in their fight against deregulation of natural gas. A government document, *People Power: What Communities Are Doing to Counter Inflation* (Washington, DC: U.S. Office of Consumer Affairs, 1981), 259–73, lists several types of strategies local groups have employed against utilities and energy producers. The concept of local groups' involvement in municipal planning for energy independence is comprehensively explored by David Morris, *Self-Reliant Cities: Energy and the Transformation of Urban America*(San Francisco: Sierra Club, 1982). A specific and highly detailed plan for a municipal authority to manage its own energy affairs is set forth by Chris Robertson et al., *Municipal Solar Utility: A Model for Carbondale, Illinois* (Carbondale, IL: Shawnee Solar Project, 1981).

CRIME: THE BIGGEST NEIGHBORHOOD ISSUE

A major study of neighborhood crime and resident reaction is that by Wesley Skogan and Michael Maxfield, *Coping with Crime: Individual and Neighborhood Reactions* (Beverly Hills, CA: Sage, 1981). Frank Browning, "Nobody's Soft on Crime Anymore," *Mother Jones*, August 1982, argues that liberal and conservative attitudes about crime have drawn much closer to each other, a new ideological trend that underlies widespread local participation in organized efforts to combat neighborhood crime. Scattered evidence indicates that police cooperation with neighborhood associations on crime issues is probably on the increase, but since police-Havenot relations have historically been tense, one should be cautious in assessing the scope of this change. Two studies of the effects of neighborhood organizing on crime problems are Gerson Green, *Who's Organizing the Neighborhood?* (Washington, DC: U.S. Department of Justice, 1979), and C. W. Kohfield, Barbara Salert, and Sandra Schoenberg, "Neighborhood Associations and Urban Crime," *Journal of Community Action*, November–December 1981, 37–44. Both agree that where neighborhood organizations create programs to deal with crime, such as Neighborhood Watch, these programs can reduce crime. Green's survey suggests, however, that many neighborhood organizations have not matched their residents' high concern for crime with successful organizing efforts.

NEIGHBORHOOD SCHOOLS

Diane Ravitch, *The Troubled Crusade: American Education 1945–1980* (New York: Harper and Row, 1983), definitively traces developments in urban education throughout the past four decades. Her work puts in perspective current concerns about the ineffectiveness of schools. Stewart Purkey and Marshall Smith offer a review of the growing "school effectiveness" literature in "Effective Schools: A Review," *The Elementary School Journal*, March 1983, 427–53. The Ocean Hill-Brownsville community control experiment is given a 10–year look back by David Bresnick, Seymour Lachman, and Lawrence Polner, *Black, White, Green, Red: The Politics of Education in Ethnic America* (New York: Longman, 1978). Carl Grant edited an anthology on new participative forms of school-community linkage, *Citizen Participation in Education* (Boston: Allyn and Bacon, 1979). Mario Fantini and Rene Cardenas, as editors, extended some of these ideas to more specific cultural settings and pleaded the case for parents as primary educators in *Parenting in a Multicultural Society* (New York: Longman, 1980). The literature assessing the impact of neighborhood organizations on schools is sparse but is led by Marilyn Gittell et al., *Limits to Citizen Participation: The Decline of Community Organizations* (Beverly Hills, CA: Sage, 1980), a gloomy evaluation of the impotence of such groups in three large cities to bring about change in school policy. Criticism of public schools is becoming a national mania, however, which is bound to affect their sensitivity to change. Books addressing the "school mediocrity" question, posed by *A Nation at Risk* (Washington, DC: U.S. Department of Education, 1983) and other reports, are flowing off the presses. A readable conservative view is Gilbert Sewall, *Necessary Lessons* (New York: The Free Press, 1983). A liberal-progressive set of proposals comes from Bruce Joyce, Richard Hersh, and Michael McKibbin, *The Structure of School Improvement*

(New York: Longman, 1983), which is notable for its conception of "Responsible Parties," authoritative committees that include representatives from community and school alike in solving school problems. The concept is similar to that described in the case study ending the chapter. Although liberals can be distinguished from conservatives by their espousal of various forms of neighborhood involvement in school affairs, conservative demands for change are helping to create a climate of acceptance for neighborhood organization initiatives. Nonetheless, Ellen Lurie's *How to Change the Schools: A Parents' Action Handbook on How to Fight the System* (New York: Vintage, 1970) remains an impassioned classic on specifically how such groups can take these initiatives.

THE ORGANIZATION AS CONFLICT MANAGER

Daniel Katz and Robert L. Kahn, *The Social Psychology of Organizations*, 2nd ed. (New York: Wiley, 1978), provide a textbook overview of interorganizational conflict theory, which is augmented by Stuart Klein and Richard Ritti, *Understanding Organizational Behavior* (Boston: Kent Publishing Company, 1980). The idea of comparing a neighborhood organization with a union probably began with Saul Alinsky himself, since he was a former labor union organizer. It was given theoretical study, however, in David O'Brien, *Neighborhood Organization and Interest Group Process* (Princeton, NJ: Princeton University Press, 1975). An excellent analysis of the conflict relation between an Alinsky organization in San Francisco and agencies it had to deal with can be found in Stephen R. Weissman, "Environmental Constraints on Neighborhood Mobilization for Institutional Change: San Francisco's Mission Coalition Organization, 1970–74," in *Community Organization for Urban Social Change: A Historical Perspective*, ed. Robert Fisher and Peter Romanofsky (Westport, CT: Greenwood Press, 1981), 187–216.

THE ORGANIZATION AS MEDIATING INSTITUTION

The concept of a neighborhood organization as a mediating institution is discussed generally in Peter L. Berger and Richard J. Neuhaus, *To Empower People: The Role of Mediating Structures in Public Policy* (Washington, DC: American Enterprise Institute, 1977). Most writings about neighborhood organizations as such have emphasized the advocacy function of the mediating institution, but implicit in these writings is the need to educate the members themselves. An example is Si Kahn, *Organizing: A Guide for Grassroots Leaders* (New York: McGraw-Hill, 1982). Forms of local government, from centralized to decentralized, that hinder or help citizen participation and especially neighborhood organization advocacy, are studied in detail in Howard Hallman,

Small and Large Together: Governing the Metropolis (Beverly Hills, CA: Sage, 1977). George Frederickson edited a collection of essays, *Neighborhood Control in the 1970s: Politics, Administration, and Citizen Participation* (New York: Chandler, 1973), that focuses on practical ways to link neighborhoods and city government. His own section of the book, entitled "Epilogue," pp. 263–82, proposed the federated partnership which is a main element of this chapter. Comparison of the public interest group with neighborhood organization was aided by several articles in *Journal of Applied Behavioral Science* 17 (1981), especially William Gormley, "Public Advocacy in Public Utility Commission Proceedings," pp. 446–62, and Jeffrey Berry, "Beyond Citizen Participation: Effective Advocacy Before Administrative Agencies," pp. 463–77.

THE PROMISE OF NEIGHBORHOOD ORGANIZATIONS FOR URBAN VITALITY

Janice Perlman, "Grassroots Empowerment and Government Response," *Social Policy*, September-October 1979, 16–21, defined the truly vital city as one in which fraternity had transcended and conjoined the often opposed ideals of equality and liberty. To her, local autonomy through localized neighborhood organizations held the key to fraternity. David Morris, *Self-Reliant Cities: Energy and the Transformation of Urban America* (San Francisco: Sierra Club, 1982), argues that since energy technologies combined with politics to deprive cities of their autonomy, a new mix of these must be employed to help them regain it. Howard Hallman, *Neighborhoods: Their Place in Urban Life* (Beverly Hills, CA: Sage, 1984), provides an extensive listing of ways in which neighborhood groups have influenced municipal decision making during the past two decades. Hallman's premise is that such organized activity is an essential element in strengthening both neighborhoods and cities. Matthew Crenson, *Neighborhood Politics* (Cambridge, MA: Harvard University Press, 1983), studied 21 Baltimore neighborhoods' informal governance structures and is less sanguine than Hallman about the potential of neighborhood organizations to bring about fraternity. Hallman's overall assessment of organized neighborhood achievements is that they represent a rough bell shape, with the majority thus far in the moderate region of effectiveness.

INDEX

Adams, John, 8, 52
Adjudication of disputes, 226–27
Advisory Neighborhood Councils, 233–35
Advocacy, 80, 138, 149, 195; with local government, 229–41; with nongovernmental institutions, 241–44. *See also* Public interest movement
Agency mindset, 242
Alienation, 19, 57, 103, 109; as atomization, 175, 250; of Havenots, 224; leading to crime, 176; megastructures as source of, 224; of neighborhood leaders, 96; of teachers and students, 189
Alinsky, Saul, 35, 83, 85, 91; aphorisms as norms, 116; attention-getting devices of, 212–13; and Back of the Yards Council, 73, 110; beyond Alinsky, 76–81; and defining issues, 114–15; and fun as antidote for stress, 117; and have-a-little-want-mores, 75; history of, 73–76; and Industrial Areas Foundation, 75; as labor organizer, 222 n.12; legacy of, 257; and organization as power, 62; organizational model of, 79, 80, 91; and People's Organization, 74, 91, 113, 116, 120; and popular education 53, 60, 110, 225; and power balances, 240; and progressive values, 228; and rationalization of motives, 110; as reformist, 208; and relations between organizers and leaders, 99–102; and status as motive, 108
Altruism as motivator, 73, 107, 109, 215, 242
Anti-redlining laws, 57, 130. *See also* Redlining
Attention-getting devices, 212–13

Back of the Yards Council, 73, 90, 110, 128, 154–55 n.10. *See also* Alinsky, Saul
Bailey, Robert, 98, 99
Behavioral Commitment Model, 110
Bernard, Jessie, 56
Big government, 12, 58
Big Oil: American Petroleum Institute, 164; independence of cities from, 170; Natural Gas Supply Association, 165
Biklen, Douglas, 243

Blight, 102. *See also* Causes of urban decline

Block clubs, 4, 39, 51, 76, 177, 179. *See also* Crime watch program, Neighborhood Watch program

Block meetings, 226

Boundary role person, 210, 212, 220

Boyte, Harry, 55, 59, 76

Bradbury, Katherine, 4

Bureaucracy, 18–20, 218, 220, 229, 243. *See also* Maximization Principle, Megastructures, Professionalism

Bureaucratic openness, 195, 198

Capital, 11–12, 48, 254; captains of, 112–13; for commercial redevelopment, 150; desertion of, 125, 129–30; in Enterprise Zones, 152, 153; for housing rehabilitation, 131–40; for municipal energy self-reliance, 167–69

Carnoy, Martin, 54, 55, 58

Cassidy, Robert, 125, 135, 245 n.7

Causes of urban decline: bureaucracy, 18–20; corporate capitalism, 11–13; government policies, 13–18; redefinition of, 7–9; symptoms of urban decline, 4–5; systemic contradictions defined, 10; theories of, 5–7

Central business district, 16, 18, 30

Centralization: of energy-gulping technologies, 159, 169; of government functions, 231–32; of school administration, 186. *See also* Bureaucracy

Chambers of commerce, 77, 90

Church, 34, 56, 76, 89, 91, 98, 111, 213, 241

Circuit breaker tax rebates, 145

Citizen action groups, 77, 95. *See also* Self-help

Citizen involvement, 109, 215, 252; in fighting utilities, 163; as result of federal initiatives, 77, 229–31

Citizen participation, 51, 52, 215

Citizen police review and advisory boards, 178

Citizens' Utility Board, 162

City manager, 30

Civil disobedience, 212

Civil rights movement, 62

Civilian patrols, 177, 183, n.11

Cloward, Richard, 9, 62, 63, 194, 211

Coalitions, 10, 52, 61, 66, 73, 75, 91, 160, 163, 241; C/LEC (Citizen/Labor Energy Coalition), 165; on crime, 181; of Democrats, 58; NPA (National People's Action), 165; on redlining, 130, South Austin Coalition, 101

Coleman, James, 187

Commercial reinvestment, 147–51. *See also* Enterprise Zones

Commitment to the neighborhood, 25, 48. *See also* Critical consciousness

Commoner, Barry, 11, 12, 159, 160

Communist Party, 35, 72

Community, meaning of, 30–35, 44

Community banks and credit unions, 134

Community control, 112, 191, 196, 233. *See also* Service delivery by neighborhood organizations

Community Development Block Grant Program 40, 131, 136, 139, 148, 155 n.24, 179, 216, 230, 236, 253

Community Development Corporation, 149, 166

Community organizer: against displacement, 140; as leader, 99–102; as neighborhood organizer, 33; as paid professional, 76, 100; and relations with leaders of the organization, 100–101; training of, 76

Community organizing, 33, 53; principles of, 74; roots of, 73; strategies of, 35, 78; as subdiscipline of social work, 71. *See also* Alinsky, Saul

Community Reinvestment Act, 131, 231

Competition, 208, 221 n.4

Comprehensive Employment and Training Act, 166, 231, 253

Concordia, 146

Conditional cooperation, 210

Conflict of interest, 209

Conflict theory, 207–14

Conservative ideology, 54, 58, 192, 199; and analysis of energy crisis, 159, 160; and approaches to crime, 176; neoconservatism, 109, 187; and urban decline, 8–9

Conservation of energy, 160, 166

Consolidation of local governments, 232. *See also* Centralization

Construction Work in Progress (CWIP), 161. *See also* Utilities

Control Data Corporation, 150

Cooperatives, 77, 133–39

Cooperation, 214, 240

Core culture, 54, 56–57

Corporate culture, 55

Corporate trusts, 14

Corporations: in agriculture, 158; as colonizers, 150; as source of support in Neighborhood Housing Services (NHS), 135; as targets of citizen action, 75; as unaccountable to society, 160, 164. *See also* Big Oil, Multinational corporations

Counter-progressive organizing, 72

Crenson, Matthew, 251

Crime: causes of, 175–76; fear of, 174–75; rates, 173, 178, 179, 182; reporting of, 173, 177

Crime control: effectiveness of localized strategies, 180–83; neighborhood-based strategies, 176–80

Crime watch program, 182. *See also* Neighborhood Watch program

Critical consciousness, 47–48. *See also* Commitment to the neighborhood

Culture of Poverty theory, 55

Cunningham, James, 46, 47, 109, 151

Curriculum, 192–93

Decentralization, 165–69, 191, 232–38

Decline of cities. *See* Causes of urban decline

Democratic culture, 51–59

Deterioration: of housing, 127; of neighborhoods, 112. *See also* Causes of urban decline

Development. *See* Commercial reinvestment

Displacement, 24, 112, 136, 140–47

Domain of concern, 219

Downs, Anthony, 4, 24, 37, 40

Easley, Linda, 119, 120

Eastside Housing Action Committee (ESHAC), 138

Economic democracy, 54–55

Economic growth, 12, 160

Economic Opportunity Act, 229

Ellis, William, 98, 223

Empowerment, 54, 61

Energy: audits, 167–68; costs, 12, 157, 159, 161, 164, 166; crisis, 157–171; infrastructure, 160; taxes on, 168; wars, 163, 165

Energy conservation. *See* Conservation of energy

Enterprise Zone, 151–54

Equal Credit Opportunity Act, 231

Escalation of conflict, 210, 213

Ethnic groups, 34, 93, 99. *See also* Race

Federal government policies hurting North, 14, 16

Federation of local governments, 232
Financial support of neighborhood or-
ganizations, 39, 121, 150, 252–56.
See also Community Development
Block Grant program, Comprehen-
sive Employment and Training Act,
Volunteers in Service to America
Fish, John, 7, 60, 64, 114, 196, 227
Fisher, Robert, 71
Fraternity, value of, 250

Gangs, 33
Gentrification, 21, 112, 119, 127, 141,
145, 146. *See also* Displacement
Gershenfeld, Matti, 86, 118
Gibbs, Lois, 92
Gittell, Marilyn, 194
Goetze, Rolf, 24, 140
Golden Mean Diagram, 142
Gorz, Andre, 208
Green, Gerson, 151
Green Amendment, 229
Greenlining, 134

Hallman, Howard, 231
Have-a-little-want-mores, 75. *See also*
Alinsky, Saul
Havenots, 9–10, 20, 25, 52, 53; against
Haves, 205–6, 221 n.4, 255; against
other Havenots, 91–92, 228; fatalism of, 53–54, 62; group life of,
93; and Have-a-little-want-mores,
75; housing crisis of, 126, 144;
leaders of, 93, 94–97, 211, 215–
16; organizations aiding, 71, 98–
99, 208; psychological alienation of,
103, 112; socioeconomic status of
187; school control by, 191–92
Haves, 9–10, 147, 205, 206, 255
Heated housing market, 141
Henig, Jeffrey, 119
Historic preservation 39, 119, 146. *See
also* Displacement, Gentrification
Hojnacki, William, 40

Holloway Tenant Cooperative, 138
Home Mortgage Disclosure Act, 130
Home-rule for cities, 13. *See also* Self-
reliance
Households, 23, 126
Housing Assistance Plan, 155 n.24
Housing code enforcement, 216, 218–
20
Housing court, 132, 219
Housing crisis, 126
Housing Opportunity Program, 155
n.24
Housing rehabilitation. *See* Rehabili-
tation
Housing reinvestment strategies. *See*
Anti-redlining laws, Redlining, Re-
habilitation, Rent Strikes, Squatting
Humberger, George, 152
Hydropower, 158, 251

Identification, with neighborhood by
residents, 40–43
Identity, as a dimension of neighbor-
hood type, 36
Ideology, 8, 44, 54. *See also* Con-
servative ideology, Leftist ideol-
ogy, Liberal ideology, Progressive
ideology
Incumbent   upgrading.   *See*
Displacement
Industrial Areas Foundation, 75
Industrial flight. *See* Causes of urban
decline
Industrial workers' movement, 62
Institutional leaders, qualities of, 241–
43
Interaction, as a dimension of neigh-
borhood type, 36
Intergovernmental relations, 13–18.
See also Municipal government
Investor-owners, 127
Issue, 114–15. *See also* Alinsky, Saul;
Community organizing; Strategy

Jacobs, Jane, 154 n.10, 174
Jefferson, Thomas, 52, 53, 249
Jencks, Christopher, 187
Jubilee Housing Development Group, 137

Kahn, Robert, 209
Kahn, Si, 63, 83
Katz, Daniel, 209
Kotler, Milton, 33, 60, 234

Labor productivity, 159
Lamb, Curt, 60, 92–98
Lancourt, Joan, 80, 111, 120, 208
Land banking, 135
Landlords, 22, 127, 128, 132, 136, 145
Langton, Stuart, 57
Lappe, Frances Moore, 158
Leader: as activist, 90–91; alienation of, 97; as disciplinarian, 227; effector as, 90, 99; elder elite as, 95–96; as facilitators, 118; general public as, 90–91; legitimizers as, 90; of neighborhood establishments, 96; neighborhood radical as, 95; respectable militant as, 95; uninvolved as, 95
Leadership: attrition of, 60, 64; context for, 85, 89, 102–4; continuum of style of, 86, 88; flexibility of, 88, 101, 119; general research on, 84–89; as representative of neighborhood, 85, 97–98, 149; styles of, 84–88; turnover of, 119, 195; urban types of, 89–90
Leftist ideology, 59–66, 211. See also Liberal ideology, Progressive ideology
Levy, Paul, 147
Liberal ideology, 54, 58, 71, 160, 187, 199. See also Democratic culture, Leftist ideology, Progressive ideology
Linkage, as a dimension of neighborhood type, 36, 38, 39
Lippitt, Ronald, 88
Little city halls, 233, 240
Local control, 44–45, 112, 236–38
Localism, 59–60, 65, 238

Madison Square Cooperative, 137. See also Cooperatives
Madisonian political view, 34
Matrix of Housing Dynamics, 143
Maximization principle, 207–9. See also Bureaucracy
Mediating institution, 35, 41, 55, 58, 65; advocacy by, 229–45; defined, 223–24; internal communication by, 225–29; school as, 199; tensions of, 225. See also Advocacy
Megastructures, 8, 65, 220, 224, 259. See also Bureaucracy
Metropolitanism, 231
Middle class, 78, 98, 253
Militancy of neighborhood organizations: Alinsky's aphorisms of, 116; as a battering ram, 64; as inadequate alone, 132; as a paradox, 61; as a source of organizational vitality, 120, 133
Model cities, 229
Models of neighborhood change, 45–49
Montessori classroom, 193
Morris, David, 34, 157, 170
Morris, Richard, 14
Multinational corporations, 8, 14, 15, 252. See also Big Oil, Corporations, Megastructures
Multiunit housing, 16, 23, 127, 136–37, 146. See also Tenant cooperatives

Municipal government, 13–18, 30, 33
Municipal solar utility. 167–70

Nader, Ralph, 77, 117
Napier, Rodney, 85, 118
National Urban Coalition, 144
Natural gas, 14, 16, 158, 164
Neighborhood: contemporary perspectives on, 32–43; government, 60; history of concept, 29–32; levels of identification with, 40–43; social functions of, 35–38; types of, 37, 41; viability of, 37, 39–40
Neighborhood change. *See* Models of neighborhood change
Neighborhood ethnography, 35
Neighborhood Housing Service (NHS) Program, 134, 135–36
Neighborhood organization: as alternative form of organization, 214; characteristics of, 76–81; as educator, 112, 227–28; future of, 256–59; goals of, 39, 78, 80, 111–14, 141, 147, 253; history of, 71–76; life cycle of, 40, 118–21; member motivation, 107–10, 163; norms of, 115–18; purpose of, 208; as reactionary, 55, 72; typology of, 195; victory by, 113. *See also* Alinsky, Saul; Leadership
Neighborhood Watch program, 178, 179. *See also* Crime watch program
New Deal, 14, 58
New Populism. *See* Democratic culture
Newsletters: nationally circulated concerning neighborhoods, 77, 161, 165; neighborhood, 225–26
Nix, Harold, 89
Nonneighborhoods, 40
Norms and rules: governing intergroup conflict, 210, 212–13; of neighborhood organization, 115–18
Nuclear energy, 158, 164

O'Brien, David, 208
Oil depletion allowance, 164
OPEC (Organization of Petroleum Exporting Countries), 159
Oppression, 53. *See also* Havenots
Organizer. *See* Community organizer
Organizing. *See* Community Organizing

Parent participation in school, 186, 192–99
Partnership programs: in commercial redevelopment, 147–54; complications in, 156 n.33, 238–41; in housing rehabilitation, 133–40; with nongovernmental institutions, 241–44; in service delivery, 237–38; tense partnerships of City Hall, 235–37
Perception, 23–25; of heated housing market, 141, 143; of place and social mobility, 33; of threat, 41
Perlman, Janice, 76, 79, 80, 103, 249, 250
Petroleum, 14, 158
Piven, Frances Fox, 9, 62, 63, 194, 211
Poletown neighborhood, 21
Police, 178–79
Police review boards. *See* Citizen police review and advisory boards
Political activist approach to organizing, 35, 72, 223. *See also* Community organizing
Political slack, 63
Poor, 53, 62. *See also* Havenots
Power: aphorisms of, 116; for neighborhood, 34; through organization, 62; relations, 208; types of, 90. *See also* Haves, Leadership
Privatism, 55, 57, 58, 209, 224
Professionalism, 100, 242–44. *See also* Bureaucracy

Progressive ideology, 8, 193. *See also* Democratic culture
Progressivism, 193
Protest, 61–65; evolving into program, 133; institutionalizing of, 59, 214, 215. *See also* Militancy of neighborhood organizations
Public authorities, 14
Public interest movement, 58, 77, 239–41
Public interest research group, 77
Public Utility Regulatory Policies Act (PURPA), 162

Quayle, Vincent, 137

Race: differences in levels of alienation, 56; discrimination in cities, 5, 30, 72, 129; and education, 191, 197; liberal attitudes toward, 57; no effects of on commitment to neighborhood, 47; and police tactics, 177–78; pride and neighborhood leadership, 97–98
Radical, 8, 95. *See also* Leader, Leftist ideology
Reagan, Ronald, 139, 151, 166, 187, 230
Redlining, 129–31; as blacklisting, 154 n.10. *See also* Anti-redlining laws
Reform, 19, 30, 71, 78, 208
Regional planning, 232
Rehabilitation, 127, 131, 136–39
Reinvestment, 17, 22. *See also* Commercial reinvestment
Renewable energy, 251
Rent court. *See* Housing Court
Rent strike, 73, 128
Residential Conservation Service, 168
Revitalization. *See* Commercial reinvestment, Rehabilitation, Urban revitalization
Rich, Richard, 108

Right-of-first-refusal ordinance, 145
Role expectations, 209–10
Romanofsky, Peter, 71
Rosenbaum, Patricia, 37, 40
Rubenstein, David, 34
Rutter, Michael, 188

Safeguard Program, 179–80
Saint Ambrose Housing Aid Center (SAHAC), 135–37
Sarason, Seymour, 101
Scala, Florence, 205, 206
Schoenberg, Sandra, 37, 40
School, 21, 33, 185–99
Self-help, 57, 77, 113, 151, 205
Self-interest, 73, 107, 215
Self-reliance, 37, 45, 153, 192, 252
Service delivery by neighborhood organization, 39, 80, 237–38. *See also* Partnership programs
Settlement house, 30, 78, 205
Shearer, Derek, 54, 55
Sinclair, Upton, 73
Slumlords, 7, 91, 127, 131
Social class. *See* Havenot, Haves, Middle class, Working class
Social fabric, 48, 153, 175, 177, 185, 209
Social Security, 16
Social work approach to community organizing, 35, 71, 223. *See also* Alinsky, Saul; Community organizing
Socioeconomic status (SES), 97, 187. *See also* Haves, Havenots
Solar energy, 167–70, 197
Spiegel, Hans, 149
Squatting, 129. *See also* Housing reinvestment strategies
Status achievement by resident, 36, 108
Strategy, 78, 117. *See also* Conser-

vation of energy, Crime control, Rehabilitation, School, Tactics
Stress, 117, 122 n.19, 207
Suburbs, 5, 17, 24
Sweat equity, 135, 166

Tactics: in commercial revitalization, 148; in housing, 128; in organizing, 116–17, 122 n.19; proxy, 75. See also Strategy
Tax Levy by neighborhood organization, 254–56. See also Financial support of neighborhood organizations
Technocrat, 132, 160
Technological imperative, 19
Tenant cooperatives, 136–39
Third parties in organizing campaigns, 80, 121, 213
Triage, 40

Unemployment, 11, 148, 167
Unemployed workers' movement, 62
Unions, 74, 78, 89; compared to neighborhood organizations, 214–17; teachers', 19, 190–92, 233; tenants', 128; schizophrenia of, 55
Urban Development Action Grant Program (UDAG), 139
Urban revitalization: meanings of, 20–22; role of perception in, 22–26

Urban decline. See Causes of urban decline
Urban renewal projects, 16
Urban vitality, 249–52
Urbanization, 13, 44, 250
Utilities, 158, 161–64

Voluntary association, 57, 66, 77, 91, 223. See also Self-help
Volunteers in Service to America (VISTA), 231, 253
Voting Rights Act, 54

Wagner Act, 214
War on Poverty, 58
Warren, Donald, 35–38, 102
Warren, Rachelle, 35–38, 102
Webb, Rodman, 53
Welfare. See Havenots, Poor
Welfare for the rich, 12
Welfare rights movement, 62
Wellstone, Paul, 211
Whistlestop Program, 177. See also Crime control
White, Ralph, 88
Win-win: case study of, 216, 218–21; in conflict theory, 61, 213; vs. win-lose, 61
Wilson, James Q., 174, 175
Winner, Langdon, 19
Women's groups, 77
Working class, 9, 23, 62, 146, 206. See also Havenots

About the Author

MICHAEL R. WILLIAMS is currently Associate Professor-in-the-College at Aquinas College, Grand Rapids, Michigan. He is the cofounder and former Administrator of the Highland Community School in Milwaukee, an alternative inner-city school. He has been president of Grand Rapids' Eastown Community Association and Council of Neighborhood Associations and is the coauthor of *Eastown!*.